THE CIVILIAN WAR

CONFLICTING WORLDS

New Dimensions of the American Civil War

T. Michael Parrish, Series Editor

THE CIVILIAN WAR

CONFEDERATE WOMEN and UNION SOLDIERS during SHERMAN'S MARCH

LISA TENDRICH FRANK

LOUISIANA STATE UNIVERSITY PRESS
BATON ROUGE

Published by Louisiana State University Press
lsupress.org

Copyright © 2015 by Louisiana State University Press
All rights reserved. Except in the case of brief quotations used in articles or reviews, no part of this publication may be reproduced or transmitted in any format or by any means without written permission of Louisiana State University Press.

Louisiana Paperback Edition, 2022

Designer: Barbara Neely Bourgoyne
Typeface: Ingeborg, text

Cover image: *Treasure Seekers,* from *Harper's New Monthly Magazine* (October 1865), courtesy of Hargett Rare Book and Manuscript Library/University of Georgia Libraries.

Library of Congress Cataloging-in-Publication Data
Frank, Lisa Tendrich.
 The civilian war : Confederate women and Union soldiers during Sherman's march / Lisa Tendrich Frank.
  pages cm. — (Conflicting worlds: new dimensions of the American Civil War)
 Includes bibliographical references and index.
 ISBN 978-0-8071-5996-5 (cloth: alk. paper) — ISBN 978-0-8071-5998-9 (pdf) — ISBN 978-0-8071-5997-2 (epub) — ISBN 978-0-8071-7817-1 (paperback) 1. Sherman's March to the Sea. 2. United States—History—Civil War, 1861–1865—Women. 3. United States—History—Civil War, 1861–1865—Social aspects. 4. Sherman, William T. (William Tecumseh), 1820–1891. I. Title.
 E476.69.F73 2015
 973.7′1—dc23
                                                                    2014043200

For Andrew,
finally

CONTENTS

Acknowledgments ix

INTRODUCTION Sherman's March and Southern Women 1

CHAPTER 1 Becoming Confederates 19

CHAPTER 2 Punishing Southern Women 48

CHAPTER 3 Working for War 76

CHAPTER 4 Confronting the Enemy 97

CHAPTER 5 Asserting Confederate Womanhood 124

EPILOGUE Shaming Southern Soldiers 148

Notes 165

Bibliography 201

Index 231

ACKNOWLEDGMENTS

I have spent most of my adult life working on this volume and have consistently had a tremendous amount of support from a large group of people, both inside and outside of academia. The project started at the University of Florida, where I was encouraged and challenged to push my ideas further. I wish that Bertram Wyatt-Brown were here to see my book in print. His friendship, encouragement, and insightful comments shaped my work and my life in countless ways. He was gracious and generous with his energy and time, and he always expressed his confidence in me and in my work. Fitz Brundage, Louise Newman, Thomas Gallant, and David Leverenz all helped this project when it was in its infancy.

Since then, many other scholars have helped me refine my ideas and incorporate new ones. I've benefited from countless conversations at my annual pilgrimage to the Southern Historical Association meetings, years of lunches at the Huntington Library, and hallway chats at several universities. I cannot thank LeeAnn Whites enough. She became my mentor and my friend after graduate school, and without her encouragement I could not have imagined finishing this book. I am similarly grateful for Michael Fellman, Gary Gallagher, Alecia Long, John Marszalek, and Joan Waugh, who all played important roles in my academic life. I have also benefited from formal and informal conversations at conferences and over meals, drinks, and desserts with Ed Baptist, Vikki Bynum, Jackie Campbell, Catherine Clinton, David Colburn, Stephanie Cole, Glenn Crothers, Clark Davis, Stan Deaton, Mary DeCredico, Ted Delaney, Jonathan Earle, Stephen Engle, Matt Gallman, Philip Goff, Marcus Harvey, Erica Johnson, Charles Joyner, Dan Kilbride, Cheryl Koos, Susan Lewis, Karen Lystra, Jim Marten, Brian Craig Miller, Randall Miller, Rebecca Montgomery, Andy Moore, Chris Olsen, Marcus Nenn, Seth Rockman, Anne Rubin, Daniel Stowell, Peter Wallenstein, Frankie White, and

ACKNOWLEDGMENTS

Anne Wyatt-Brown. I would also like to express my appreciation to the members of the Tucker Society and various "readers" at the Huntington Library. Thanks, too, to Rand Dotson and Mike Parrish for sticking with me and pushing me to write a better book. I would also like to thank them for their careful reading of the manuscript and for their solicitation of an outstanding anonymous reviewer. I also appreciate the work of my very perceptive and thorough copy editor, Jo Ann Kiser. In junior high, Veda Mara Levin encouraged my love of writing and taught me how to express myself. At the University of Massachusetts, Amherst, Stephen B. Oates revived my love of history and the Civil War and encouraged me to pursue it in graduate school.

The staffs at several libraries helped me by pointing out manuscript collections that might prove useful and regaling me with family stories about Sherman's March. I would especially like to thank Dick Shrader at the Southern Historical Collection of the University of North Carolina, Henry Fulmer at the South Caroliniana Library of the University of South Carolina, Elizabeth Dunn at the Rare Book, Manuscript, and Special Collections Library of Duke University, and Dale Couch at the Georgia Department of Archives and History. I would also like to thank the rest of the staffs at those institutions as well as those at the Atlanta History Center, the Special Collections Department in the Robert W. Woodruff Library at Emory University, the Hargrett Rare Book and Manuscript Library at the University of Georgia, the Georgia Historical Society, the Library of Congress, the Henry E. Huntington Library, the South Carolina Department of Archives and History, the South Carolina Historical Society, and the University of Florida Libraries. I am also grateful for financial support from an Andrew W. Mellon Foundation fellowship at the Henry E. Huntington Library, a Women's Studies Research Grant from Duke University, and an Albert J. Beveridge Grant from the American Historical Association.

For giving me places to stay when I was on the road and for their continued friendship, special thanks go to Amy Manning, Stan and Debbie Deaton, Donna and Mark Fleishman, Peter Hartog, Lynne and Roger Irvine, Jennifer and Jay Langdale, Jim and Maxine Perlmutter, Sherry Seitlin Kornfeld, Pat Solley, and Keith and Tara Spolan. My amazing friends, especially Elizabeth Gainer, Vanessa Guzzi, Sherri Kasper, Emily

ACKNOWLEDGMENTS

Leventhal, Susan Lichtstein, Amy Manning, Brenda Rosen, Deborah Roth, Leslie Sokol, and Melissa West, all kept me smiling and mostly sane.

I feel fortunate to have both married into and been born into a wonderful family. Their constant love helped me get through everything. I am so lucky to have them in my life. My mother- and father-in-law, Judie and Paul Frank; my brother- and sister-in-law, Gary and Gail Frank; and my niece and nephew, Sarah and Ryan, have treated me as if I had been born a Frank. Emily Judem read the entire manuscript and made excellent suggestions. My parents, Marilyn and Howard Tendrich, taught me to believe in myself and follow my dreams. I can never thank them enough for being such wonderful parents and friends to me. My mom went far beyond the call of duty by accompanying me on research trips and being a great research assistant. My brother, Jon, has always cheered me on. I wish I could have taken my grandparents, Shirley and Jack Seitlin and Helen Tendrich, up on all their offers of help. I am especially grateful to the three little speed bumps who slowed my work down and made me take time to appreciate everything. Daniel, Noah, and Shayna are the lights of my life. Their love of reading and learning makes everything worthwhile. Their hugs are even better. I'm glad they think the Civil War is cool. Although I did not use the title Daniel suggested—"Sherman's Somewhat Crazy March and the Details Behind It"—I'm glad I can finally show all three of my children what I've been working on for their entire lives.

Andrew has been the best of everything since I met him. I can't imagine my life without him as my best friend, cheerleader, chef, sounding board, psychologist, editor, research assistant, proofreader, traveling companion, live-in comedian, fellow child-herder, and husband. He knows more about Sherman, Southern women, gender, and the Civil War than he ever wanted to know. His unfailing confidence in me and in my work kept me going. I know my work is better because of him. I would not want to do it without him. I love him everything.

THE CIVILIAN WAR

INTRODUCTION

SHERMAN'S MARCH AND SOUTHERN WOMEN

They regard us just as the Romans did the Goths and the parallel is not unjust.
—William T. Sherman to Ellen Ewing Sherman, January 5, 1865

On February 24, 1865, wealthy slaveholder Mary Maxcy Leverett was relieved to report that "the long week of agony is over." She and her family in Columbia, South Carolina, had faced an ordeal unmatched by anything they had experienced before and something that they could never have prepared to encounter: the invasion of their homes by Union soldiers. Although it was widely reported that "terms were, private property respected, women & children unmolested," she wanted her son to know that those "terms" were a sham. The "wretches" had disregarded the prohibitions about women and their possessions and had instead "rushed . . . into our house to pillage." The destruction of her private property took all forms. Not only had the soldiers "smashed open desks . . . broke open drawers with axes [and] asked for keys to corn house & smoke house," but they also entered the feminine inner sanctum of the home, the bedrooms. She was horrified that they had "crept under the bed" and especially mortified that they did not even leave her "a second suit of underclothes." They also confiscated many seemingly trivial domestic items, all of which made her personally feel the sting of the raid. They left with "the comb with which I comb my hair" and they "broke open my work box & stole my scissors." When she appealed to Union officers for help, they taunted her and "showed me the old State House flag with a look of exultation & one of them argued hotly with me to prove it all our own fault." Her day continued with repetitions of the "same riotous scenes." Despite the fact that she "was on my feet all day, a tremor all over me," Leverett tried to keep calm. She was "determined they should not see I was afraid."

Other slaveholding Southern women endured similar scenes of personal humiliation as Yankee "demons" destroyed domestic property in Leverett's Columbia. She detailed countless events that transpired around her. "As the houses burnt down one after another the terrified women & children rushed into the Asylum for safety surrounded by these yelling devils, who tore open their trunks & gave to negroes or tore to atoms." Even the Ladies' Asylum—literally a place of sanctuary—offered the women little protection. Enemy soldiers taunted and hassled the white women who fled there: "the fiends raged curseing, screaming up and down . . . swearing they were going to blow up the Asylum that night." The five hundred terrified women who took shelter in the Asylum feared for their lives, and one woman reportedly "died of fright." Other women took to the woods for safety, but were still harassed by the "wretches," who sneered at them: "Ladies, it is a very cold night, why don't you go into your [burning] city to warm yourselves?"

When Sherman's men left Columbia, Leverett and many of her peers viewed the war and the Confederate cause through the prism of the Union's dishonorable behavior and their personal shame at having had strange men rifle through their personal belongings. Leverett and other slaveholding women wanted to spread the word about the outrageous events in Columbia. "Our men *must know* how we have been treated." She appealed to white men's sense of honor and manliness, with the assumption that knowledge of the Union army's treatment of Confederate women would invigorate Southern soldiers. "If our men never fought before, tell them I say they must do it now: if they give up, or their knees shake, I won't count them as men, but as dogs who deserve to, deserve to die." As for her dedication to her nation, she reported an exchange she had with a Union soldier. When asked if she was ready to give up, she said, "No! It would make us more determined & drive every man into the field with feelings more embittered & intense than ever. It was a *good thing* for us." When Yankee soldiers suggested that the Southern men needed to "come home to take care of their families," she disagreed. After all, she said, the women "would take care of ourselves, that I had suffered (pointing to our sacked house) but was willing to suffer. I could bear calamity."[1]

INTRODUCTION

Stories like this one, told frequently by both elite Confederate women and Union soldiers during the march, fill the contemporary historical record of Sherman's campaign. All along Sherman's 1864–65 march through Georgia and the Carolinas, Confederate women and Union men faced off in heated domestic confrontations. This book privileges these types of stories and demonstrates that they are critical to understanding the campaign. Whereas most scholars have focused on "Sherman neckties" and "Sherman's sentinels" as the best physical evidence of the destructive campaign, *The Civilian War* demonstrates that the most revealing elements of the campaign are instead found in these confrontations in slaveholding women's parlors and bedrooms, between soldiers and civilians, between men and women. Sherman's March brought soldiers into the homes of the enemy as part of the official ambitions of the campaign, creating personal battles between Yankee men and those they deemed Confederate sinners. These domestic battles shaped the outcome of the war, its historical legacies, and the fate of the nation.

In late 1864, Union general William Tecumseh Sherman, with sixty thousand seasoned soldiers under his command, set out to crush the Confederacy's ability and will to continue its war of rebellion. After capturing and occupying Atlanta, Georgia, in September, the Union troops began marching east in November. At the end of the March to the Sea and after a brief occupation of Savannah, they continued their campaign into the Carolinas at the beginning of 1865. By the time the campaign ended on April 26, 1865, near Durham Station, North Carolina, Sherman had inflicted more than $100 million in physical damage and had earned the scorn of Confederates for his approach to the civilian population.[2] Having secured the surrender of Confederate general Joseph Johnston, the Union proclaimed the march a success. The campaign, commanders asserted, had fulfilled its two public and interrelated goals: to break the will of Confederates and to destroy the material and human resources supporting the rebel military.

Sherman's troops marched through the heart of the lower South, purposefully cutting through the farms and plantations of the Confederate home front. This chosen path of destruction, which commanders designed

3

to target the families and households of the lower South's wealthiest slaveholders and political leaders, led to a myriad of interactions between Northern soldiers and elite Southern women. Throughout the campaign, the actions of Union men generally conformed to a mode of warfare specifically designed to take aim at the class and gender of those in their chosen swath of the Confederate home front, filled as it was with wealthy slaveholding women. Although they generally avoided physical contact with the elite white women they encountered, Union soldiers found and employed countless ways to strike at their enemies' femininity and livelihoods. Sherman's men, as has often been described, lived by confiscating the supplies of the Southerners in their path, and they destroyed much of what they could not take with them. This assault, though, went far beyond foraging for food and burning supplies and homes. Union soldiers also ravaged the interiors of the homes they entered, went into bedrooms and other private areas that were especially restricted from strange men, verbally insulted women, threatened rape, destroyed personal items, and otherwise unleashed an unprecedented direct assault on domestic life on the Southern home front. In most instances, these actions formed part of a plan that Sherman and his troops articulated prior to and justified throughout the campaign—one that would assert the aggressively masculine power of the Union over the passively feminine South.

Elite slaveholding women, as much as Confederate military resources, stood at the center of William Tecumseh Sherman's famous campaign through the Southern heartland. Throughout the campaign, domestic warfare tactics shaped the behavior of Northern soldiers. Sherman and his men marched east out of Atlanta with the intention of punishing the slaveholding class, who, in their minds, caused the war. They embarked on their campaign with the knowledge that the enemies they faced were primarily wealthy white women, whose defeat required tactics appropriate to their station and sex. Sherman designed his march to address the presence of female civilians, his soldiers repeatedly made decisions that accounted for the presence of hostile women, and the success and failures of the campaign largely resulted from the responses and experiences of this unconventional enemy. By waging a "domestic war" specifically designed for the gender, class, and race of these civilians, Sherman

INTRODUCTION

hoped that he could destroy slaveholding women's ability and desire to continue supporting the war. Confederate women faced the enemy on their own terms, responding with specifically feminine forms of defiance. Working with assumptions about wartime standards of respectability and how they imagined Union soldiers would treat them and their bodies, these women defended themselves and their property. Sherman's March would not have been as successful as it was if the soldiers had not taken into account the female presence in the areas they invaded. Sherman designed the campaign to break the will of those elite female Confederates who most supported the war and also to destroy the ability of Confederate men to fight it. Taking these gendered aspects into consideration, this study follows Sherman's lead with its focus on the wealthy slaveholding women in the area of the South that he targeted.

The campaign on women reflected neither cruelty nor vindictiveness on the part of Union soldiers. It did not, as many Lost Cause memorialists later declared, target innocent women. Sherman directed his men to bring the war to slaveholding women because he understood that they had, in part, brought the war to the Union and had sustained the Confederate war effort.[3] For starters, Sherman and the Union leadership recognized elite white women's roles in initiating the Southern rebellion during the secession crisis. When the war began, slaveholding women encouraged men to enlist in the Confederate army and then kept them on the battlefield with supplies and letters of support. These women's continued dedication to the Confederate war effort through both material and moral support became increasingly problematic as the Union worked to hasten the war to an end. As a result, United States commanders made the home front and its slaveholding female inhabitants an important part of their battle plans.[4] Sherman worked to bring the war home to elite women in Georgia and the Carolinas. He recognized that he was dealing with a hostile female population and treated it as such. After he captured Atlanta, he expelled the civilians, most of whom were women and children. In this eviction, he acknowledged women and children as the enemy and refused to be swayed by their gender. Sherman made his appreciation of white Southern women's dedication to the Confederacy and involvement in the war effort clear early in the conflict, explaining to his brother, Ohio senator John Sherman, that "the entire South, man, *woman,* and child are against us, armed and determined."⁵ Sherman conceived of slaveholding Southern women as Confederates, rebels, and enemies, and he treated them accordingly.

Surprisingly, historians of Sherman's March have marginalized the centrality of Confederate women. With few exceptions, scholars have portrayed the campaign as an attempt to destroy the ability of the Southern military to fight. Scholars frequently discuss civilians, but these civilians too often appear in narratives and interpretations as stories of personal interest rather than historical importance. Civilians are in the way of Sherman's war rather than an integral part of his method of war. In most narratives, the occasional skirmishes with Confederate soldiers—which happened with less frequency as the campaign grew longer—receive far more attention than the more common interactions with female civilians.⁶ In the most significant work on Sherman and the home front, *When Sherman Marched North from the Sea,* Jacqueline Glass Campbell describes Sherman's March as "an invasion of both geographic and psychological space." Using Savannah as her starting point and incorporating women into her work, Campbell examines the second half of the campaign as an attack on the home front that was primarily shaped by changes in geography and environment. Campbell argues that the increased destruction and anger of Union soldiers toward the female enemy in the Carolinas resulted from the increasingly difficult terrain. Although she explores some of the interactions between invading soldiers and white Southern women in the Carolinas, she misses an opportunity to see how this campaign was premeditated and rooted in the people rather than the place.⁷

Bringing gender and the experiences of elite women to the forefront of an interpretation of Sherman's March provides a new means for military historians to understand wartime damages. Recent scholars have struggled to determine the extent of damage inflicted on Southern civilians, often engaging in what amounts to social scientific debate over how much physical damage was incurred.⁸ Rather than count destroyed homes or literally assess damages, *The Civilian War* instead demonstrates how gender norms turned typically overlooked acts into unpardonable insults. Elite Confederate women generally understood as normal the theft of food, the destruction of factories, and even the freeing of slaves during wartime invasions. Larger affronts occurred when Union soldiers

INTRODUCTION

took axes to pianos, stole private diaries, smashed china sets, ran their hands through lingerie, paraded around mockingly in ladies' gowns, and otherwise took self-guided tours of bedrooms, private chambers, and other areas of homes that were off-limits to strange men. Southern women accepted some acts as wartime realities and viewed others as evidence of Yankee barbarity. This perspective refines historian Mark Grimsley's widely held distinction between "hard" and "total" war.[9] In the case of Sherman's March, the tactics employed were not restrained by a percentage of effort but rather by the rules of gender.

Recent assessments of Sherman's March have increasingly, and in some ways correctly, pointed to the ways that the campaign's destruction has been overstated. Indeed, as much as Sherman declared that he would proceed by "smashing things to the sea," Sherman's soldiers did not burn every town, tear up every railroad, or ransack every home.[10] Atlanta would burn, but it was more the exception than the rule for a campaign that publically declared its intent to destroy the Confederacy's ability to continue the war. Sherman, the literature proclaims, waged war on the home front but in a restrained manner. Grimsley, in perhaps the most important reassessment of the march, argues that Sherman waged "hard war" rather than total war. This terminology, used by contemporaries to describe Sherman, is "flexible enough to include operations aimed at the destruction of enemy economic resources . . . forced evacuations, or confiscation of property without recompense." In addition, it captures the idea of tactics that result in the "erosion of the enemy's will to resist by deliberately or concomitantly subjecting the civilian population to the pressures of war."[11] Joseph T. Glatthaar, in an even greater revision of the conventional wisdom of widespread and indiscriminate destruction, asserted that "in general, Sherman's army treated Southern civilians well."[12] Although Sherman's troops destroyed South Carolina, they "did not set fire to [Georgians'] homes, except in the case of prominent Confederates, whose homes universally received the torch," and in North Carolina Union soldiers "ceased their policy of destruction."[13] Most recently, Mark Neeley sees a "cult of violence in writing about the Civil War" and proclaims that the wartime damage and death has been greatly exaggerated.[14]

These approaches have their merits, as many Southerners in Georgia and the Carolinas escaped with their homes and private property intact.

These attempts to portray a less damaging campaign, however, ignore the ways that Sherman targeted elite Confederates of the slaveholding class and used tactics specifically designed for their gender. Furthermore, a study of the degree of physical damage to buildings does not get at the heart of the psychological destruction visited on the Confederate home front. Scholars' dismissal of feminine complaints of destruction—the loss of their wedding gowns, diaries, handkerchiefs, and other domestic items—as frivolous and inconsequential minimizes the importance of what women experienced at the hands of enemy soldiers. Although not directly tied to the pursuit of the Confederate war, the ransacking of a slaveholding woman's private letters and sentimental items was intimately tied to an attempt to destroy her confidence and support of the Confederacy. Glatthaar, for example, notes that soldiers "came to the conclusion that ravaging homes was as effective as burning them to the ground" and that their destruction of these homes included "everything of financial or sentimental value within the home." Yet, he does so without exploring the implications of the "sentimental" destruction.[15] As a result, his reassessment of the damages focuses on the masculine effects of the march—the loss of what he deems as the economically valuable items such as livestock, crops, and buildings. Bringing gender to the forefront of Sherman's March reveals a more complicated story. Although at first glance it may seem as though Confederate women were upset over the loss of frivolous items, they more precisely expressed their anger over Sherman's troops' knowing destruction of those items that defined white female privilege in the American South. Such actions demonstrated that Union soldiers would not respect the presumed respectability of elite slaveholding women. Union soldiers did not merely scatter handkerchiefs to the winds; to their elite female enemies these delicate items represented an unforgivable crossing of boundaries.

Although contemporary observers and modern scholars have tirelessly discussed the "destructive war" or "hard war" that Sherman waged, most have failed to recognize his gendered ambitions. Sherman designed his campaign to physically destroy the Southern landscape and assert Northern domination over the South. Few historians acknowledge the centrality of slaveholding Southern women and domesticity to Union tactics in the 1864–65 campaign. Instead, most focus on the official military objectives of the march to destroy the Confederacy's ability to provide

INTRODUCTION

supplies to its army as well as the morale of its supporters. With few exceptions, scholars have conflated the two goals, assuming that Union attempts to destroy material resources constituted the sole means of crushing the spirits of the "rebels" who supported secession and the Confederacy. In addition, their assessments have invariably defined the Confederate supporters in the path of Sherman as ungendered, or even male, "civilians." As a result, they treat the campaign as a conflict between men on the battlefield as they ignore the presence and power of the wealthy and largely female civilian population. Because Union troops faced little sustained resistance from the Confederate army, most analyses of the march focus on the ease with which Sherman and his men progressed through the South and asserted the Union's military advantage. Participants, too, played down women's place in Sherman's March. For example, although he helped make war on the civilian enemy and faced the female population's ire, Union officer Henry Hitchcock minimized women's role as enemy combatants. Despite experiences to the contrary, he asserted that during the March to the Sea *"we* have met . . . no opposition."[16]

The prioritization of what happened while troops were between cities, towns, and homesteads precludes an exploration of the resistance that elite Southern women exhibited toward their enemies. By turning women into passive victims, scholars have left the impression that the North actually invaded a quiescent South. In reality, the destruction of lives and domestic property, which Sherman's March exemplified, profoundly shaped the Civil War experiences of Confederate women and men. The invasion itself cannot be understood without an understanding of whose space was invaded, how Yankee soldiers viewed them, how slaveholding women handled the incursion, and how Confederate soldiers reacted to the despoiling of their homeland. Gender illuminates the undertones of Sherman's campaign on the wealthy white Southern home front. It also shows elite women as a significant aspect of Sherman's campaign—both as targets and as participants.[17]

Even as they ignore women, however, most studies of Sherman's March recognize that the 1864–65 campaign had everything to do with power. Scholars' explorations of power as it related to the campaign emphasize a detached military and political strategy to show the South the North's superior strength.[18] Early in the war Sherman understood the utility of defeating the people rather than just the armies. Tellingly, Sherman himself made the connection between the military campaigns and a demonstration of power explicit when he acknowledged that despite the fact that he "[could] not change the hearts of those people of the South," he would "make war so terrible . . . [and] make them so sick of war that generations would pass away before they would again appeal to it."[19] He believed that Confederates had brought this punishment upon themselves. In early 1864, he commented that "a people who will persevere in war beyond a certain limit ought to know the consequences."[20] In 1864, Sherman had an opportunity to execute his ideas and give Confederates what he saw as a much deserved and forceful display of Northern male dominance that would lead them to acknowledge Union power. He designed his Georgia and Carolinas campaign to show the strength of the Union armies. Sherman explicitly stated that the campaign, designed to "demonstrat[e] to the world . . . that we have . . . power," would be "proof positive that the North can prevail" and would no doubt end the Southern war effort. Southerners would be forced to recognize Union power and from then on continually wonder about the North's "willingness to use that power."[21] Sherman hoped to intimidate all Southerners, male and female, with a forceful display of Northern male dominance.[22]

The Civilian War demonstrates how, with Sherman's March, the Union launched a gender-specific military campaign on the home front, one that encompassed an active female civilian population and focused on the trappings of their domestic worlds. Yankee soldiers specifically honed in on the world of elite Southern femininity, a world that was exceptionally privileged in its command of both human and material possessions. Throughout the march, Union soldiers treated elite Southern women as enemies, albeit feminine ones, and no longer allowed them the protections afforded by race, class, or gender during peacetime.[23] These interactions were governed in part, by Sherman's desire to "make a raid that will make the South feel the terrible character of our people."[24] According to Union soldiers' refashioned idea of slaveholding women as enemies, female Confederates became a population in need of subduing. Sherman himself made this goal clear: "This movement is *not* purely military or strategic, but it will illustrate the vulnerability of the South."[25] Furthermore it would make the "inhabitants feel that war & individual Ruin are synonymous terms."[26] Sherman and his soldiers understood

INTRODUCTION

the gendered nature of their attack on the Southern home front and willingly brought the war home.

Union soldiers' engagement with hostile slaveholding women does not discount the physical damage they wreaked upon the Confederate landscape. On the contrary, the destruction of the lower South's economy complemented the domestic warfare waged on its inhabitants. As Sherman explained, the goal of the campaign was "the utter destruction of its roads, houses, and *people*."[27] In an effort to destroy the Confederates' ability to wage war, Sherman's soldiers freed thousands of African slaves as they demolished miles of railroad tracks, acres of cotton plantations, and various factories and storage facilities. They also watched with glee as parts of Atlanta, Columbia, and other towns burned. The creation of Sherman neckties—the nickname given to the railroad tracks that Sherman's men heated and bent so they could not be easily repaired—should not be separated from the destruction of real neckties and other articles of fancy clothing and domestic items. If, in gendered terms, the railroad represented the ability to wage war, the bedroom represented the willingness to sustain the fight.

This work also builds upon a progression of scholarship that uses gender and culture to reinterpret battlefields and home fronts in ways that minimize, if not blur, the distinction between the two. For more than a generation, scholars have brought to light the important role of female soldiers, nurses, spies, and government workers.[28] Many, if not most, Civil War historians embraced these studies of wartime women, though, without changing the fundamental narrative of the war. Female nurses cared for male soldiers; female soldiers pretended to be men in order to act in the realm that mattered most; female spies helped men make better (or worse) battlefield decisions; and female government workers freed up *man*power for more important tasks. Although the authors of these pathbreaking accounts offered new narratives of the war that hardly segregated women out of them, many historians remain content to include women as the supporting cast and reserve the leading roles for men.[29] Surprisingly, many scholarly accounts of the war explore the experiences of civilians without adequately acknowledging the numeric dominance of women in this population and the ways that this reality shaped the war itself.[30]

The traditional narrative is crumbling, even if it is doing so very slowly.[31] Scholars of the African American experience have increasingly privileged the role of enslaved men and women, instead of just enlisted African American men, in the war effort. Enslaved African Americans, in these interpretations, did not need to enlist in the Union army or serve as nurses in order to shape the outcome of the war.[32] Other challenges to the traditional narrative have come from reinterpretations that treat the Civil War as, in LeeAnn Whites's words, a "crisis in gender." Whites's work, published in 1995, was "based on the premise that one critical vantage point has indeed been almost entirely absent from [the academic debates over the Civil War]: *gender.*" As Whites stressed, this absence is especially surprising in Civil War scholarship because "it is hard to imagine any activity that has been more gendered than the conduct of war." Whites insightfully explored how the Civil War both revealed and altered gendered ideas and roles in a Georgia town.[33] Whites's work on gender and the war followed and inspired a new group of scholars intent on asking new questions about the Civil War as well as connecting women and gender with the most important questions that traditional military historians have asked about the war, such as causation, effects, and causes of victory or defeat. By integrating men, women, and gender into single accounts where claims on manhood and womanhood need to be asserted and defended, scholars have demonstrated how gender and the war shaped each other.[34]

This approach becomes especially important when exploring battles and campaigns that took place on the home front. Consequently, Sherman's March offers an opportunity to examine how gender shaped the course of a military campaign, from the perspectives of both soldiers and civilians. If Sherman's March is indicative of the war as a whole, it further demonstrates the need to apply Whites's observation to all aspects of a war in which the home front and battlefront often blurred. From this military offensive's planning through its implications, and whether examined from the Confederate or Union perspective, gender shaped the behavior of everyone involved in and affected by it. Union officials designed Sherman's March with gender in mind as they planned an attack on a home front filled with elite women. Attacks on domesticity and womanhood were not unintended consequences of a march through the home front or the collateral damage that occurred as the Union

INTRODUCTION

destroyed the Confederates' ability to wage war. Instead, the confrontations between Yankee soldiers and slaveholding women were intentional and inseparable from the events and tactics that military historians traditionally emphasize. These confrontations also illuminated soldiers' understandings of manliness and masculinity. The response of Confederate soldiers to the home front campaign is best understood through the lens of Southern manhood and honor.[35]

During Sherman's March, Confederate women and Union soldiers had little choice but to confront each other. *The Civilian War* contends that in these engagements soldiers and civilians expected that notions of gender would restrain each other's behavior. Confederate women hid valuables and weapons under their skirts, in their bedrooms, and in their babies' cribs, and they demanded the protection afforded to "respectable women." When face to face with the enemy, they also responded with the feminine weapon of words, heaping vitriolic tirades on those they saw as ungentlemanly invaders who did not belong in their homes or bedrooms. At the same time, these women rarely formed volunteer militias or defended their homes with physical violence. On a few occasions they formed female home guards and carried guns under their skirts, but they only did so in case Union men breached the code of respectable wartime conduct by engaging in acts of physical or sexual violence. When these fears did not materialize, the weapons remained hidden. Gender similarly restrained Union men and created war tactics specifically designed for the privileged female enemy. Careful not to breach certain rules of warfare and etiquette, Union soldiers generally refrained from physically attacking white women's bodies. Instead, using methods designed to strike at the feminine and elite white identities of their home front enemy, Sherman's soldiers inflicted the hardships of war onto the various manifestations of Confederate womanhood. They burned homes, the geographic epicenter of womanhood in the American South. Even when the soldiers left the buildings standing, they often destroyed the domestic elements that made the house a home. Adding insult to injury, Union soldiers frequently ransacked bedrooms, tore up ladies' dresses, rummaged through women's "unmentionables," ransacked kitchens and cupboards, pillaged the relics of dead relatives, freed domestic and field slaves, smashed pianos, and otherwise destroyed various vestiges of elite white women's world. Rather than the actions of unrestrained men in the chaos of war or the foraging necessary to feed an army on the move, these actions were deliberately employed to defeat psychologically enemy women and men of the Confederacy. Northern men understood the sanctity of women's space and used it to their advantage.[36]

The distinction between the nature and the extent of damage explains why so many slaveholding women in the lower South remained steadfastly committed to the Confederate cause when their prospects seemed most dim. *The Civilian War* contends that elite Southern women largely refused to yield to "Satan Sherman and his imps," an enemy who violated what they imagined as the basic rules of polite society.[37] Confederate soldiers often came to a different conclusion, choosing to abandon the fight in order to return home to protect their families. This explanation, which is offered in the epilogue, complicates interpretations of Confederate morale by historian Drew Gilpin Faust and others who have argued that the war ended when women demanded that their husbands return home.[38] Sherman's campaign ultimately proved successful. Although it did not destroy Confederate women's will to fight, it achieved its desired ends. Despite the devotion to the Confederacy by women who faced Sherman's men, Southern men on the battlefield saw the invasion as an insult to their manliness. They felt strongly the failure of their inability to protect their ladies from the barbarians of the North and, as a result, many lost the will to fight.

The enduring loyalty of Confederate women to the Lost Cause creates a methodological issue for scholars of the war and this study.[39] Many records of the war were written and published years, if not decades, after the fighting ended. The authors of these memoirs wrote the war to reflect desired memories and to suit their unreconstructed late nineteenth-century ambitions. They reflect what Faust labeled the "century-old legend of female sacrifice."[40] As a result, this volume avoids using memoirs and other accounts that were written a significant time after the events discussed unfolded. Instead, *The Civilian War* relies on hundreds of contemporary journals, personal correspondence, and official documents to tell the story of the march and its effect on those it touched. Fortunately, many civilians and soldiers left extensive journals describing the events and people around them. In addition, slaveholding women and both Union and Confederate soldiers left behind countless letters detailing the campaign. Official letters between military commanders detail the

INTRODUCTION

campaign's purpose and path, but so do letters that commanders and soldiers sent home to their families and friends. In addition, to describe their experiences Confederate women wrote lengthy letters to family members who were on the battlefront and elsewhere on the Southern home front. They wrote these letters to reassure loved ones as to their safety and also to let them know about the enemy's tactics. In addition to avoiding memoirs and the problems of memory, *The Civilian War* does not allow slaveholding women or Union soldiers or Confederate soldiers to dictate a singular version of events. Instead, whenever possible, the volume uses the words of one to corroborate the behavior and words of the other. Often the Union and Confederate viewpoints are not very far apart. For example, Confederate women frequently described how they mouthed off to the enemy soldiers; Union soldiers expressed disgust and dismay at the vocal defiance they faced from elite Southern women. The integration of both viewpoints helps create a fuller picture of the attitudes and events of the campaign. It also helps avoid the glorification of one side or the other by exaggerated accounts of personal behavior. Taken together, these records offer a full picture of the personal and military aspects of the campaign.

Rather than presenting a chronological narrative of Sherman's March, *The Civilian War* analyzes the campaign as a series of experiences. Several of the chapters highlight the perspectives of elite Southern women as they awaited, experienced, and then dealt with the aftermath of the invasion. Chapter 1 explores how slaveholding women in Georgia and the Carolinas readied to confront Union troops. Recognizing that the line between home front and war front had blurred, white women continued to draw upon their beliefs that the home afforded some protection. As they prepared for the imminent approach of Sherman's troops, elite Southern women's consciousness of themselves as Confederates strengthened. Chapter 2 places the gendered motives and tactics of Union troops at the center of the campaign's basic narrative. It contends that Sherman specifically designed his campaign through Georgia and the Carolinas as a comprehensive assault on elite Southern domesticity that would "cure her of her pride and boasting."[41] Sherman's campaign moved

15

through the plantation South particularly focusing on making wealthy slaveholding women feel the horrors of the campaign. Chapter 3 explores how, as Sherman's troops neared, elite Confederate women in Georgia and the Carolinas displayed their regional loyalty through increased work for their nation. By moving beyond the written rhetoric of the women, this chapter demonstrates how slaveholding women actively supported the Confederacy as they raised money, encouraged enlistment, sewed uniforms, rolled bandages, nursed wounded, and performed many other tasks that contributed necessary materials and labor to the war effort. Chapter 4 examines the personal interactions between Union soldiers and female Confederates during Sherman's March. In these confrontations slaveholding women discovered that their gender and class provided less protection than they had anticipated. Consequently, the Union attack on Southern domesticity and homes forced elite women to defend both their regional and gender identities. Successfully adapting their femininity to one that included a defense of their homes and their nation, slaveholding women made clear their belief that Sherman and his troops were inhuman, uncivilized, and capable of almost anything. Chapter 5 explores the aftermath of the campaign. It contends that Sherman and his men left more than physical destruction and ruin in their path; they also left bitterness, hatred, and Confederate patriotism in their wake. The invasion of the domestic sphere during Sherman's campaign failed to force elite white Georgia and Carolina women to abandon the nation that they had helped to create. Instead, it magnified elite women's Confederate patriotism as it reinvigorated their sense of the irreconcilable differences between Confederates and Northerners. The march created in Confederate women "a hatred that *knows no change,* and [a people who] can *never forget* what they have done, even to the tenth generation."⁴² The march helped ensure Union victory, but it could not, as Sherman told his wife, "break the pride of the [women of the] South."⁴³ It was despite continued support on the home front for the war that the Confederate military ultimately surrendered. *The Civilian War* concludes by explaining the actions of Confederate men with the logic of nineteenth-century gender norms. Sherman's March may have been more successful in its indirect attack on Confederate soldiers than it was in its direct assault on the nation's slaveholding women. Although physically removed from the domestic destruction on the home front, soldiers from Georgia and the

Carolinas felt the psychological brunt of the attack. In short, the campaign destroyed Southern men's sense of honor and their confidence in their ability to protect their homes and families. It consequently forced Confederate soldiers to come to grips with the fact that they could not protect Southern womanhood from the onslaughts of war.

Tom Taylor, a Union soldier who "witnessed a scene of destruction and woe," assessed Sherman's March as "a black page for American history!" Sherman's March, he recorded in an 1864 diary entry, would long be understood as he saw it at the time, as an attack on helpless civilian women and children. Taylor described in detail how foragers "[entered] the premises and after robbing family of every thing to eat, deliberately [proceeded] to break jars, dishes, furniture &c. until not more than a dozen half sashes were left and not a single piece of furniture left undamaged." The soldiers did not stop with the destruction of the kitchen and the living space, however. They moved to the private and feminine spaces where they "then robbed the beds of their bedding, wardrobes of their clothing and cut open mattrasses even to the one on which the little children slept on their crib." All this destruction constituted what Taylor considered an "inhuman and fiendish act" that continued as the soldiers drove "the lady big with child, her innocent, little children and her aged mother from the house." To humiliate the women of the household, they even took "the graduating diploma of Miss Bryan . . . tore the ribbon and seal from it and cast it on the floor."[44] Taylor's assessment of the march as a "black page" proved partially accurate. Although many Americans do not share Taylor's conclusions about the march's place in American history, they share his opinion of women's place within its narrative. Since 1865, most scholars of the Civil War, and of Sherman's March in particular, have glossed over Confederate women's experiences and active participation in the war. Assuming that Southern women passively suffered through a horrible ordeal over which they had little control, scholars have spent little time on the complexity of female rebels' motivations and experiences. However, a closer look at Sherman's March reveals slaveholding women as ardent and active Confederates. Their place at the heart of the campaign allowed them to understand its implications in ways that most historians have not. One woman noted the significance early in the campaign. "How that march through those *feminine foes* in Georgia will read in History! The cry of those ruined households will sound along the ages."[45] As another Confederate woman noted, female rebels did not stand quietly by as noncombatants while Union soldiers ransacked their homes. Instead, they began a campaign of their own, vowing that as lifelong Confederate women they "[would] *never* submit to *Yankee* dominion."[46]

CHAPTER 1

BECOMING CONFEDERATES

In October 1860, North Carolinian Catherine Edmondston could not stop thinking about the upcoming presidential election. She could not have envisioned the turmoil and bloodshed that would follow, but she recognized the incredible stakes involved. No matter how she looked at it, the impending election threatened her privileged status as a slaveholder. As she saw it, all of the likely scenarios seemed troublesome. Stephen A. Douglas, she boldly and perhaps misleadingly proclaimed, was as "bad as Lincoln" as they both would "undermine the South & Slavery!"[1] She knew one advocated popular sovereignty and she deemed the other an abolitionist, but she considered them both equally hostile to her interests. Although women could not vote, she carefully followed politics and obsessed over the election that threatened her personal status. Her husband's and her Halifax County estate included 1,894 acres, and they owned eighty-eight slaves. They had much to lose. Whereas national politics and the interference of abolitionists worried Edmondston, the possibility of war did not. As the election approached, Edmondston's words echoed the Fire Eaters' radical calls for disunion. Like the most vocal secessionists, she declared that "if S C did secede & there was any attempt made to coerce her, I would go to South Carolina & load guns for her men to shoot!"[2]

Lincoln's election magnified Edmondston's anxieties about the future, and like many other North Carolina planters she concluded that her state had no option but to secede from the Union. When North Carolina dragged its feet on the issue and seven other slaveholding states formed the Confederacy, Edmondston impatiently wanted to be part of the excitement. She especially felt the exclusion during the February inauguration of Jefferson Davis as Confederate president, and her state's refusal to join South Carolina and others soured her on North Carolina's political leaders. She could not understand why her state had not yet joined her "sisters in blood, in soil, in climate & in institution."[3] Edmondston continued to voice her political opinions and follow the secessionist deliberations, and she finally got her wish in May 1861 when North Carolina seceded and joined the Confederacy.

Edmondston spent the entire war as a civilian and on the home front—a place widely considered separate from the ghastliness of the war front. From there, she and other elite women advocated for the Confederate cause, raised money, gathered supplies, and otherwise supported the war effort, presumably without risking physical harm. As the war progressed, though, she watched as the distance between the battlefield and home front narrowed. With battles frequently being fought in and near Southern towns and farms, many Confederate families faced Union soldiers who entered the home front. Rather than resolve the political issues that threatened her status as an elite slaveholder, the trajectory of the war began to threaten her directly.

Edmondston's awareness of her increasingly precarious situation resulted from her continued desire to gather news about the war. In her diary, she recorded details that included troop movements, battlefield news, and Confederate prospects. Some of these details corresponded with the fates of family members and neighbors, but many of them had to do with her interest in the Confederacy itself. As she read the news, Edmondston realized that the Union increasingly made war on elite women. When the Union imprisoned Rose O'Neal Greenhow and Eugenia Levy Phillips for espionage activities in July 1861, Edmondston decried their "vile treatment" at the hands of the enemy. She was outraged that elite women, of backgrounds similar to her own, could be treated so poorly.[4] She likewise condemned Benjamin Butler's 1862 Woman Order in New Orleans, which held that any woman who did not show respect to Union soldiers would be treated as a prostitute, as the result of "cold blooded barbarity."[5] In 1864, when Philip Sheridan's troops razed Virginia's Shenandoah Valley, she saw it as further evidence of the Yankee war on women. Sheridan's campaign outraged her because it had specifically targeted those who should have been safe in wartime but instead "the cries of houseless women & children alone mark his track."[6]

In November 1864, Edmondston began to watch the campaign that she would personally confront. Although she would have had no reason to think that William Tecumseh Sherman and the Union army would ultimately enter her town, she carefully followed their activities in Atlanta. She despised his "infamous" eviction of women and children from the city and considered it to be inhumane and uncivilized. After all, it explicitly violated the distinction between home front and war front by turning one into the other. She expected that this betrayal of the rules of war would galvanize Southern support for the Confederacy and guarantee "resistance to the death from every Southern man, woman, & child in the future."[7] She could not imagine an alternate scenario as she concluded that the eviction of Atlanta's women represented the continued attempt of the Union to bring the war directly to elite Confederate women. Edmondston, in particular, bemoaned the fate of "women & children, for it is on them that the magnanimous Yankee nation makes war."[8]

Although Catherine Edmondston and many other elite women considered the Civil War to be their war, generations of scholars neglected to include them as active participants in it. Scholars excluded women's participation in politics and the war effort from the conversation because they could neither vote nor serve in the military. In recent years, Catherine Clinton, Drew Gilpin Faust, and George Rable have led a generation of scholars to bring women out from the shadows in order to demonstrate their vital roles in the Confederate and Union war efforts. New works, as LeeAnn Whites and Alecia Long's *Occupied Women* demonstrates, show "women as direct players in the conduct and outcome of the war." Society may have officially restricted nineteenth-century women from politics and the battlefield, but as Whites and Long and other scholars have shown, Civil War women rarely remained on the margins. Instead, they found ways to take part in politics and other public aspects of life. Women did not sit on the sidelines or on pedestals, but instead they played an integral part in decisions during both peace and wartime.[9]

The slowness of the incorporation of women into Civil War scholarship may have partially resulted from the prevailing belief that the female home front and male war front were distinct entities. Nineteenth-century Americans certainly embraced this belief. Despite the home front destruction experienced in earlier American wars, nineteenth-century Americans clung to the assumption that wars took place on battlefields, far from the security of the feminine domestic sphere. Men willingly went off to battle to protect their wives, mothers, and sisters, and the glory earned on the battlefield became mythic on the home front. The death of loved ones, the most common consequence of war to affect women and children, became an honor instead of merely a hardship.[10] Similarly, antebellum Americans, especially those in the South, often considered it worse to experience the shame of a relative who avoided military service than the grief resulting from wartime casualties. At the same time, the violence and gore of war remained on the battlefront and did not often interrupt the peace of the domestic household. Women's increasing participation in the Confederate war effort and changes in Union military policies turned the idea of a separate home front on its head and redefined the nineteenth-century concept of warfare.[11]

From the very beginning of the war, Confederate women helped conflate some of the distinctions that traditionally separated home front and war front. Many slaveholding women embraced the idea that they were responsible for the morale of their new nation and that their households were essential to fighting the war. As their states seceded, prepared for war, and sent men off to fight the Yankees, many elite Southern women became involved in the business of the Confederate war effort. When the war continued into its fourth year, their developing identities as Confederate women and their confidence in their increasingly public roles in wartime grew stronger even as Union general William Tecumseh Sherman's troops approached their homes and farms in 1864 and 1865. Just as importantly, they recognized that they had become military targets and adapted themselves to deal with a campaign designed to attack their domestic and feminine worlds. Events leading up to the Georgia and Carolinas campaign clearly demonstrated that the Civil War had eased and erased most of the prohibitions that previously separated women and domestic life from the harshest realities of battle. Confederate women realized that their participation in the war as proponents of secession, suppliers of food and clothing, and defenders of the home front had allowed Union soldiers to see them as enemies in their own right. Confederate women, cognizant of the ways in which Sherman's troops treated their domestic enemies, readied for a battle of their own.

As the Civil War approached, the lives of elite Southern women became more focused around and circumscribed by the home. This transformation occurred with the rise of the middle class and the separation of the male workplace from the home as well as with the rise of an elite slaveholding community.[12] Ideas about domesticity and the ideals of "true womanhood"—which stressed piety, purity, and submissiveness—did not merely confine white women to the home and domestic chores, but also empowered them.[13] Many white women used assumptions about femininity in order to participate in an increasingly masculine public domain. They took on positions as teachers, writers, and reformers that played on public notions of "feminine" qualities.[14] In this manner, although not always in the public eye, white women engaged in public life.[15] In addition, the idea of separate spheres granted women, especially among Southern elite families, control over the domestic aspects of their lives. White women ran households and raised children as they saw fit. As the holders of the keys to all rooms, stores, pantries, and bureaus, slaveholding women controlled the domestic activities of their households. Those chores that they did not do themselves they directed others, especially domestic slaves, to do for them.[16]

The Civil War forced all Americans to reevaluate white women's visible place in society.[17] Politics consumed local communities, and the waging of the war required the active participation of households. White women also reshaped their roles as they dealt with wartime shortages and the deaths of loved ones. They became active participants in the battle for Southern nationhood and targets for enemy armies.[18] Because the enemy recognized them as "busy and responsive, in the face of an occupying military presence" and as participants instead of as harmless bystanders, Union soldiers dealt with Confederate women as active rebels and enemies.[19] This progression from civilian to female enemy grew out of the realities of life during the Civil War; Southern women could not avoid participation when soldiers fought battles in their backyards and when even the wealthiest families faced shortages. From the outset of the fighting Confederate women refused to accept a passive role, and they demonstrated their political awareness through their words and actions. As they personally encountered the hardships of wartime life, slaveholding women shouldered more active roles in the fight for independence.

As such, the Union increasingly engaged them as enemy combatants throughout the Civil War, using tactics specifically designed for feminine adversaries.

White Southern women's active participation in the public sphere predated the war. Many women initially drew attention to themselves as "rebels" and Confederates when they voiced their opinions on sectional issues and then on secession. Far from sheltered, politically ignorant ladies as they have often been portrayed, many Southern women paid close attention to the political events around them. As Elizabeth Varon and other historians have demonstrated, nineteenth-century women frequently engaged in the political discourse of the day.[20] They read the news and discussed it in depth with friends and family of both sexes. They also began keeping extensive journals in the 1850s and 1860s to record what they knew to be historic events.[21] Antebellum white women did not have access to ballots, so they voted with their actions. Women, who had entered the realm of politics in varying forms in previous years, used their influence and abilities to push the men of their families to act in the political realm during the sectional crisis. When the secession crisis came to a head in 1860, elite white Southern women had much to say on the issue. They especially paid close attention to the contentious presidential election facing the nation. For example, Georgian Dolly Lunt Burge assumed that the 1860 election "may be the last presidential Election Our United Country will ever see."[22]

White women around the South filled the galleries of secession debates, wore ribbons and other accessories to proclaim their loyalties, wrote editorials and letters in support of their positions, and otherwise demonstrated their political acumen in the 1850s and early 1860s. In these ways, white women engaged in and expanded the political sphere in order to actively participate in it. During the secession crisis, white women of all classes, who could not exert their influence or express their political opinions through voting, nevertheless acted in ways that clearly demonstrated their involvement in politics. South Carolinian Leora Sims rejoiced that she lived in the state capital because she could attend debates and listen to the speeches. Sims, who hoped that her friend Harriet Palmer's "southern blood is as fiery as mine," professed herself a "regular fire eater."[23] As self-proclaimed patriotic Southerners, many white women pushed their husbands toward secession after Lincoln won the 1860 presidential election. By appealing to their husbands' sense of familial duty and honor, elite Southern women encouraged men to echo their political sentiments and vote for secession.[24]

After Southern conventions voted for secession, many elite white women applauded their states' decisions to leave the Union. For example, as other states began to follow South Carolina's lead, Emma Holmes wrote that she was "doubly proud . . . of [her] native state, that she should be the first to arise and shake off the hated chain which linked us with Black Republicans and Abolitionists."[25] Holmes was not alone in her anti-Union sentiments. White women across the South longed to join South Carolina and break free from the United States. On January 3, 1861, Georgian Anna Maria Cook ardently hoped that her state would join South Carolina in secession.[26] When Georgia finally seceded, another elite woman rejoiced that "the very name of *Georgian* is of itself a heritage to boast of." She had "always been proud of my native state but never more so than now."[27] Slaveholding women around the South similarly applauded the ultimate secession of their states. Although the horrors of war would dampen some of these women's initial enthusiasm, many took an active and educated part in the movement to separate South from North. Mary Boykin Chesnut justified her support of secession as an outgrowth of her upbringing. Because her "father was a South Carolina Nullifier," she boasted that she "was of necessity a rebel born."[28] Elite white Southern women's political and historical knowledge gave them the confidence both to voice their opinions to the men of their family and to know that their husbands, fathers, and brothers would listen to these ideas.

Elite women's participation in the secession movement may have been restricted to words and symbolic acts, such as donating jewelry, but their roles in the public realm grew when men moved to the battlefield to exchange gunfire rather than insults. White women's early celebration of Confederate military success would ultimately lead to more concrete support of the Southern war effort. Drucilla Wray celebrated the Confederate capture of Fort Sumter after the first shots in what would become a lengthy war were fired: "Hurrah for Carolina!!! and her noble sons."[29] Once the hostilities began, white Southern women made themselves essential to the Confederate war effort by encouraging men to enlist. In this endeavor they drew upon the power of their femininity. Women taunted, cajoled, and shamed men into eventually joining the Confederate forces. They appealed to the manhood and honor of white Southern men and urged them to fill the ranks of the military because, as Mrs. Allen S. Izard of South Carolina asserted, "I sh[oul]d hate a *man* who w[oul]d flinch, even f[ro]m martyrdom for his Country."[30] Men who refused to enlist often found themselves snubbed by the ladies.[31] Published poems similarly demonstrated white women's dedication to the recruitment of soldiers for the Confederacy. One patriotic poem created a conversation in which a woman encouraged her sweetheart to enlist to prove his love to her: "If you love me, do not ponder, / . . . Join your country in the fray. . . . / Be her own and my defender— / Strike for freedom to the last."[32] Throughout the South, female Confederates increasingly lent their voices and persuasiveness in support of their nation's call for action.[33]

White women with family members on the front lines often had an urgency to their vehement support for the war against the North. Georgian mother of three Charlotte Branch wrote a poem to her sons urging them to fight:

> Strike for the mother that gave you birth
> Your native home and fires . . .
> Press hard the savage foe
> Nor pause until . . .
> Their treacherous flag lies low.[34]

Protecting Branch's "native home" ultimately demanded that she sacrifice two of her sons at the First Battle of Manassas in 1861. However, their deaths did not discourage her. She continued to write supportive letters to her only surviving son as he fought on against the "savage foe." She also continued to work for Southern independence.[35]

Slaveholding women's wartime involvement resulted from an intense patriotism, their recognition of the privileges afforded by slave labor, as well as a perceived difference between themselves and "Yankees." Early in the war, Confederate women recognized the pointed animosity of their Union foes. In response to white Southern women's assumptions about the enemy soldiers, rumors of exaggerated horrors spread throughout the region. "Every day," South Carolinian Emma Holmes wrote, "brings fresh accounts of the demoniac fury & hatred of the Northerners toward the Southerners & South Carolinians especially." The grossly exaggerated rumors held that "men even suspected of sympathy with the South are murdered in cold blood."[36] Nothing seemed too horrible to attribute to Northerners, especially since many Southerners increasingly saw themselves as racially, ideologically, and culturally separate from their wartime enemies. Southern women considered Union soldiers "Sumner-like reptiles of the North" and celebrated the political separation of North and South. These staunch female Confederates wanted no connection with the "miserable fanatic set" of Yankees.[37] As the war lengthened, and battle tactics changed to what many white Southern women understood as uncivilized, their sense of difference from Northerners and their celebration of Southern independence grew stronger.

The progression of Union tactics from an early wartime focus on the battlefield to direct assaults on Confederate civilians led Southerners increasingly to view Northern soldiers as "demons."[38] The enemy presence in militarily occupied areas could be tolerated as the consequences of war, but Southern women frequently complained that Union soldiers took things too far.[39] When, in 1861, the Union imprisoned a group of Southern women and their young daughters in Washington, D.C., men and women across the Confederate states voiced their outrage.[40] In November 1861, Rose O'Neal Greenhow, a Confederate spy and one of the arrested women, proclaimed in the *Richmond Whig* that Union actions illuminated "the cruel and dastardly tyranny which the Yankee government has established at Washington." Greenhow played upon nineteenth-century ideas about gender as she expressed her hope that "the incarceration and torture of helpless women, and the outrages heaped upon them . . . will shock manly natures and stamp the Lincoln dynasty everywhere with undying infamy." Enraged by their arrest, but confident of their place in history, the women in custody saw themselves as female martyrs to the Confederate cause. Greenhow recorded her story because she believed that her "sufferings [would] afford a significant lesson to the women of the South, that sex or condition is no bulwark against the surging billows of the 'irrepressible conflict.'"[41] Similarly, as she prepared for her internment, Eugenia Yates Levy Phillips wrote, "This day has ushered in a new era in the History of the Country, one which marks the arrest and imprisonment of women, for political opinions!" The women's bravery and sacrifice became clearer, she continued, as they "prepared with courageous hearts, inspired with the thought that we were suffering in a noble cause, and determined so to bear ourselves, as not to shame our southern countrywomen."[42] Both Greenhow's and Phillips's words demonstrate that despite their actions, these women assumed that their sex placed them beyond the scope of punishment. They ascribed to the belief that women should always be protected. The imprisoned women proclaimed that Union actions crossed gender boundaries. They subsequently played upon their imprisonment to inflame further Southern patriotism and demonstrate the necessity of war and total separation from the North.

Elite women in Georgia and the Carolinas confirmed Greenhow's and Phillips's assessment of female imprisonment and rallied against what they saw as Federal tyranny. For Mary Boykin Chesnut, wife of South Carolina Confederate senator James Chesnut, the incident demonstrated the inhumanity of Union soldiers. In her estimation, Northern men had unfairly singled out white Southern women as easy prey, because "*these* times make all women feel their humiliation in the affairs of the world." Their wartime vulnerability resulted from the fact that "women can only stay at home, and every paper reminds us that women are to be violated, ravished, and all manner of humiliation."[43] Chesnut recognized that women could be attacked in many ways—they could be "ravished," even without physical rape. Accustomed to protection as a result of their femininity and white privilege, slaveholding women across the Confederacy realized that the change in military tactics increased their likelihood of being personally threatened in some way. With their husbands, brothers, sons, and fathers at the battlefront, these women would have to protect their purity through their own ingenuity. As the war progressed, they found more reasons to fear for their safety as well as new ways to protect themselves and their nation.

The imprisonment of Southern women in 1861 foreshadowed the breaking of gender boundaries in the future. In May 1862, reports of Major General Benjamin Butler's actions in occupied New Orleans further excited Confederate tempers. After the women of the city repeatedly avoided and attacked the Union soldiers there, Butler issued his infamous General Order 28. Butler's attempt to subdue and control the Confederate women in New Orleans, the "Woman Order" laid out the situation and the punishment: "As the officers and soldiers of the United States have been subject to repeated insults from the women (calling themselves ladies) of New Orleans . . . it is ordered that hereafter when any female shall, by word, gesture, or movement, insult or show contempt for any officer or soldier of the United States, she shall be regarded and held liable to be treated as a woman of the town plying her avocation."[44] News of the order spread quickly across the South, where it was met with shock and disapproval. White women and men denounced it. Confederates viewed "Beast" Butler's improper discussion of and treatment of white women as both unforgivable and inexcusable. Even during wartime, elite women expected that men, including the enemy, would treat them with respect and protect them.[45] From South Carolina, Mary Boykin Chesnut condemned Butler for "turning over the women of New Orleans to his soldiers!" She was appalled that "this hideous cross-eyed beast orders his men to treat the ladies of New Orleans as women of the town. To punish them, he says, for their insolence."[46] Butler's unforgivable actions, she later wrote, were surprisingly uncivilized, even for a Yankee. "We hardly expected from Massachusetts behavior to shame a Comanche."[47]

After reading Butler's order, North Carolinian Catherine Edmondston similarly decried his actions. Although she claimed that she could not "find words to express [her] horror and indignation," Edmondston adamantly denounced Butler, and, by association, all Northerners for their "cold blooded barbarity." Butler's actions were so horrible, she raged, that "we no longer will hold any intercourse with you, ye puritanical, deceitful race, ye descendants of the Pilgrims, of the hypocrites who came over in the Mayflower." She saw hypocrisy in Butler's actions. Although Northerners might claim "*piety*" and "civilization" and their "fancied superiority," Edmondston saw their actions as the opposite. As a result, Edmondston insisted that "we are none of you, desire naught from you. We detest you!"[48] The "Woman Order" similarly provoked Georgian Gertrude Thomas to denounce Butler as someone whose name "will be branded with the reputation of being the most vile loathsome of all God's creation." Acknowledging what she saw as an unprovoked and sexualized attack on Southern ladies, she also remarked on the insulting order's galvanizing effect on Confederate soldiers. "Had our brave men required an additional incentive for valour they have it furnished in the appeal to protect the honour of their women."⁴⁹ For those women who would later confront Sherman, Butler's order had already proven the barbarity of Union tactics and the levels to which Union soldiers would sink.

Thomas's hope that the order would encourage Southern men to continue their fight against the Union mirrored the words of prominent Confederate officials. Commanders insightfully played upon the honor of white Southern manhood and the sexualized tone of the order to provoke further anger and to unite the Confederacy against a common enemy. Confederate general P. G. T. Beauregard, for example, called upon the "men of the South" to retaliate: "Shall our mothers, our wives, our daughters, and our sisters be thus outraged by the ruffianly soldiers of the North, to whom is given the right to treat at their pleasure the ladies of the South as common harlots?" He encouraged the men of the South to "drive back . . . those infamous invaders of our homes and disturbers of our family ties."⁵⁰ Similarly, Louisiana governor Thomas O. Moore proclaimed that "the annals of warfare between civilized nations afford no . . . instance of infamy" similar to Butler's "Woman Order." He hoped that the unforgivable order would steel the men of Louisiana to drive the Northern troops out of the state. Proclaiming "to the world that the exhibition of any disgust or repulsiveness by the women of New Orleans to the hated invaders of their home and the slayers of their fathers, brothers, and husbands shall constitute a justification to a brutal soldiery of the indulgence of their lust," Moore justified women's actions and called for Confederate men to support them. Butler's order, he continued, could not end female defiance in New Orleans because "contempt and abhorrence" were natural reactions to Federal officers and soldiers. Further, "the spontaneous impulse of their hearts must appear involuntary upon their countenances and thus constitute the crime for which the general of those soldiers adjudges the punishment of rape and brutalized passion." Moore called upon all Louisianians to fight for their women. They "must arm and strike, or the insolent victors will offer this outrage to your wives, your sisters, and your daughters." Southern soldiers were not only defending their homes, but they had to protect "the jewel of your hearths—the chastity of your women." Moore, like others around the Confederacy, played upon the fear of Union rape of white women to spur all of the men of the South to action.⁵¹ Confederates so reviled Butler for his treatment of Southern ladies that there was a price put upon his head.

In 1864, Union policy shifted to one directly aimed at the Confederate home front and its female civilian population as enemies of war. In September, United States general Ulysses S. Grant ordered General Philip H. Sheridan to "do all the damage . . . you can" to turn "the Shenandoah Valley [into] a barren waste."[52] In addition, Grant hoped that the soldiers on this campaign would "eat out Virginia clear and clean as far as they go, so that crows flying over it for the balance of this season will have to carry their provender with them."[53] Sheridan and his men took these orders to heart, seizing or destroying all flour, grains, and livestock as well as burning civilians out of their homes. While carrying out these orders, few soldiers sympathized with the plight of enemy women. "I do not believe war to be simply that lines should engage each other in battle, and therefore do not regret the system of living on the enemy's country," Sheridan remarked. After all, he continued, elite Southern "women did not care how many were killed, or maimed, so long as war did not come to their doors, but as soon as it did come in the shape of loss of property, they earnestly prayed for its termination." Sheridan pointed directly to Confederate women as military enemies when justifying his advance on the home front. "As war is a punishment, if we can, by reducing its advocates to poverty, end it quicker, we are on the side of humanity."[54] Like Sherman, Sheridan believed in the utility of bringing war to the Confederate home front and the slaveholding women who occupied it. Hoping to bring the war to an end, both men denied slaveholding women their protected status and instead engaged them as enemies in their own right. This method of "domestic war" guided Union actions throughout the South beginning in 1864.[55]

The Union's tactical shift to direct attacks on the Confederate home front brought elite women, who clearly recognized their new situation, to center stage of the Civil War. No longer protected by their gender, their class, or the presence of their men, these slaveholding women learned to adapt to battle-like conditions. Forced to prepare to engage the enemy face to face, slaveholding women became active participants on the war front. Southern women in Georgia and the Carolinas had paid close attention to the progression of Union tactics as they changed in Washington, D.C., New Orleans, and Virginia. Their awareness of what was happening across the Confederacy, especially in the Shenandoah Valley, led elite Southern women to understand the Union's crossing of gender boundaries. Consequently, many slaveholding women had learned what to expect from Union soldiers by the time Sherman's troops began their campaign in Georgia and the Carolinas even though the women still hoped that they were wrong. This knowledge allowed Confederate women to prepare for a direct assault on Southern domesticity and domestic space in Georgia and the Carolinas, even if they still assumed themselves somewhat protected from the onslaught of enemy soldiers.[56]

Catherine Edmondston recognized the implications of Union intentions in Virginia and other campaigns, and she despised the new tactics. In her opinion, Grant's order "for barbarity, equals anything yet done in this most barbarous of all wars." His directive "'to leave the [Shenandoah] Valley such a waste that next year a crow flying across will have to carry his own rations with him'" appalled her. Edmondston's initial disbelief of Grant's "barbarous" orders changed as she observed the policy in action. She continued her journal entry with horror. "His Lieutenants are carrying it out to the letter!" She recorded reports that Sheridan's men had destroyed farming tools and burned countless mills and barns, as well as "wheat, oats, & corn enough to maintain Early for three months." To add to the damages, Sheridan's men ate thousands of Southern sheep and had "driven off stock & horses in such quantity that there has been as yet no account taken of them!"[57] Apparently the men were carrying out to the letter the order to make sure that the valley was "laid entirely waste, everything which can support life to be destroyed and all the stock of any kind to be driven off or killed."[58]

As she reflected on Union activities across the South, Edmondston understood the extensive implications of Grant's domestically destructive policy. In her mind, Union actions against white Southern women demonstrated the despicable nature of Northern commanders. She declared Sheridan "a monster!" whose actions confirmed him as a "fit associate for Butler and Sherman!" and "a disgrace to humanity!" She was shocked that "such conduct is tolerated by a nation who *calls itself Christian!*"[59] Edmondston's fury at Sheridan's attack on domesticity clearly comes across in her journal. In the Shenandoah Valley Sheridan "destroyed everything before him. Blood & carnage, smoking ruins, the cries of houseless women & children alone mark his track."[60] Sheridan's destruction of civilian property, especially the homes, took the Civil War to a new level. However, in the eyes of elite Confederate women the loss of property paled in comparison to the Union disregard for gender boundaries. The attack on civilian women was the most troubling aspect of the new warfare for all Southerners, including Edmondston.[61] As she paid close attention to reports of Sheridan's destructive path through the Shenandoah Valley as well as that of Sherman's actions in the Deep South, Edmondston mentally prepared herself for attack. Sherman's men would later head toward Edmondston's plantation, but by that point she thought she knew what to expect from the "monster."

Despite the news out of the Shenandoah Valley, white women in Atlanta, the first to face Sherman's new "domestic war" campaign, underestimated what was in store for them. Although women in Georgia and the Carolinas understood from previous Union actions that they would not be ignored or protected as civilians, they did not anticipate Sherman's tactics. As a result, the forced eviction of women and children from the captured and occupied city shocked those who encountered it. Not only did they consider Sherman's orders inhumane, but they also objected to the timing. From Ravenswood, Georgia, one woman denounced the September evacuation of Atlanta. She considered it "dreadful for women and children to be turned out of doors homeless," and she saw the expulsion as particularly harsh because it occurred at the start of winter. She stressed that in the "darkened annals of history" there were no others who, like the Union, "wage[d] war upon helpless women and children."[62] For Gertrude Thomas, Sherman's evacuation of Atlanta demonstrated her own precarious situation. Although she had originally assumed that she would stay in Augusta if the Yankees captured the town, "the exiles of Atlanta has taught me that a different destiny awaits me if Sherman reaches here." And Thomas "firmly believe[d]" that the arrival of Sherman's troops in Augusta was *only a matter of time.*"[63]

Catherine Edmondston despised the conduct of the Union Army in Atlanta. She condemned Sherman's evacuation order as "so infamous that a Russian example must be sought if we would find a paral[l]el amongs[t] civilized nations." She fumed that "he finds it for the interest of the U S that *every inhabitant* should be banished from Atlanta & its vicinity." Instead of its subduing the Confederates, Edmondston expected Sherman's forced evacuation of Atlanta to strengthen the Southern cause, just as it had her personal patriotism. In her mind, Sherman could only expect "resistance to the death" from his enemies.[64] Many of her fellow

Confederates shared Edmondston's shock and disdain at the eviction of Atlanta's civilians. Until this point in the Civil War, armies had rarely officially ordered residents out of the cities that they occupied.[65] This departure from military precedent emphasized to many white women the lengths to which the Union would go to win the war and further demonstrated the differences between the two regions.

Sherman recognized the disgust of Southerners across the Confederacy in response to his evacuation of the fallen city, and he gloried in the reaction. "The people of the South have made a big howl at my moving the families of Atlanta."[66] However, the Southern reaction did not soften him to the plight of Confederate women and children. Sherman responded to complaints from the Atlanta city council showing no sympathy for those who faced the brunt of his orders. Instead he blamed the Confederates for bringing war to the domestic sphere. He justified his actions by referencing "the vindictive nature of our enemy."[67] Sherman's assessment of Atlanta's civilian population, including its women, as a powerful enemy heralded things to come. No longer could the privileges of race and gender keep elite female civilians out of the direct path of war, but they instead made these women targets. Slaveholding women in Georgia and the Carolinas learned from the Atlanta experience and increasingly prepared themselves for the worst as the troops approached. Sherman's activities in Georgia combined with previous Union actions toward Southern women gave Confederate women a clear understanding of Union intentions toward them as enemies. These female civilians subsequently readied themselves as best they could for the horrors of a gendered battle.

After watching Union attacks on civilians increase in intensity, Confederate women tried to prepare themselves for a direct assault on domesticity. As Sherman and his troops moved across Georgia in the autumn of 1864, slaveholding women recognized the danger of their position as female civilians. The presumed weakness of the female sex became a constantly discussed topic as Confederate women realized that they were left to defend themselves against an enemy who seemed to acknowledge few boundaries. However, this knowledge did not discourage them. In a letter to her husband, one Georgia woman explained, "we were all a set of helpless females without a man even to go to for advice." Instead of letting their situation become a liability, these women "had to think

& act for ourselves & we had no time to be afraid."[68] Elite women took up the challenge of fending for themselves and worked to protect their homes and families. Another Georgian, Loula Kendall Rogers, similarly acknowledged the path of destruction sure to follow Sherman's capture of Atlanta and the precarious position of female civilians. They were "very much troubled about what to do if the Yankees should get any nearer," especially after hearing of Atlanta's fate. When considering her own options, Rogers recognized both her power and powerlessness in the situation: "I do so dread to leave the beloved home of my childhood, to be plundered and burnt by the hated race." Although she felt a sense of personal danger as a woman in the path of Union soldiers, she also realized that her presence might protect her and her family's property and prevent enemy soldiers from burning and raiding her home.[69]

Knowledge of Atlanta's capture and Union military power did not guarantee that elite women would surrender to their fears by leaving their homes or submitting to Northern troops. Many elite women refused to give in to the dreaded enemy at any cost. After the fall of Atlanta, Minerva McClatchey recorded that "the Federals . . . say that we must go." However, the enemy's demands had little effect on McClatchey, who, true to her war-like name, "told them I should not leave my house while there was a roof over my head unless Genl Sherman 'ordered me personally and preemptorily to do so.'" She remained adamant, declaring, "This is my home[.] I have a right to stay at it[.] God has given me that right." She further stressed the inhumane and uncivilized warfare pursued by the Union: "If Genl Sherman chooses to order me away, I shall obey—that is his lookout—not mine."[70] Warfare, she assumed, should never preclude the proper treatment of elite white women. McClatchey was not alone in this belief. As she worried about a Union attack on her home in Augusta, Catherine Rowland harshly denounced Sherman's actions. The destruction of feminine civilian property, she asserted was "stronger evidence than ever of the vile, mean, treacherous, black hearts of our enemies" who showed no shame as they "destroy women's wardrobes and . . . tear their clothes to pieces."[71] These men had gone far beyond the confines of "civilized warfare," at least as nineteenth-century white Southern women conceived of it. Although thousands of women fled their homes in favor of other places, many, like Rogers, understood the protection that their presence gave to their homes. After Union troops had marched through Georgia and South Carolina, Mary Maxcy Leverett noted that "they burned every house that no one was in on every road leading from Columbia toward N. Carolina."[72]

The expectation of a Union attack haunted many Southern women after Atlanta's fall; they feared not only for their own safety but also for that of their families. One Athens, Georgia, woman's recurrent dream in October was "that the Yankees had come here again and . . . that they took father pris[o]ner." She was "very glad it was only a dream & hope it will never happen."[73] Widespread uncertainty of Sherman's intended path combined with rumors and knowledge of the destruction and terror his troops brought understandably rattled many Confederate women.[74]

In preparation for Union attacks, slaveholding women worked to get their valuables out of the projected path of enemy soldiers. They knew that if Sherman's troops arrived in their towns, the enemy men would likely burn their homes and ransack their possessions. In November 1864, M. A. Lark asked her mother to take care of her treasures. She was "fearful" that the Yankees would come to Augusta and destroy her belongings. "If their is any danger of them coming there . . . please go down and get my best things . . . get all you can."[75] Other elite women who believed they lay in Sherman's path also worked to protect their property. Some buried their clothes with more valuable items such as silver and jewelry.[76] Not only did they want to protect their possessions for their own use and survival, but they also saw the Northern soldiers as undeserving of such treasures.[77]

Southern white women's fears for the safety of their domestic possessions extended not only to those of monetary value but also to those of sentimental worth. Consequently, they looked for ways to conceal their letters and diaries. In Georgia, Loula Kendall Rogers feared the loss of her journals, which would allow the enemy to get a glimpse of her sacred inner thoughts. If they seized her journals, she asserted, she wanted them to know her "honest sentiments toward Yankees." Any soldier who intruded on her domesticity and read her private thoughts would be treated to Rogers's fiery opinions. "If this book should ever fall in their hands," she wrote in November 1864, "I want them to know that *I hate, loathe and abhor the very scent, sight & name* of a *Yankee* with all my *heart, soul, mind, and body.*" Rogers further asserted that these were no shallow boasts of patriotism but that "this assertion I would stick to if they were to point a thousand bayonets at me at once."[78] In North Carolina, Catherine Edmondston dreaded the idea of having her innermost thoughts revealed to the enemy. "And now, old friend, you my Journal, for a time good bye! You are too bulky to be kept out, exposed to prying Yankee eyes and theivish Yankee fingers." To prevent her story from being exposed, her journal would "go for a season to darkness & solitude." She continued to record her thoughts, but it would "henceforth be kept on scraps of paper, backs of letters, or old memorandum books which I can secrete." Edmondston knew that the "bumming officers would seize upon the 'Journal of a Secesh Lady—a complete record of a daily life spent in the Southern Confederacy from July 1860 to April 65'" and enjoy thumbing through it. If they discovered her journal, she knew she would feel horrible seeing her private thoughts "thus dragged from the recesses of private life & for aught I know published for the amusement of a censorious, curious, and critical public."[79]

Other Confederate women had similar concerns for the fate of their correspondence. One Georgia woman worried about the approach of Union troops in early 1865 and about what to do with her letters. Although she would "hate to burn them," she "would not have them [Yankees] get hold of some of them for the whole Confederacy."[80] At least if she destroyed the letters herself, the enemy would not get to read these personal missives. Similarly, days before Sherman's troops arrived in Columbia, South Carolina, Emma LeConte "destroyed most of my papers but have a lot of letters still that I do not wish to burn." She knew she would have to do something soon, however, because she did "not care to have them share the fate" of those of her kinswomen in Liberty County "which men read and scattered along the roads." To avoid this, LeConte resolved to "try to hide them."[81] By concealing their journals and letters, elite Southern women hoped to find protection for their private records of Confederate domestic life. White Southern women's fears of the consequences of allowing their diaries and letters to get into enemy hands proved to be justified. Along the path of Sherman's March Union soldiers scattered women's letters across the landscape and even sent them north for the amusement of family members and for publication in newspapers.

Knowledge of destructive Union practices did not paralyze Confederate women with fear as Sherman and his men had hoped. Instead, many prepared to defend their homes and families as best they could. Using whatever means available, slaveholding women determined to prevent the Northern army from desolating the Southern home front and terrorizing civilians. As Sherman and his troops neared the coast of Georgia late in 1864, a group of white women in Savannah banded together to protect their city. Left to their fate by departing Confederate soldiers, these women refused to give up and instead took matters into their own hands by creating their own military regiment, the "Lawton Protectors." Savannah, left without sufficient military defenses, was "about to be invaded by the Ruthless hoards of the North." This group of women refused to stand by quietly as Yankees destroyed their homeland. Without enough white men to protect them, they resolved to do whatever it took to avert their destruction. They clearly laid out their plan as well as their motivations for undertaking such an unusual action. They "determined like the Spartan women of old, to form our-selves into a military coraps [i.e. corps] and to die upon our thresh holds, Rather than yeald to the damned invaders one inch of Georgia's soil." To protect themselves and their homes, they offered officials "our services and demand arms." In this declaration, these Savannah women illuminated their hatred for the enemy and willingness to die, like men, for their nation. Like "the Spartan women of old," they would bravely take up arms against the enemy. Faced with the reality of a direct assault by troops, this group of women stepped outside of antebellum gender conventions to respond to Sherman's attack on domesticity. Left to fend for themselves, they rallied and created their own military defense for their homes and families. The creation of the Lawton Protectors exemplifies Confederate women's willingness to take extreme measures against the war on the Southern home front.[82] Another Confederate woman asserted that Augusta's women should be armed to defend their homes since the men were not there to do so. "Let each one put her mark on one at least of the foe, as they put their brutal feet on our streets or with doors defended by faithful servants, from the windows make her feeble arm felt."[83]

After reading voluminous reports of Union destruction in Georgia, South Carolina's elite women anticipated and prepared to face the brunt of Union fury. Through letters, newspapers, and word of mouth, white women closely followed reports of Sherman's troops' burning and evacuation of Atlanta as well as their subsequent march through Georgia.

Made anxious by the news of the soldiers' destruction of homes and personal property in Georgia, and fearful of personal attacks, women in the Carolinas prepared for a direct assault as best they could. Many women correctly assumed that Sherman and his troops would head to South Carolina from Georgia to attack the first state to secede. Fearing that she would no longer be protected by virtue of her sex or race, Eliza Josephine Trescot acknowledged, "I fully appreciate the danger that threatens us; and at this time, I think the feeling of safety would be the sweetest in the world. My heart sickens at the thought of the Yankees." Furthermore, her confinement to the home front because of her sex made the situation all the more frustrating. She did not want to believe the rumors, but understood that "the expectation of all the humiliations and insults and barbarities that have been heaped upon the unfortunate women, in the power of the Yankees seems too dreadful ever to be realized, yet we have no reason to believe ourselves more worthy of being exempted from these calamities than others."[84] As early as September 1864, Trescot suspected not only that her state would not escape Union destruction but also that, as the "seedbed of secession," South Carolina would face the brunt of Union vengeance. Confident that she would face the fury of Northern soldiers, but not exactly sure how far the enemy men would go in their treatment of women, Trescot prepared for the worst. After Savannah's capture, Pauline DeCaradeuc felt similarly. She confidently wrote, "it can't be long now ere our state is overrun by the enemy."[85] Another South Carolina woman revealed her concerns to her aunt in January. "We have already been told what treatment we are to expect at his hands, even worse than Georgia, No mercy is to be showed us at all."[86] Confederate women accurately predicted that if Sherman and his troops headed to the Palmetto State, they would feel the fury of the enemy.

Female South Carolinians also realized that the Union soldiers specifically aimed their campaign at elite white women and the trappings of domesticity. In January 1865, as Sherman feinted to Charleston, one woman feared that if they stayed at home "a parish of helpless women all alone," she would face "the cruelties, and insults of lawless raiding parties." Despite these fears, "we have all determined to remain where we are for the present and if it must be so that our dear City shall fall, then we will all go there and meet our fate." This decision, she insisted, "is not the hasty conclusion of a few, but nearly every one... in our neighbourhood." This group of women would willingly remain in the path of danger to show their loyalty to the Confederacy. During wartime, she explained, "we all have to make sacrifices, the time is near at hand, when we too, are to suffer as our sister States have done."[87] Although she knew from newspapers and letters that women had faced the brunt of Sherman's destruction in Georgia, this Confederate patriot readied herself to confront Union troops.

Other elite South Carolina women acknowledged their vulnerability on the home front and their continued confidence in their nation. Playing upon her assumed feminine weakness, Louisa Pearce recognized that "we poor females must await the issue be what it may." She feared that the "State will be overrun by these Vandals who have no limit to their depredations, their outrages and insults." From Melrose, she noted that the civilians "[were] left, a community of females, of old men and children—to be invaded by those hateful Yankees, and not a soldier to raise an arm to defend us!" Despite this, she reassured her friend that there was no "fear or panic among us." Instead, they continued to support the Confederacy and bear their hardships: "Every face is as quiet and every duty as energetically performed, as though there was not a Yankee in a thousand miles of us." None of the residents had evacuated in the face of invasion, but instead the "country is filled with refugees from the lower part of the state." Pearce asserted "there is a cheerfulness that can only belong to a people who have confidence in the protection of God to our just cause, and to the bravery of a people who will *never* submit to *Yankee* dominion." As for herself, she "would rather be a subject [of] England, of France—even of *Russia,* than a *free* (?) citizen of *their* vile government!"[88]

Elite South Carolina women embraced an increasingly vehement form of Confederate patriotism as they anticipated Sherman's invasion, confident that the general and his men wanted vengeance on the cradle of secession. Many commented fearlessly on the inevitable destruction and horrors fated for their state. After Sherman had captured Savannah, Kate Crosland, like many of her neighbors, expected that Sherman would head his troops into South Carolina once he finished with Georgia. He would then punish the Carolina home front. "Know that while the great Sherman sits on what he imagines is the dead carcass of Georgia, he vows to spare no age, sex or condition in this noted rebel state where first we breathed the pure free air and saw the sweet light of heaven." She knew that "it is here their malice will rage fiercest." She continued her rant against the enemy, painting Sherman and his troops as devils. "[Will] not Satan laugh and hurry back to his brimstone quarters to tell what great and wondrous things he has learned from the Yankees? and the fiends will dance after him in high glee." Crosland still believed Savannah would find a way to defeat the invaders. "Surely Georgia is not dead she must hear the mama's cry of her fair daughters driven to a mad house by brutal outrage and she *will* drive the insolent foe from her soil or perish *all* in the conflict."[89] Crosland could not believe that the people of Savannah would give up the fight for their state and the Confederacy. As a proud South Carolinian and Confederate, she could not imagine giving up on her nation or her state. Crosland, like many of her countrywomen, condemned Northern behavior and prepared to withstand the Union attack. Unlike the men of Savannah, who fled before the Union threat, these women refused to surrender to the Union or its "uncivilized" tactics.

Other female South Carolinians lacked confidence in Georgia's ability to drive out the invader and feverishly prepared for what they perceived to be Sherman's inevitable arrival. The invasion, which had earlier in the war seemed unthinkable, became something expected by all. S. C. Goodwyn revealed her fears to her husband. The implications of the "dreadful news" of Savannah's capture worried her. She assumed that the enemy would head to South Carolina and that "if Sherman gets on this soil the outrages in Georgia will be nothing to what they will do here."[90] Others saw more clearly the consequences of the loss of Savannah, especially without a fight. "With the fall of Savannah," Grace Brown Elmore realized, "all our hopes of escape from the horrors of war have vanished, we feel almost as sure of Sherman's reaching Columbia before long as if he were already here." Consequently, "every one is preparing for his reception, all valuables are being removed or hidden." As she readied for the Union raiders, Elmore emphasized what she assumed were Sherman's intentions toward South Carolina. Sherman, according to one account, told a woman that "hitherto I have endeavored to restrain my men, but when I pass to Carolina my orders shall be every man for himself."[91] Recognition of these intentions did not dissuade Elmore from her staunch loyalty to the Confederacy. She and other white South Carolinians had no illusions about the Union troops' desire for vengeance: "Oh the terrible wrath that is to be expended on us. We are Carolinians that is our crime, what will be our doom."[92] Despite her certainty of the horrors that would arrive with Union troops, Elmore remained at home.[93] Knowledge of Union retaliation for secession did not surprise or discourage Confederate women. It instead emboldened them to fight to protect their country and their families.

In addition, Sherman's approach did not keep many slaveholding women from expressing an undaunted loyalty for Confederate South Carolina and the expectation that their state would behave honorably in the face of the enemy. More than fear or femininity, honor and patriotism governed Confederate women's responses to the imminent arrival of Union soldiers. Mary Gayle Aiken recognized "that the Yankees will not show much mercy to S. Carolinians," but she refused to abandon her nation or her home.[94] In her wartime diary, Emma Holmes explicitly asserted her allegiance to her nation, its tenets of honor, and her pride in her state. Disdaining Savannah's surrender to Sherman, she expected better from South Carolina. "I trust Charleston will become one grand sacrificial altar & funeral pyre before her soil is polluted by Yankee tread," Holmes exclaimed. Furthermore, "I shall blush for Charleston, were it left standing." Instead, "Every spire & housetop should lift its flaming finger to Heaven in supplication to its high tribunal, as well as to proclaim to the world that death is preferable to dishonor."[95]

Other slaveholding women agreed and also condemned Savannah's surrender. Writing to her aunt, South Carolinian Sarah Tennent lambasted Savannah for her weakness. "Has not the conduct of Savannah been most disgraceful, and shameful?" Tennent refused to believe that the same dishonorable fate might befall her state. She expressed her "hope and trust that Charleston may not follow her example." After all, it would be "humiliating for Charleston the hot bed of Secession, the first to take up arms in defense of her rights . . . to go quietly back into the detested Union." She did not believe that this would come to pass. "Savannah might but Charleston never." Even before she personally confronted Sherman's troops, Tennent could not reconcile the sacrifices of war with the possibility of defeat and reunion. She assumed that the Confederacy could never go "quietly and submissively back into the Union; after so much blood shed." She could not envision reunion because of the "thousands of precious lives that have been laid willing sacrifices on their Country's altar, the many desolated homes, the sufferings, hardships, and privations we have all undergone for our Country's cause." In particular, Tennent stressed "the horrible manner in which we have ever been treated by our diabolical foe" as reason why the two warring countries could never again be one. As she put it, "the thought is too humiliating it cannot be so.["][96]

Confederate women in Georgia and the Carolinas did not confine their expressions of patriotism to private correspondence or journals. Some also expressed their patriotism and reiterated their expectation of protection to their government officials. In December 1864, one South Carolina woman wrote to Confederate president Jefferson Davis expressing her concerns about the impending advance of Sherman's troops toward her home state. She acknowledged that everyone in the state was "very anxious respecting Sherman's advance," because, "should he get into S[outh] Carolina our fate will be most deplorable." Like other South Carolinians, this woman understood that the Union military would show no compassion for the residents in the "seedbed of secession." She especially feared Sherman's troops because of her vulnerability as a woman. "[Sherman] has treated the ladies of Geo. most shamefully[,] and if possible will treat us worse in Carolina." Despite the costs, this woman and others like her proclaimed that they could "bear up under it all could we only have a hope that Sherman will be stopped in his wicked course." She made one last plea to Davis on behalf of her patriotism. "I therefore hope you will do for us what you can in this sad dilemma and stop the advance of our vile enemy. In behalf of my native State I entreat you to think of us."[97] Confederate women's loyalty, she assumed, should assure them the respect and protection of their nation. Despite fears for her personal safety, she continued to support her nation and expected it to support her.

In January 1865, a group of Charleston women publicized their Confederate loyalty in a letter to the *Mercury*. In this public format, they disdained rumors that the city would be given up to the enemy after four years of fighting. "We have listened with grief and horror inexpressible to the hints of abandoning to our foes, without a struggle." Although they knew the human costs, these women used their privilege and gendered position to urge the leaders of Charleston to "fight for every inch, and if our men must die, let them die amid the blazing ruins of our homes; their souls rising upwards on the flames which save our city from the pollution of our enemy." The dishonor of surrender, they asserted, was not an option. Instead, "if Charleston, defended to the hour, must . . . fall, let the Governor and her homes—to sound of the guns of our forts, as they send out their last defiance to the baffled foe."[98]

The realization that Confederate soldiers could do little to protect women from Union soldiers fostered a dread of sexual assault across the Southern home front. Slaveholding women understood that Union soldiers used tactics specifically designed to outrage female enemies, and many feared that they would be singled out for the greatest of all outrages. Some Confederate women worried that they would become targets for Union attacks in part because their sex made them especially vulnerable. Catherine Edmondston hoped that there would be some salvation for "women & children" because she understood that "it is on them that the magnanimous Yankee nation makes war."[99] In the opening months of the Civil War many would have scoffed at the possibility of white soldiers raping white women. However, by the time Sherman's troops reached South Carolina in 1865 elite Southern women believed the enemy troops capable of anything. After all, the escalation in tactics had shown that Union soldiers often ignored gender conventions in favor of a full attack on the domestic enemy and rumors of rape circulated. The line of acceptable behavior was, at best, unclear. As Grace Brown Elmore bemoaned, "Have not this people taught us how impotent is the weakness and helplessness of women, have they not made us know that upon us will they wreak their vengeance by the most frightful and wicked of crimes." Elmore especially pointed to the actions of the men who had clearly violated gender boundaries in their campaigns. "Have not their Butlers, their Rosecranz[es], their Burnsides and their Shermans appeared but as arch fiends." These men, Elmore lamented, eagerly "let loose upon us the all passions & wickedness of man. Oh well they know how to avenge themselves, on women, what she values more than all things, the loss of which would be living death."[100] Elmore feared that the escalating war against white Southern women would eventually result in the worst attack of all—rape.

Other elite Southern women remained confident that Union soldiers would not completely disregard gender norms and saw their sexuality as a weapon of resistance. They consequently prepared to hide valuables on their person, hopeful that the crossing of gender boundaries by Union soldiers would not extend to disrespect for women's bodies. These Confederates believed that Union men would respect the sanctity of Southern womanhood and made plans to take advantage of it. In her journal, Emma LeConte noted that she was "hastily making large pockets to wear under my hoop skirt—for they will hardly search our persons."[101] Another woman revealed like precautions in a letter to her husband. "I woke the children and put on them two suits of underclothing and their dresses and wore the same quantity myself."[102] In addition, as Union soldiers approached, some women slept in their clothes to protect both their property and their virtue.[103] Although Confederate women understood the destruction Sherman's troops would bring to their state, they still hoped that polite behavior might prevent the enemy soldiers from completely violating them.

Fearing that Union troops would destroy all personal items they found in Southern homes, slaveholding women scrambled to find hiding places for their valuables. They often chose secret spots, assuming that certain areas would be safe from plundering troops. Frequently these "safe" places focused around the assumed inviolability of a lady's private chambers and person. In many cases, women hid their food, silver, personal correspondence, and other treasures in bedrooms. In February 1865, after Sarah Jane Sams heard "a rumor . . . that the Yankees are but six miles from here," she immediately began looking for ways to protect her property. To prepare for the anticipated invasion, "Bet, Ma and myself have been busy all day removing our provisions from the cellar and the pantry into our bedrooms hoping they may be more secure." In defense of their domestic items, these women "emptied the cotton out of one of our mattresses and filled it very nicely with all of our cloth, blankets, sheets and gentlemen's clothing, sewed it up like a mattress and put under the rest." She recognized that these precautions might prove useless, and Union soldiers might breach her private space. "Whether they discover it will be proved by tomorrow I fear."[104] Although she hoped that these gendered spaces would not be violated, Sams knew that the standards of warfare had changed in recent months. Even so, she still expected that the invading armies would follow the conventions of peacetime society and not desecrate the privacy of a woman's bedroom or tear open a mattress. She, like many of her elite countrywomen, demonstrated her confidence in gender boundaries with her actions. Sams let her husband know that she had hidden "my jewelry . . . also your important papers." As a result, "My room looks more like a commissary room than a bed room."[105] Others used similar tactics. Charlotte St. Julien Ravenel described her attempt to protect her property from the approaching Union invaders. She and Pennie were up into the early morning hours "putting a way things in a mattrys we opened the cotton and put the things between."[106] Despite what she had heard about the Union attack on women, Ravenel naively believed some gender boundaries would not be crossed. She continued to trust that gentlemen would not force their way into a woman's bedroom.

Antebellum gender conventions, which allowed slaveholding women to assume that their bodies and bedrooms were inviolable, also led them to understand an invasion of their homes and bedrooms as a violation. Consequently, they often used the rhetoric of rape when describing the horrors that they expected to face upon Sherman's arrival in their towns. Columbian Emma LeConte described her interpretation of enemy actions in a year-end entry in her diary. "[Union troops] are preparing to hurl destruction upon the State they hate most of all." Furthermore, "Sherman the brute avows his intention of converting South Carolina into a wilderness. Not one house he says shall be left standing and his licentious troops whites and negroes shall be turned loose to *ravage* and *violate.*"[107] Some white Southern women were not surprised by what they saw as depraved behavior from the Yankees. Georgian Matilda Champion acknowledged the inappropriate words and behavior of the approaching Union soldiers, while asserting the failure of such tactics. "I am not astonished to hear of Gen. Sherman saying he could buy the chastity of any Southern woman with a few pounds of coffee. He would find himself woefully mistaken if he were to try that."[108]

The progression of Union tactics in the first four years of the Civil War destroyed Confederate women's assumptions that home front and gender prescriptions would protect them no matter how they supported their nation. The 1861 imprisonment of women, "Beast" Butler's Woman

Order, the expulsion of Confederate women from some Missouri counties, Sheridan's Shenandoah campaign, and the early reports of Sherman's March demonstrated that white women no longer occupied a privileged status as protected noncombatants. The line between home front and war front blurred, and, out of necessity, Confederate women prepared for the impending confrontation with Union troops. In doing so, slaveholding women looked to nineteenth-century gender norms to protect them from the very violations of these norms. They hoped Union soldiers would restrain themselves from treating them as enemies and would acknowledge the privileges they had as a result of their class and gender.

CHAPTER 2

PUNISHING SOUTHERN WOMEN

After four months of fighting in the Georgia heat, Union general William Tecumseh Sherman's forces finally captured Atlanta on September 1, 1864. Confederate troops fled, leaving more than one thousand civilians in the railroad city. Southern women, children, and mostly elderly men remained in their homes, wondering what life in occupied Atlanta would be like. Many likely tried to imagine a future under the watch of enemy soldiers and perhaps gathered information from their neighbors about experiences in other occupied parts of the South. They may have read or heard stories about Butler's occupation of New Orleans, the Union's siege and capture of Vicksburg, or any one of the countless Southern towns and cities that the Union controlled before the war ended. As they contemplated a future of food shortages, curfews, and restricted mobility, Sherman's next move completely blindsided them. On September 8, 1864, he ordered the eviction of all civilians from Atlanta. The general insisted that families had no place in the Union command post that Atlanta had become. In addition, he declared that he refused to feed, clothe, shelter, or otherwise support this hostile and dependent feminine population. Sherman turned the citizens of Atlanta into refugees.

Sherman's Special Field Orders, No. 67, as it was officially known, generated protest from Confederates inside and outside of Atlanta. It violated the rules of war as understood by many observers, Confederate and otherwise. Sherman may have agreed, but months earlier he had proclaimed that "in war we have a perfect right to produce results in our own way, and should not scruple too much at the means, provided they are effectual."[1] The mayor of Atlanta complained to Sherman about the unfairness of such harsh treatment of Southern women and their families, but Sherman was not moved by Southern protests. After all, he asserted, "War is cruelty, and you cannot refine it; and those who brought war on the country deserve all the curses and maledictions a people can pour out." An enemy was an enemy, male or female. He would not be moved by pleas for sympathy. As for the outcry at his evacuation orders, "you might as well appeal against the thunder-storm as against these terrible hardships of war. They are inevitable, and the only way the people of Atlanta can hope once more to live in peace and quiet at home is to stop this war, which can alone be done by admitting that it began in error and is perpetuated in pride." In Sherman's mind, elite women's role in the Confederate war effort justified the eviction of civilians, most of whom were women. He ignored their pleas for clemency, throwing their own actions back in their faces. "Now that war comes to you ... you deprecate its horrors, but did not feel them when you sent car-loads of soldiers and ammunition, and moulded shells and shot, to carry war into" other places. White women's active role in supporting and supplying Confederate soldiers, he claimed, validated the Union's treatment of them as enemies. If this breaking of social norms resulted in victory, the ends justified the means. As Sherman asserted, "I want peace, and believe it can only be reached through union and war, and I will ever conduct war with a view to perfect an early success."[2]

Sherman's understanding of slaveholding Confederate women as enemies shaped his plans for the Georgia and Carolinas campaign. No longer willing to leave women outside of the boundaries of warfare, Sherman pursued a campaign that used gender ideas to undermine his female enemies rather than to protect them. Sherman recognized the vital role that elite women continually played in sustaining Confederate soldiers on the battlefield, and he vowed to strike at the geographic and metaphoric heart of the Confederacy. In bringing war home to female civilians, Sherman and his soldiers hoped to destroy Confederate support and to bring about a rapid end to the Civil War.

Sherman, along with many other Union leaders, blamed elite slaveholders for secession and for leading the United States into a bloody civil war. Although he and others acknowledged that many nonslaveholders enlisted in the Confederate army, Sherman also recognized that secession and slaveholding were closely intertwined. If the South wanted to fight a war for slavery, Sherman wanted to wage a war against slaveholders. As a result, he and other Union soldiers often expressed bitterness toward slaveholders and toward the war that they caused and prolonged. Although many issues shaped the attitudes of Sherman and his soldiers—from the frustrations of marching through tough terrain and heavy rains to food shortages, exhaustion, racism, and homesickness, for example—it is no coincidence that soldiers wreaked the greatest damage on families of Confederate officers, prominent secessionists, or large slaveholders in general. Consequently, they aimed their destructiveness at the South's elite, punishing slaveholders for causing and continuing a deadly drawn-out war. Even after several years of war, these families had the most material goods to lose, and Sherman's men took special care to slow down long enough to inflict damage and heap insults on wealthy families and to teach them that "secession means something more than a holiday parade."[3]

By marching through the Southern home front and specifically through its slaveholding strongholds, Sherman's troops had little choice but to confront Confederate women. For various reasons, the Confederate home front had become women's domain, both numerically and ideologically. By late 1864, the Confederate draft expanded to include white men between the ages of seventeen and fifty, draining away most of the white men from local communities in Georgia and the Carolinas. Although young boys and elderly men remained at home, many white Southern women assumed most of the roles traditionally assigned to men in the nineteenth century. As a result, during the Civil War white Southern women often controlled production, supplies, money matters, slave discipline, and day-to-day farm life. Many of them not only ran households but also ran the factories, farms, and schools. In this manner, the Southern home front became women's sphere and any attack on the home front became by definition an assault on white women.[4] Union soldiers took this new reality into consideration as they launched their offensive in Georgia and the Carolinas, specifically attacking those items they felt would most affect elite women's loyalty to the Confederacy. To pursue an effective home front campaign, Sherman and his men had both to refashion elite Southern women as enemies and to treat them with the tools that Northern troops felt would be most damaging to a female enemy.

Sherman designed a campaign that would wreak the greatest damage, psychologically and physically, on the wealthy Confederate home front and its female occupants. Before and during the march, Sherman publicly warned elite white women that they would not be spared the horrors of war. In January, he made clear in gendered terms his desire to make all Confederates suffer. "To the petulant and persistent secessionists, why, death is mercy, and the quicker he or she is disposed of the better." He, however, did not intend to show any mercy. After all, he continued, "Satan and the rebellious saints of Heaven were allowed a continuous existence in hell merely to swell their just punishment. To such as would rebel against a Government so mild and just as ours was in peace, a punishment equal would not be unjust."[5] Sherman intended to capitalize on the gender of his female targets in the hopes of overpowering and subjugating the Southern home front. In wonderfully gendered language, he promised to "make Georgia howl" through the utter destruction of its roads, houses, and people and show the South its powerlessness.[6] Doing so, he assumed, would crush civilian and military confidence in Southern troops, especially in the invaded areas, and result in the surrender of the Confederacy. In the process, Sherman's March launched an attack on Southern domesticity akin to a sexual assault on the South as a whole.[7] Union troops and white Southerners recognized this reality. Slaveholding Southern women, as well as their men on the battlefield, saw the invasion of the Confederate home front as both a military and a personal offense. They bemoaned the campaign's crossing of boundaries believed sacred by "polite" nineteenth-century society. Thresholds and bedrooms were assumed inviolable, yet Union soldiers purposefully invaded them throughout the campaign.

The decision to destroy domestic Confederate property had as much to do with a desire to hurt the Confederate war effort as it did with the purpose to break the will of the South and thereby, as Sherman asserted, "cure *her* of *her* pride and boasting."[8] Union troops received orders to destroy items that directly assisted the Confederate war effort, and these guidelines led them into the houses of slaveholding women in Georgia and the Carolinas. Throughout the march, they stole food, fine clothing, silver, and jewelry, while they destroyed the houses that white women governed. Sherman's orders to "forage liberally," gave his men relatively free rein on the home front. In addition, he gave wide license to his commanders concerning the treatment of the Southern home front and its female civilians. To them he "intrusted the power to destroy mills, houses, cotton-gins &c." Although Sherman asserted that "no destruction of such property should be permitted" when the army went "unmolested," he frequently gave exceptions to the rules. "Should the inhabitants . . . manifest local hostility, then army commanders should order and enforce a devastation more or less relentless according to the measure of such hostility."[9] As a result of the ensuing ambiguity and a general desire to address the morale of slaveholding women, the ransacking of Southern homes and property during Sherman's March occurred regularly. Although reports of physical rape of white women were rare, the seemingly unrestricted actions of Union soldiers created anxieties among slaveholding women across the South in regard to their personal safety as well as to their property. By invading women's domain, Sherman and his men crossed a line of propriety held sacred by elite Southerners and Northerners.

Unlike some of his men, Sherman did not merely justify his assault on female Confederates as punishment for their ardent support of the war. It was a tactic designed to achieve military ambitions. Sherman firmly believed that he could eliminate this group's participation in the war by aggressively attacking women's domain. Before the campaign through Georgia and the Carolinas began, Sherman recognized elite white women and other civilians as vital participants in the Confederate war effort. In his discussion of the treatment of presumed noncombatants in Alabama in January 1864, Sherman asserted that behavior, not sex, determined civilians' classification. He was willing to leave alone the women, children, and noncombatants who "remain in their houses and keep to their accustomed business their opinions and prejudices can in nowise influence the war, and therefore should not be noticed." However, he continued, "if any one comes out into the public streets and creates disorder, he or she should be punished, restrained, or banished."[10] Sherman continued using this rationale in his Georgia and Carolinas campaign. As long as slaveholding women acted as ladies, they would be treated as such. However, if their behavior became "unruly," Sherman stressed their hostility over their femininity.[11]

Furthermore, acting with nineteenth-century assumptions that "true" women behaved consistently within the "cult of domesticity," Sherman assessed that if he brought the war to female civilians, their support for the Confederacy would inevitably crumble, as would the South. After all, women, he thought, belonged in the home where they could focus on domestic matters. Sherman viewed all women, including his own wife, through this lens. Commenting on her potential participation in Chicago's Sanitary Fair, a local fundraiser for the United States Sanitary Commission, he let his wife know that he did not "approve of ladies selling things at a table" because "it merely looks unbecoming for a lady to stand behind a table to sell things."[12] Sherman clearly believed that women—strangers or family members, Northerners or Southerners—should behave in particularly gendered ways.[13]

According to such logic on gender roles, only the strongest of men could endure wartime horrors and the heightened masculinity of soldiers; women could not possibly survive them. In addition, an invasion of the home front would deny Confederate women their ability to exercise power in the domestic sphere. Major Henry Hitchcock, one of Sherman's key aides, articulated this aspect of his commander's plan, noting that "the mere fact of [the march] is bound to have a powerful influence of itself: it shows the real hopelessness of their 'cause' first to those who suffer, and to the people of 'The South,' and then to all the world."[14] The march, then, would demoralize the slaveholding women it directly affected, as well as the Southern soldiers fighting to protect their homes and families. Indeed, Hitchcock explained, "the [march's] express purpose [is], in fact, of teaching [Southern] people that war means ruin and misery, & that 'their Government' cannot protect them."[15]

Sherman's gendered offensive against Confederate women began prior to the March to the Sea. After a four-month campaign for Atlanta, Confederate forces evacuated the city on September 1, 1864. Sherman and his troops took control of it on September 2, allowing Southern forces to escape. In a letter to Henry Halleck, Sherman detailed his plan "to remove all the Inhabitants of Atlanta." Sherman predicted the outcry, but would hear nothing of it. "If the people raise a howl against my barbarity & cruelty, I will answer that War is War & not popularity seeking. If they want Peace, they & their relations must stop War."[16] Subsequently, in establishing Atlanta as a command post for Union operations, Sherman issued Special Field Orders, No. 67, on September 8, 1864, to "[vacate] all except the armies of the United States." This order resulted in the forced departure of Atlanta's more than 1,500 civilians.[17] Despite protests from Confederate officials and civilians that this action violated an unstated and highly gendered code of conduct, Sherman stressed the necessity of evacuation, insisting that "the use of Atlanta for warlike purposes is inconsistent with its character as a home for families."[18] Furthermore, and perhaps more importantly, Sherman was "not willing to have Atlanta encumbered by the families of [his] enemies."[19] He saw no reason to divert resources from his men in order to support the slaveholding Georgia women who had promoted and prolonged the war. A hostile civilian population would not only impede military activities, Sherman asserted, but its presence would also unnecessarily burden the Union army, who would have to feed and shelter Confederate women and children. He cared little that his enemies had labeled him "Sherman the Brute."[20] As he told his wife, Ellen, "I would have been a silly fool to take a town at such cost, and left it in the occupation of a helpless and hectic People."[21] He further justified his actions with paternalistic language, reasoning "it is a kindness to these families of Atlanta to remove them now at once from scenes that women and children should not be exposed to." Furthermore, he asserted in a response to John Bell Hood's protestations that "the 'brave People' should scorn to commit their wives and children to the rude barbarians who thus as you say violate the Laws of War, as illustrated in the pages of its dark History."[22] Personally, he was relieved to no longer have "women boring me every order I give."[23]

Despite widespread agreement with and support of Sherman's evacuation policy in Atlanta, many Northern soldiers grappled with the moral implications of the eviction of white women. Some Union men struggled to reconcile how they presumed they should treat "respectable" women with the necessities of war. For example, Ohio army surgeon J. Dexter Cotton revealed to his wife his somewhat ambivalent support for the order and justified it without reference to military tactics. "It seems very hard," he explained, "but serves them right for most of the *women* of the south are generally stronger secess[ionists] than the men."[24] In the end, Cotton decided that, despite their class and gender and the protections that normally accompanied them, these Confederate women deserved to be ousted from their homes and stripped of their property because they helped initiate and continued to support the rebellion. Another Yankee soldier, H. D. Chapman, "did feel sorry for the women and innocent children." However, he did not let his sympathy get in the way, and instead justified the order because "our army is here and must be fed."[25]

As soldiers generally defended the evacuation of Atlanta's civilians as "military necessity," they often acknowledged that revenge motivated it. In his response to a letter protesting the order of evacuation, Sherman revealed his intertwined war aims: he wanted to exact vengeance on traitorous Southerners, as well as to end the war. Southerners protested that his policy wreaked havoc on families and turned gender ideals upside down. It would not be proper, they insisted, to expel women and children from their homes. Sherman did not agree. As he stressed, "war is cruelty." Sherman wanted female Southern civilians, like their male counterparts, to feel the consequences of secession. Sherman made clear that his wartime policies would not be adjusted to accommodate contemporary gender prescriptions. Elite white women could expect harsh treatment like that Union soldiers directed at Southern men as long as they remained hostile to the Union. Support for Sherman's actions in Atlanta resounded across the North. Sherman noted that "a howl was raised, but the President and Secretary of War backed me, and now all recognize the wisdom & humanity of the thing."[26] His wife Ellen was "charmed" with his evacuation of Atlanta. She pointed to the Confederacy's "insolent women" as "responsible for the war." She further applauded the order because it would force elite Southern women "to feel that [war] exists in sternest reality."[27] Even to Northern women, female Confederates had become more identified with their regional loyalties than with their gender.

Once he had established Atlanta as his command post, Sherman attempted to destroy General John Bell Hood's Confederate forces. He then determined to march his troops across Georgia to demonstrate the power of the federal army. Sherman further proposed that he cut off his supply and communication lines and live off of the wealth of Confederate households as he and his troops marched across the South. He described to his wife how his soldiers were "practicing . . . the art of foraging and . . . take to it like Ducks to water." He was pleased to note that "We wont starve in Georgia."[28] This tactic would allow him to pursue the devastation of the Southern countryside without having to protect railroads or supply trains. At the same time, it would separate the Confederacy from its own supply lines. Specifically, he "propose[d] to act in such a manner against the material resources of the South as utterly to negat[e] Davis' boasted threat and promises of protection."[29] These boasts, of course, were part of a larger set of patriarchal assurances that the Confederate government and army would take care of the women of the South. Sherman's plans and actions would prove to elite women that neither their government, their soldiers, nor their gender could protect them anymore.

Before their departure from Atlanta on November 15, 1864, Sherman's troops burned everything of military importance in the city—depots, shops, factories, foundries, and machine shops. According to official Union reports, only war-related businesses and factories were destroyed by fire. Unofficial records kept by soldiers, however, confirmed the contemporary reports written by Southern civilians that focused on the widespread destruction of homes and personal property caused by departing Union troops. "Many houses had been burned & all day long the fires kept increasing in number," soldier E. P. Burton recorded in his diary. "The sight was magnificent & melancholy in the extreem, I think by dark all the public buildings & stores with many of the residences must have been destroyed."[30] William Gibson observed the civilian results of the destruction: "The fields were filled with women and children, half-naked refugees from their burning homes."[31] Another Union soldier similarly recorded how military necessity and domestic destruction went hand in hand. "The work of destroying the city of Atlanta which our Gen has ordered, still continues. Directly North of where we are I see a beautiful residence wrapped in flames." As the soldiers "advanced through the City the smouldering ruins of once beautiful homes met our gaze on every hand."[32] The white women of Atlanta, already insulted by their eviction, watched their domestic lives go up in smoke.

The aggressive assault on the domestic world of elite women continued as Union troops left Atlanta and marched east through Georgia. Leaving Union generals George H. Thomas and John M. Schofield with sixty thousand soldiers to deal with Hood's Confederate troops in Tennessee, Sherman's men began their March to the Sea on November 15, 1864. To effectively forage, destroy, and demoralize the Georgia countryside, Sherman divided his troops into two wings, a left (northern) wing commanded by Henry W. Slocum and a right (southern) wing under Oliver O. Howard. Although the officers and soldiers began the 285-mile march toward Savannah with little knowledge of the plan or their destination, they confidently moved forward at Sherman's command and took note of the social status of the communities they faced. The troops marched from ten to fifteen miles each day, foraging and destroying Confederate property along the way. Union soldiers recorded a 40- to 60-mile-wide swath of destruction strewn with evidence of their presence—railroad ties twisted around trees in "Sherman neckties," houses almost entirely razed by fires with only "lone chimney-stacks, or 'Sherman's Sentinels,'" left standing, burned crops, and otherwise trampled countryside.³³ "The amt of propperty destroyed by the army is immense," Union soldier Edward Allen recorded. "Rail roads seemed to be our especial skill and the way we tore up and burned the Georgia Central beats all."³⁴ The soldiers carefully followed Sherman's orders to "break up that railroad . . . so that every rail will be disabled." The general wanted "each bar of iron actually twisted, either around a tree, or with one of the hooks."³⁵ In addition to destroying the transportation routes, Allen wrote, "depots, public building[s] and building[s] that were not so public shared the same fate of the RR. Each Corps (4 of them) left a black streak to mark its way over the sacred soil."³⁶ As this report reveals, although the soldiers had official orders to target and destroy railroads, mills, and other places or items that supported the Confederate war effort, they bragged about their ability to destroy a much wider range of Confederate property, including domestic property.³⁷

A lack of compassion for wealthy slaveholding women existed throughout the Union ranks and for the duration of the march. As the troops made their way through Georgia, James Leath observed that "the people are left in a very destitute and suffering condition." The dire straits in which he put Confederate civilians did not bother him, however. "If they all starve to death I shall not be surprised, neither will I care," he wrote. Leath's callousness, like that of other Union soldiers, may be attributed to his views on the war. Confederate civilians, women included, deserved what they got because it was "a horrible state of affairs [that] they had brought upon themselves."³⁸ Edward Allen gloried in Sherman's orders and justifications for the evacuation. He encouraged his parents to read the letters about the "removal of the women & children of Atlanta." These letters, he boasted, "are so good, just the sentiments of his whole army." Because Sherman was "not afraid to treat . . . [Confederate women] as they deserve," the soldiers praised him as "the man we like to fight under."³⁹ Another man rejoiced "we are under command of General Sherman and will destroy all before us."⁴⁰ Union troops agreed with their commanders that the attitudes and wartime roles of Confederate women warranted whatever hardships the army brought upon them.

Compassion for enemy women rarely altered Union soldiers' behavior toward elite white women. In the eyes of Union soldiers, elite Southern women deserved no special, protective treatment. When recording a confrontation with the wife of a railroad agent in Madison, Georgia, Horatio Chapman tellingly noted that although he "almost always [had] sympathy for the women," this particular one elicited no such response. Not only did she have a "large and elegant mansion," but also "she was a regular secesh and spit out her spite and venom against the dirty Yanks and mudsills of the north."⁴¹ Part of this animosity may have resulted from class envy, but Union soldiers also insisted that Confederate women, as vocal nationalists and slaveholders, deserved punishment for their rebellious, secessionist natures. In many ways, elite women's participation in the war negated their gender or at least the protection it usually entailed.

The desire to erode the morale of elite, slaveholding Southern women as well as a focus on destroying the Confederacy's material support resulted in a route through a rich agricultural area of Georgia. It offered fertile opportunity for good eating and high spirits among the soldiers. After feasting on sweet potatoes, poultry, pork, and other camp rarities, Delos Van Deusen bragged, "we didnt leave plenty" for the civilians.⁴² Most Northern soldiers simply rejoiced in the bounty shared during the campaign. Throughout the trip from Atlanta, there was a constant influx of "foragers bringing in all manner of stuff and in all Shapes & conditions." As a result, "all the Boys enjoyed the trip hugely."⁴³ Another man noted, "We had a very nice time while on the march plenty to eat and did not march very hard."⁴⁴ As many soldiers wrote, throughout the march the troops "subsist[ed] almost entirely from the enimey's country."⁴⁵

As they moved across the Southern countryside, Union soldiers worked to keep excess supplies away from Confederate soldiers and slaveholding civilians. They gleefully "destroyed all we could not eat, stole their niggers, burned their cotton & Gins, Spilled their Sorghum, Burned and twisted their Roads and raised Hell generally as you know an army can when 'turned loose.'" Furthermore, the soldiers "lived on the fat of the land finding endless supplies of Sweet Potatoes, Poultry, Hogs, Sheep, Cattle, Sorghum, Syrup, Honey &c yes and plenty of Peanuts to eat on the way."[46] It was "a continuous thanksgiving."[47] Although they "only had 4 days rations issued . . . in the whole march" many soldiers reported that during the campaign they "lived better than ever before" on "evrything that a rich planters place could afford." The bounty of the land proved plentiful as "in some places as much as 3,000 . . . bushels of sweet potatoes would be consumed in one night." Even the towns offered good fare. Charles Brown described the meal in Milledgeville, Georgia. The troops "had 5 chickens 1 turkey (the largest I *ever* saw.) the hind quarter of mutton a ham, about 25 lbs of cap honey 1/2 gal. of Syrup, all the pan cakes we could eat. warm buiscuit & evry thing in proportion."[48] Furthermore, the soldiers gloried in their foraging efforts. One described "some of the nice things we had to eat" including molasses, sweet potatoes, meats, and chicken. He then mocked "those Georgians" as "clever people to have so many good things ready for us."[49] From Savannah, Sherman noted that because the troops "came right along living on turkeys, chickens, pigs," not only did he not have to feed them, but "Jeff Davis will now have to feed the people of Georgia instead of collecting provisions of them to feed his armies."[50] Not only had he succeeded in supplying his own troops and limiting what was available to Confederate troops, but he had also brought suffering to the wealthy civilians in his path. He hoped these measures would end their support for the Confederacy.

In another tactical measure, Sherman spread his men across a forty- to sixty-mile-wide path to keep Confederate soldiers and civilians anxiously wondering where he was heading. One soldier described the path as a "black streak behind us about 50 miles wide."[51] Another observed that, "for forty miles in width, the country throughout our whole line of march is a desert."[52] The distribution of Union forces kept Confederate troops thinly spread trying to protect a wide area and consequently prevented high casualties. Although there were several skirmishes with Confederate troops on the March to the Sea, Union casualties for the entire campaign numbered only 2,200. Union forces easily captured Milledgeville, Georgia's state capital, on November 23. There, in addition to general looting and destruction, the Union soldiers held a mock legislature to "repeal" the state's secession ordinance.⁵³ Once again, as part of Sherman's psychological tactics, soldiers worked to humiliate Confederate women and men to demonstrate the power of the Union army.

Although Sherman had designated a specific group of men as official foragers for his army and directed them to gather only food and supplies for the troops, "Sherman's Bummers" as well as other soldiers often seized personal property as souvenirs of the campaign and as an additional way to hurt their female enemies.⁵⁴ Sherman's commanders recognized the possible outcomes of attacking female enemies. As one commented, "The dictates of humanity must at least be observed," because "no good can result to the cause of their country from indiscriminate destruction of property or burning of the homes of women and children."⁵⁵ However, the soldiers rarely listened to these admonishments or orders. Women's clothes, letters, linens, jewelry, silver, household furnishings, sewing supplies, baby clothes, and dishes often became spoils of war. None of these items would directly help the Union or Confederacy militarily, but their theft and destruction struck at the heart of women's lives.⁵⁶ According to some of Sherman's men, few homes escaped the foraging. "House Robbing has become universal," Union chaplain John J. Hight wrote. "I do not mean all of the men rob houses, but all the houses are robbed."⁵⁷

Union soldiers seized whatever they could get their hands on from Confederate civilians. They "went into Private houses and took what they wanted," Michael Dresbach observed as his unit approached Savannah. "Some got Silver Pitchers and Plate of considerable value[.] One of the Boys dug up a Box that was Buried in the field containing $60,000 Confederate money[.] Another found one containing 2 gold watches and $260 in coin there is a great deal found that we do not hear of."⁵⁸ As the men headed toward Savannah, William Gibson recorded that he "destroy[ed] a vast amount of cotton, wine, Brussels carpets, mahogany furniture, china ware, silver plate, etc., etc., of untold value." He gleefully noted that "the owner had just sent them from Savannah to his country residence *for safe keeping*."⁵⁹ Edward Allen left a detailed description of the loot obtained after the Union captured Columbia, South Carolina. "Every concurable article that one could imagine, must, was to be found in our camp, clothing, bed clothing, such splendid coverlids, qui[l]ts, & sheets, musical instruments violins guitars, music box." The soldiers took whatever they could carry, "& had not pianos been quite so heavey you might have seen many of them there." They also carried away food items like "Flour meal sugar, butter, all the yankee notions usually found in stores." The soldiers had appropriated so many things that Allen realized "it would take too much time, candle & paper to mention or even try to mention all that was there."[60]

Some soldiers sent the domestic treasures they confiscated to loved ones in the North. However, they dropped much of the very fancy, but heavy, booty along the roadside as the march continued. Edward Allen noted that "most all was left—destroyed except small articles of value easily carried by one of the boys."[61] Charles Brown alerted his family as to the gifts he would be sending home as well as to the ones he had lost. As did most of the souvenir hunters, Brown primarily saved domestic items. "I have some selections of Rebel music to send," he wrote to his parents and sister, "a good selection & [you] shall have the first best lot." In addition to the music, he took "some jewrlry from the house of Reb. Gen. Irwin. [whose] house was plundered from ground to Shingles & burnt."[62] John Herr planned to send home the lightweight curiosities along with the treasures he had appropriated including "a few heads of rice so you can see how it looks in the Straw[, and] . . . a vest that I captured."[63] In their letters home and in their personal diaries, Yankee soldiers proudly detailed the domestic trinkets they had taken from slaveholding households.

Confederates could do little to stop Sherman and his men as they marched through Southern towns, plantations, and farms. Union troops faced negligible organized military opposition as they marched east through Georgia. William J. Hardee took control of Confederate troops in Georgia on November 17, 1864, but like his predecessor he could not stop Sherman's progress through the state. Acknowledging his powerlessness, Hardee unsuccessfully focused his energy and forces on protecting the port of Savannah. Sherman and his troops cut through most of the state by December 10, 1864, and demanded the surrender of Savannah a week later. When Hardee refused, the Union forces began a siege of the city, but left Confederate troops free to evacuate. Hardee and his men abandoned Savannah on December 21, escaping across the river into South Carolina. Subsequently, Sherman took control of the city with its two hundred artillery pieces, ammunition, and approximately thirty thousand bales of cotton. On December 22, 1864, Sherman sent President Abraham Lincoln a telegram announcing the accomplishment: "I beg to present you as a Christmas Gift the City of Savannah with one hundred and fifty heavy guns and plenty of ammunition: and also about twenty five thousand bales of cotton."[64] The soldiers proudly recalled their triumphant campaign: "36 days ago we were standing near Atlanta Geo watching the angery flames devouring Building after Building[.] [T]o day we stand here at Savannah Master of over a Hundread fields which was bought and Paid with Freemans Blood." In addition to the immediate consequences, this soldier also reflected on the larger significance of the march. "Here we have ended what I think will go down in History and be told over and over again as one of the greatest acheevements on Record."[65]

Throughout their home front attack, Union soldiers targeted slaveholding families, who they considered instrumental in Southern secession. Sherman provided justification for this action when he commanded that soldiers should "discriminate between the rich, who are usually hostile, and the poor and industrious, usually neutral or friendly."[66] Sherman believed that everyone shared his antipathy toward the slaveholding class: "No man will deny that the United States would be benefited by dispossessing a rich, prejudiced, hard-headed, and disloyal planter."[67] The troops complied with their commander's wish to punish elite slaveholding Southerners. In Georgia, soldiers devastated wealthy slaveholder Howell Cobb's plantation and did not "feel much troubled about the destruction" because he was "one of the *head devils*." Hitchcock relished the attack on Cobb, noting that he "has four or five other plantations, and 500 to 600 negroes in all."[68] One soldier observed the specific punishment of elite Southerners and wrote during the march that "the Army are renting their spite on everything destructible & our line is marked each day by dense columns of black smoke curling up from the former residences of the 'chivalry.'"[69]

Union soldiers left their mark on the South's domestic landscape. After ransacking homes, many defaced the remaining buildings. "Almost every house in town is more or less damaged," Confederate officer Andrew McBride complained from Jonesboro, Georgia, to his fiancée. "The walls of most of them completely covered with charcoal autographs of Yankee celebrities such for instance as this on the door of your house 'Patrick Boyle 90 Ind Vol Infty.'" Other Union soldiers were more personal in their epithets. "Just under Patricks name, I found 'Miss Ada is tha pritist girl in town.'" Graffiti of Union insults covered other walls. The soldiers "volunteered or tendered a good deal of advise to President Davis and Genl Hood and to rebels generally." McBride included examples: "'Jeff,—relinquish your efforts to establish a new Confederation' [signed] 'Abe'" or "'Genl Hood: you didn't expect us to come in at the back door, did you?'"[70] Through graffiti, Union soldiers left lasting displays of their victories and heaped further insults upon Confederates.

On multiple occasions, Union soldiers took advantage of the domestic luxuries within the homes of the Southern elite, striking directly at the heart of women's domain. Pianos, a mark of wealth and privilege, frequently became targets of Union destruction. "Some of our soldiers are very reckless and smash everything that comes in their way. One fellow played on the piano while his comrades danced a jog on the top of the instrument and then he drove an axe through it."[71] Throughout the march, soldiers engaged in similar celebrations in their enemies' parlors. When updating his sister on the state of affairs, Union soldier Charles Brown highlighted the nonmilitary items that the troops destroyed. "You might see all sorts of scenes" along the march, including "boys pounding Piano keys with their Hatchets to see who could make the most noise." Others had contests where they would "pile up a pile of plates & 'order arms' on them to all who could break the most." The actions of other soldiers directly struck at the heart of femininity. In these situations, some of the Northern men would "see who could dress themselves in the best suit of womens clothes & then make the lady of the house play for them to have a cotillion & if the music did not suit slash their hatchet through the top of the piano to improve the time."[72] The scenes did more than taunt and humiliate the Southern ladies who witnessed them. By mimicking and mocking slaveholding women, the enemy men also flaunted the false sense of security that these items provided elite women. In addition to the physical damage caused by the drunken festivities, the Northern soldiers specifically trampled on the markings of domesticity and femininity to strike at white women's privileged place.[73]

Once in control of Savannah, Sherman set about demonstrating to the city's residents that a peaceful surrender and return to the Union would protect Southerners from Union wrath. To contrast his treatment of residents in Savannah to that of rebellious Atlantans, Sherman opened his headquarters to whoever wanted to visit. He also allowed the local government to continue functioning and made sure that food came into the city to feed the residents. At the same time, however, Sherman justified the tactics that he had employed up to this point. "This may seem a hard species of warfare, but it brings the sad realities of war home to those who have been directly or indirectly instrumental in involving us in its attendant calamities."[74] A surprised Sherman admitted that his campaign, designed to "take some conceit out of [Southerners]," had not completely succeeded. In Savannah, he noted, "although I have come right through the heart of Georgia [the women] talk as defiantly as ever." Sherman expressed astonishment that the elite women of Savannah "remain, bright and haughty and proud as ever. There seems no end but utter annihilation that will satisfy their hate of the 'sneaking Yankee' and 'ruthless invader.'"[75] Despite the military importance of his campaign, Sherman noted the reactions of female Confederates. He had assumed that, as women, they would give up in the face of domestic warfare. When they did not comply, he persisted in his attack on the home front, taking it from Georgia up into the Carolinas, where he assumed the slaveholding women to be even more unrepentant rebels. Despite evidence to the contrary, Sherman found his tactic so effective that he later advised other commanders to use similar home front raids. He explained to George Thomas that "perfectly practicable and easy" raids "will have an excellent effect." Sherman apparently missed the galvanizing effect of his campaign on white Southern civilians. Instead, he claimed "it is nonsense to Suppose that the People of the South are enraged or united by such movements. They reason very differently." Perhaps it was wishful thinking when Sherman asserted that slaveholding women "see in [the movements] the Sure and inevitable destruction of all their property, they realize that the Confederate armies cannot protect them, and they see in the repetition of such raids the inevitable result of starvation & misery."[76]

After his capture of Savannah, Sherman continued in his policy to make war "*terrible beyond endurance*" and thereby secure Confederate surrender. To do so, Sherman and his commanders eschewed taboos involved in crossing the increasingly blurred wartime gender boundaries. As Union troops understood it, Confederate women's vocal enmity further opened the door to allow women to be treated as hostiles instead of as a protected group. Henry Hitchcock expressed his desire to retaliate against what he saw as the South's intentional provocation of war in a letter to his wife. "Our enemies have shown themselves *devils* in the spirit which ever began this most unprovoked and inexcusable rebellion." As a result of women's continued defiance "there is nothing for it but 'to fight the devil with fire.'"[77] A Union army chaplain with Sherman similarly justified the assault on women. "So far as the *women* are concerned, we might as well spare our pity, for they are the worst secessionists, and why should *they* not suffer?" he asked. "Would you now spare them a proper amount of suffering? We say no. Let them understand that secession means something more than a holiday parade."[78] The chaplain's statement reveals an animosity toward Southern women not only as secessionists but also as frivolous and overly privileged girls who, he assumed, saw secession and war as nothing more than spectacle. Another Union chaplain came to an equally harsh conclusion about Confederate women. Although "the ladies, at some of the houses, are represented as intelligent, beautiful, and rebellious," their charms made no difference to him. They were still Confederates. "A pretty traitor is no better than an ugly one—male or female. Many of the officers are boiling over with sympathy for those pretty female rebels, but I have none."[79] For this man of the cloth, female provocation of secession justified the harsh treatment of female Southern civilians and their domestic treasures. To repay the South for its provocation of war, Union soldiers, as one of them described, made the "the effects and ravages of war . . . noticeable everywhere." In Savannah, as John Glidden noted, "very few civilians and ladies are to be seen. . . . Martial Law is supreme in everything."[80] If the "devilish" Southerners insisted on continued support of their misguided and malicious cause, Union troops remained equally determined to punish them for their actions.

Although emancipation was not necessarily the goal of the march, Sherman's soldiers freed thousands of the slaves that they encountered on Georgia and Carolina plantations as they destroyed the trappings of slavery, such as cotton fields, gin houses, plantation homes, and agricultural equipment. Bringing down the Southern elite required a destruction of their way of life and labor system—slavery. For many Northerners, the emancipation of slaves was less about freedom for everyone and more about punishing slaveholders. From Savannah, Sherman issued Special

Field Orders, No. 15, on January 16, 1865, granting freedpeople full control of the Sea Islands as well as coastal land thirty miles inland from Charleston, South Carolina, to Jacksonville, Florida. Many Southern blacks followed the Union troops, often to the chagrin of white soldiers, hoping to gain their freedom in the ranks of the Union. Some served as spies for Sherman's army. Others cheered as the Union troops passed by. Although some officers were kind to the escaped slaves who followed the army, others allowed racist attitudes to govern their actions. From the viewpoint of white women, the emancipation of their slaves compounded the Union's assault on domesticity. The absence of enslaved blacks, who served as the foundation for elite leisure and symbolized the privilege of whiteness, further minimized white women's domestic control on the home front.[81]

As he contemplated his march into South Carolina, Sherman justified his home front campaign and hoped to improve upon his successes in Georgia. As he understood it, "We are not only fighting hostile armies, but a hostile people," and as a result "must make old and young, rich and poor, feel the hard hand of war, as well as their organized armies." He basked in the success of "this recent movement of mine through Georgia" which "had a wonderful effect in this respect." He continued his war on the home front, with confidence in his tactics. "I think before we are done, South Carolina will not be quite so tempestuous."[82] Sherman understood that "the whole army is crazy to be turned loose in Carolina," but he did not mind. He acknowledged that "with the experience of the past 30 days [in Georgia], I judge that a month's Sojourn in South Carolina would make her less bellicose."[83] For his part, Sherman wanted to "punish South Carolina as she deserves . . . and devastate that State in the manner we have done in Georgia."[84]

When he left Savannah on February 1, 1865, Sherman again spread his troops across a forty-mile-wide stretch to leave Confederates guessing at his destination and to inspire fear. Each corps continued its destructive journey along different routes. Still unsure of their final destination, the soldiers assumed they were headed toward South Carolina and welcomed a sojourn in the Palmetto State. The soldiers in Sherman's army, like their commander, did not hide their desire to wreak vengeance on the state of South Carolina. John Herr gloried that "we will Show old South Carolina a trick that She never saw before[.] we will make her suffer wors[e] then she did the time of the Revolusionary war." Union troops would do this to "let her know that . . . it isened so sweet to seceds as she thought it would be." Other soldiers agreed with Herr, who recorded that "nearly every man in Shermans army say they are in for disstroying every thing . . . in South Carolina I dont know but I think Sherman will disstroy every thing that is of no value to us." As a result, he thought that, "ere long you will heare of Shermans Army sweeping through S.C. like a hericane."[85] Although there was no official confirmation of their destination, O. M. Poe realized that they were heading to the Palmetto State: "Wo to South Carolina! We are on her borders, ready to carry fire & Sword into every part of that State, and there is not one in all the length & breadth of the land to stay our hands."[86] Sherman's men eagerly prepared to destroy South Carolina, the "mother of treason."[87]

Union soldiers' thirst for vengeance on South Carolina did not go unnoticed by Confederates. In early February 1865, Union soldier Edward Allen recorded his interaction with a Confederate soldier at Petersburg, Virginia, who "deplores the idea of letting Sherman pass through Ga and enter S.C." The Southern soldier, according to Allen, condemned Sherman's imminent entry into the Palmetto State. He asserted that "[Sherman] ought not by any means be allowed to enter for says he: '*they have a grudge against our state*.'" Allen wholeheartedly confirmed Southern fears. "Never spoke rebel truer! they have got a grudge, and S Carolinians will *all* know it before long."[88]

The soldiers' intentions toward the Palmetto State were not unknown to, or repugnant to, their commander. Prior to entering South Carolina, Sherman acknowledged, "The truth is, the whole army is burning with an insatiable desire to wreak vengeance upon South Carolina." He did not disagree with his troops' goals: "I almost tremble at her fate, but feel that she deserves all that seems in store for her."[89] After all, "Carolina herself taunted us with poltroonery and cowardice and forced us the contest."[90] Hinting at the treatment the Palmetto State would receive, Sherman reportedly told a woman in Savannah, who wanted to return to her native South Carolina, "You will be going, madam, out of the frying pan into the fire. My army is composed of some of the most lawless ruffians upon earth." He also reportedly acknowledged that "here in Georgia, I can with difficulty control them, but when I enter South Carolina I shall neither be able nor desirous to do so. You have heard of the horrors of war; wait until my army gets into South Carolina and you will see the reality."[91]

Officially ordered or not, Union soldiers all knew that "poor South Carolina must suffer now. None of the soldiers are storing up mercy for her. Her deluded people will now reap the full reward for all their folly and crimes."[92] Regimental commanders did little to stop their men's desire for vengeance on the Palmetto State. Some even fanned the flames. Edward W. Allen noted that when the orders were read, they included reminders that "S.C. was the state where the seeds of rebellion were first sown & ripened into feint." The orders also let the soldiers "understand that we were not to be so closely restricted as through Ga. ie, allowed more priviledges."[93] Destruction of the first state to secede would demonstrate to the South the consequence of rebellious actions as well as the North's superior power. Union tactics in South Carolina, in particular, targeted the seedbed of secession "to crush the last particle of wind out of the Confederacy."[94]

Federal soldiers believed that the rabid rebels in South Carolina, most of them slaveholding women, deserved whatever hardships they experienced. As a result, as they entered South Carolina, Union troops consciously punished the inhabitants by burning homes, ransacking bedrooms, and publicly humiliating elite women. "The well-known site of columns of black smoke meets our gaze again," Union officer George Ward Nichols observed. "This time houses are burning, and South Carolina has commenced to pay an installment, long overdue, on her debt to justice and humanity."[95] Sebastian Duncan similarly recorded that it was "almost as though there was a Secret organization among the men to burn Every thing in the State for thus far . . . houses, in Some way, get on fire & nearly all we have passed thus far are in ashes."[96] As the soldiers made their way northward through South Carolina, they burned at least a dozen towns. Parts of Gillisonville, Grahamville, Hardeeville, McPhersonville, Springfield, Robertsville, Lawtonville, Barnwell, Blackville, Midway, Orangeburg, and Lexington all went up in flames. The soldiers watched "South Carolina . . . getting badly scorched" with satisfaction.[97] As men and as Northerners, Union troops put rebel women in their place.[98]

Union troops continued to attack slaveholding households as they marched through South Carolina. Upon entering the seedbed of secession, they went in search of specific secessionists, "asking 'Is this the home of Mr. Rhett?' and 'Is that the dwelling of Mr. Middleton?'" In addition, certain slaveholders were "pulled about and struck" by the invading soldiers. They also specifically destroyed the family homes of well-known planters Dr. John Cheves and Maxcy Gregg, and that of Columbia mayor Thomas Jefferson Goodwyn.[99] One Union soldier noted that "the poor people are respected by the soldiers and their property protected." On the other hand, "the rich are persecuted when caught and their barns, gins & houses fall victims to the invaders match."[100] This tactic did not go unnoticed by elite Southern women in the area. Pauline DeCaradeuc described how the soldiers raged against her class and her family. The soldiers let her know "that they had to arrest and shoot every influential citizen in S.C., every mover of secession." Such intentions put her family in danger. The soldiers further told her they could see "from the accumulation of wealth, the quantities of food, books & clothes in this house . . . that they knew Father was wealthy, literary, & influential, & they had heard enough of him." As a result, they wanted "to make an example of him."[101] As did his soldiers, Sherman saw the attack on slaveholders as a fit punishment.[102]

The burning of the outlying areas of South Carolina would pale in significance to what awaited Columbia and Charleston. Intent on destroying what they saw as the "cradle of secession," the "hotbed of rebellion," and the home of "the authors of all the calamities that have befallen this nation," Union soldiers displayed little mercy when they entered Columbia on February 17. Sherman's triumphant troops let loose their anger toward the Confederacy and Confederates but believed that *"their punishment is light when compared with what justice demanded."*[103] A group of soldiers foreshadowed the fate of South Carolina's capital as they entered the city singing, "Hail Columbia, happy land, / If I don't burn you, I'll be damned."[104] The soldiers were not disappointed. By the time the Union troops left Columbia, "the Capital, where treason was cradled and reared a mighty raving monster, [was] a blackened ruin."[105] Other reports concurred. "When our army left [Columbia] there was little left to mark the site except a blackened map of smoking ruins."[106] This "pile of ruins," they hoped, would be "a warning to future generations to beware of treason."[107] In the end, fire destroyed approximately one-third of Columbia. Although contemporaries debated who initially set the blaze, Union soldiers clearly felt satisfied by the result. Sherman held that his men had no role in the burning of the city, but acknowledged that "[Union soldiers] not on duty, including the officers who had long been imprisoned there, rescued by us, may have assisted in spreading the fire." In any case, they "indulged in unconcealed joy to see the ruin of the capital of South Carolina."[108] Union colonel Oscar L. Jackson "believe[d] it was not done by order but there seems to be a general acquiescence in the work as a fit example to be made of the capital of the State that boasts of being the cradle of secession and starting the war."[109]

While in Columbia, Sherman and his troops recognized that they had unleashed an unprecedented assault on its white civilians, most of them female. Women, many soldiers reasoned, deserved harsh treatment because of their culpability for the war. Union soldier Edwin Bowen recorded an encounter with an elderly Southern woman who begged for mercy after Union soldiers took her corn and food. Although Bowen claimed to have felt some pity for the woman's situation, his verbal response to her did not reflect it. Instead, he told her that he needed the corn. With what comes across as a sarcastic comment on her role in the war, he further dismissed her complaints, assuring her that "'God will not forsake the richeous.' She must look to him."[110] Similarly, Charles S. Brown described an incident along the march in which an individual soldier asserted his power by forcing Southern women to beg. There are men "that would stand & have a woman kneel to them & beg for Gods sake to leave enough for her children in the house." Even women's humiliating entreaties did not ensure that the soldiers would comply with their requests. After forcing the women to kneel, Brown remarked, the soldiers would "turn from them with oaths & take the last morsel of food."[111]

As they had throughout the march, Northern soldiers frequently expressed their desire to make slaveholding Confederate women pay for their role in the Southern war effort and to simultaneously use them to hurt that effort. In Columbia, Union lieutenant colonel Jeremiah W. Jenkins, provost marshal of the invaded city, explained the actions of the Union army: "The women of the South kept the war alive—and it is only by making them suffer that we can subdue the men."[112] Jenkins saw the utility in attacking Southern domesticity as a way to punish both contemptuous female civilians and Confederate soldiers. Union troops saw a need to punish misbehaving Southerners, despite their gender or age, for their roles in the Civil War. As a result, soldiers even extended their hostility to white Southern children. Men who during peacetime served as fatherly protectors of all youngsters considered them enemies during the Civil War. As he took blankets away from children in Columbia, one Union soldier said "let the d——d little rebels suffer as we have had to do for the past four years."[113] Once they had determined civilians of all ages and sexes to be enemies of the United States, Union soldiers treated them as such.[114]

As they marched northward, Yankee soldiers continued to plunder domestic items from slaveholding households and leave them along their path. From South Carolina, an Illinois soldier commented on the waste. "Articles of silverware, that have been carried along, are thrown into the road, where the heavy wagons crushed out all semblance of anything useful, and the tired and thirsty soldier, relieved of his burden, passes on."[115] Although Sherman officially opposed the wholesale plunder of Southern property, he rarely punished offenders and applauded the effects that the looting had on the Southern civilian population. George M. Wise, a lieutenant on the march, insisted that despite the stated orders, Sherman intended the widespread devastation, especially against the "fair" sex. "Sherman is the most relentless enemy the South has in the Union Army, and when a word from his lips would have stopped the universal devastation he would not speak that word, but said simply to the pleading fair ones of Columbia 'It is your own fault.'"[116]

On several occasions, Sherman made a direct connection between his war on elite women and his desire to crush the fighting abilities of the Confederate army. In the process, he demeaned the Confederate government and drew on concepts of manhood to criticize his enemies. He told his wife that although "the poor women and children will starve," it was not his fault. He continued, telling her that he had told Confederate women in Georgia that "if Jeff Davis expects to found an empire on the ruins of the South, he ought to afford to feed the people."[117] Writing from South Carolina in February 1865, Sherman made a similar statement. He dismissed complaints from Confederate commanders about his policies for "warring against women and children" as "petty nonsense." It was not his job to provide for and protect Southern women. That responsibility belonged to Southern soldiers. "If they claim to be men they should defend their women and children and prevent us reaching their homes."[118] Sherman repeated this explanation to his wife, once again insisting that

Southern men were to blame for the hardships felt by elite women and mocking their inability to do so. "The People along our Road will have nothing left wherewith to Support an hostile army," he explained. He told her not to pity the women, however, "as I told them their sons & brothers had better Stay at home to take Care of the females instead of running about the Country playing soldiers."[119]

Charleston fared no better than Columbia after its surrender. After Confederate forces fled on February 17, U.S. forces under Brig. Gen. Alexander Schimmelpfennig entered a city that had little military equipment left. He mimicked Sherman's approach, and the evacuation did not protect the city or its civilian population from a full-scale assault. With the military provisions already destroyed, the soldiers focused their vengeance on domestic targets. They ransacked homes, terrorized women, and otherwise made their presence and power known. This domestic assault fulfilled the long-standing wishes of Union soldiers. Sherman, for example, had already received word from Halleck expressing his hope that if Charleston were captured "by some accident the place may be destroyed, and if a little salt should be sown upon its site it may prevent the growth of future crops of nullification and secession."[120] United States troops had no problem complying. As one soldier noted, "The army burned everything it came near in the State of South Carolina" because "the men 'had it in' for the State." As a result, the army's "track through the State is a desert waste."[121] Edward Allen showed no surprise or remorse for his countrymen's treatment of the two cities. "The soldiers have had such a hatred for Columbia & Charleston that it is no wonder they burned it [Columbia]."[122] Sherman's satisfaction with the results was evident. He proudly claimed that "any one who is not satisfied with war should go and see Charleston, and he will pray louder and deeper than ever that the country may in the long future be spared any more war." The commander wanted the city to remain untouched as a monument to the horrors of war and the strength of the United States Army. "Charleston and secession being synonymous terms, the city should be left as a sample, so that centuries may pass away before that false doctrine is again preached in our Union."[123]

After leaving Columbia, Union soldiers burned Camden, Winnsboro, Lancaster, Chesterfield, and Cheraw, "[leaving behind] . . . a howling wilderness, an utter desolation." They hoped this would prevent South

Carolina from "ever [wanting] to seceed again."[124] James Stillwell noted that "there is scarcely anything left in our *rear* or *trac[k]s* except pine forests and naked lands and Starving inhabitants. A majority of the *Cities, towns, villages* and *country houses* have been burnt to the ground."[125] As they entered North Carolina, many Union troops rejoiced in their accomplishments. One soldier, Jesse Bean of Minnesota, wrote a commemorative poem as "we bid adieu to S. Carolina leaving our Marks of revenge behind us to Show the Generations to come." His poem mocked "the fate/ Of the first Rebel State/ That Seceded from the Union." In the poem, Bean bragged that Union soldiers had "set Columbia on fier" so that the conquering forces could "let them know where we went." Furthermore, he asserted that the destruction of livestock and property "was all for the benefit of South Carolina."[126] Union soldiers certainly felt satisfaction at the results of the domestic campaign in the Palmetto State.

Sherman shaped his military tactics in North Carolina to account for a civilian population that was poorer than that in South Carolina and rumored to have Unionist tendencies. As they entered North Carolina on March 8, Sherman acknowledged his troops' wanton destruction in South Carolina and directed his officers to "instruct your brigade commanders that we are now out of South Carolina" and that soldiers should now "deal as moderately and fairly by the North Carolinians as possible."[127] Although most historical accounts hold that Sherman softened his tactics in the Tarheel State, his troops continued in their course of both targeted and widespread destruction.[128] Their vandalism began almost immediately upon the troops' entrance into the state when soldiers began setting fire to North Carolina's pine forests by lighting patches of congealed sap. They also torched the turpentine, tar, and rosin factories that they encountered along the state's streams. One Union soldier observed that North Carolina's pine forests "made the handsomest fire . . . especially the smoke as it rolled up in huge back volumes." It was, he continued, "splendid." As Union soldiers "blazed their way through" the state, North Carolina stank of burning turpentine.[129]

Confederate troops could do little to impede Sherman's "domestic war" policy in North Carolina, where Union troops continued to employ tactics designed for a privileged female enemy. When Union troops captured Fayetteville on March 11, they destroyed the local arsenal and mills, tore up railroads, and foraged liberally. They also terrorized the civilian population and destroyed much personal property, perhaps because they found "the city of Fayetteville . . . offensively rebellious."[130] After recounting all of her material losses, one woman in Fayetteville complained that the Union soldiers "spared nothing but our lives."[131] Several Union officers made similar observations. From Fayetteville, Dexter Horton noted, "our march over the country has been like the blighting pestilence, for we have taken or turned upside down everything before us."[132] Despite reports in several newspapers "that our treatment of citizens is good," one soldier warned, "don't believe a word of it."[133] Even Sherman acknowledged the level of destruction. "Poor North Carolina will have a hard time for we sweep the country like a swarm of locusts." This destruction did not trouble Sherman. Although "thousands of people may perish," he believed that his march would succeed because "they now realise that war means something else than vain glory and boasting." Sherman believed that as a result of his tactics in Georgia and the Carolinas, "if Peace ever falls to their lot [Southerners] will never again invite War."[134]

Sherman ordered the left wing under Slocum's command to march out of Fayetteville on March 15, 1865. Within two weeks of Sherman's April 13 entrance into Raleigh, after battles at Averasboro and Bentonville and after General Robert E. Lee surrendered his Army of Northern Virginia to Union general Ulysses S. Grant, Joseph Johnston surrendered his Confederate troops to Sherman at Durham Station, North Carolina. The assault on the Southern home front had come to an end. Sherman's men returned to what Illinois soldier Charles W. Wills described as "our good behavior," which included "no foraging, no bumming rails, or houses, and nothing naughty whatever."[135] Indeed, once orders to cease foraging were given, Sherman's troops immediately complied. Such an immediate change in behavior illuminates the ability of Sherman and his fellow officers to govern their troops when desired, and it demonstrates the spirit of permissiveness of the commanders throughout the march. One of the men on the campaign, Allen Morgan Geer, observed the remarkable change after Johnston's surrender. "Very striking is the difference between this march and all others previous. The people remain contentedly at home, men are plenty, a safety guard is at each house and our soldiers make no effort to forage or destroy."[136] Sherman clearly controlled his troops' actions.

PUNISHING SOUTHERN WOMEN

Sherman designed and pursued his march through Georgia and the Carolinas as a comprehensive assault on the slaveholding Southern home front and its domestic trappings. Intending to break the will of the Confederacy by destroying it on both the psychological and physical levels, Union soldiers ransacked Southern homes, paying special attention to the markers of domestic life and femininity. They looted and burned homes, tore apart bedrooms, scattered private letters across fields, danced on pianos, and destroyed women's fancy dresses and undergarments. They also stole jewelry, china, silver, and candlesticks. Elite slaveholding families, considered instrumental in Southern secession and the coming of war by their enemies, bore the brunt of the attack. Those soldiers who initially felt twinges of pity for their civilian targets soon learned to mute these feelings and concentrate on women as the "strongest rebels." This animosity toward Confederates, as well as the tacit consent of their officers, allowed them license to ransack the home front as they terrorized and taunted their female enemies.

Sherman and his soldiers assumed that their campaign against the Southern home front and its female occupants would prove an easy success; surely, "the weaker sex" would quickly and passively surrender to the power of an aggressive invading army. Much to their surprise, an easy victory would not prove to be the case. Many elite Southern women refused to take the invasion of their domestic sphere quietly. Acknowledging that Northern troops had adjusted their policies to allow for an attack on femininity and domesticity, Confederate women rethought their position on the home front. As rumors spread of the impending invasion, Confederate women prepared themselves and their homes to weather the storm. Having found the means to merge their gender and regional identities in ways that allowed them to fight for their nation, they refused to submit. Sherman would not so easily "cure [Confederate women] of [their] pride and boasting."

CHAPTER 3

WORKING FOR WAR

In January 1865, as Union troops headed toward the capital of secession, the elite women of Columbia, South Carolina, opened a fundraising bazaar to aid the Confederate cause. After four years of supporting and sacrificing for the war effort, and months of gathering items for sale, these women would not be deterred by the fact that "the enemy are knocking at our doors."[1] With state sanction, the women decorated the State House with elaborate displays that highlighted the virtues and symbols of the Confederacy and its eleven states. They covered the state booths "with a canopy of lace & crimson trimmed beautifully with evergreens and [surrounded] with the shield of each state and a large flag drooping over the whole canopy."[2] Every detail worked to emphasize the connection to Confederate soldiers, as the bazaar's setup represented a series of military encampment tents. Columbia's elite women planned all aspects of the bazaar and used their close proximity to danger to encourage donations on behalf of the soldiers. Women solicited friends around the Confederacy for gifts of money and items for sale.

The crowds for the Columbia Bazaar—which began on January 17—exceeded the planners' expectations. As Emma LeConte proudly recorded, "Our great Bazaar opened last night and *such* a jam!"[3] The offerings at the Columbia Bazaar were varied and indulgent. Tables held extravagant desserts, fancy dolls, homespun items, tobacco pouches, cutlery, jewelry, and scarce foods. Some booths also offered attendees entertainment in the form of fortune telling, raffles, and other amusements. Attendees willingly paid inflated prices to participate in the spectacle and to obtain the luxuries and delicacies, with each purchase publicly demonstrating their support for the Confederate war effort. Despite being forced by Sherman's approach to close after only five days instead of the intended two weeks, the bazaar raised between an estimated $150,000 and $350,000 for the Confederacy's sick and wounded soldiers. The organizers gloried in the fact that the advance of Union troops did not prevent the bazaar from being "a complete success."⁴

For the planners of the Columbia Bazaar and many of its participants, the event was the latest of a steady series of public actions to support the Confederate cause. From the very beginning of the war, these elite slaveholding women worked with the belief that the war could not be waged without their steadfast support. They knew that their husbands and sons could not sustain the fight without the material and psychological sustenance they received from home. Victory, the women assumed, was partially on their own shoulders. In 1860 and 1861, they had encouraged secession and then helped encourage the enlistment of soldiers. When the war began they sewed uniforms and created bandages for their men. They wore homespun often, restrained from eating delicacies that were common in peacetime, and for four years sustained their material and moral support even as they became increasingly aware that they were in the direct line of Union hostility.

The elite white women who confronted Sherman in late 1864 and early 1865 played an active role in the Confederate war effort long before the general and his troops physically entered their lives. They did not remain on the sidelines of the war as they and their "protectors" often declared in later years. These slaveholding women supported secession in 1860 and 1861 and made the Confederacy a central part of their lives and duties for the next four years. Believing that fighting for independence was the only honorable course of action, they urged their countrymen into battle against the Yankees. With men focused on their military obligations, Confederate women faced several daunting tasks of their own. During the war, white women fulfilled many traditionally male tasks, including managing plantations, working for the government, and overseeing slaves. In addition, they coped with the war-related demands on the home front as they became nurses, ran makeshift hospitals, provided clothing, prepared food, and sent letters of moral support to the battlefront to support their soldiers. Although these tasks forced privileged white Southern women to redefine themselves and their place in society, the women willingly engaged in these efforts in order to show their support for the Confederacy and the soldiers. Wartime tasks allowed elite women of the South to create and promote a sense of female Confederate identity and nationalism.

As the Civil War lengthened and the enemy directly threatened their domestic sphere, many elite Southern women bolstered their regional loyalty through increased work for their nation. Slaveholding women willingly, and sometimes eagerly, took on previously male responsibilities in the name of a developing sense of Confederate womanhood. Their increased roles in the nation allowed white women to develop a shared sense of Confederate identity and camaraderie with others across the South. As a result of these opportunities, elite white women did not, for the most part, lose heart or their feminine identity. Instead, their deep-seated Southernness prepared them to move into new roles that emphasized their loyalty to the Confederacy. The wartime behavior of white Southern women reveals an enthusiasm for the Confederacy as well as a willingness to merge regional and gender roles to make countless sacrifices for their nation.

Sherman's March scarcely marked the beginning of wartime hardships for white women in Georgia and the Carolinas. As earlier scholars have repeatedly demonstrated, white Southern women assumed various duties to meet wartime needs at the outset of the Civil War. They took on increased responsibilities as plantation mistresses, slave overseers, nurses, seamstresses, teachers, fundraisers, spies, soldiers, and writers. They helped raise military regiments, worked on farms, took over businesses, worked for the government, formed female home guards, and lobbied politicians. Women provided much of the clothing, food, supplies, and medical care that their men on the battlefield required for survival. In addition, many willingly sacrificed luxury items and turned to home manufacture. When necessary, white Southern women did whatever was needed to support the Confederate war effort, whether or not it conformed to traditional, or peacetime, gender norms.[5]

Elite Southern women did not necessarily cast off the trappings of femininity to support a long-term war effort. Instead they found ways to adapt their roles as ladies into those as Confederates. When the war broke out, for example, white women throughout Georgia and the Carolinas began working to equip the military. Catherine Edmondston of

North Carolina explained that throughout the South "the Cloth for . . . Uniforms & Tents is purchased by individual subscription, not waiting for the State to equip its men." Such an operation required "thousands of Ladies who never worked before [to be] hard at work on coarse sewing."[6] These elite women, like Edmondston, willingly toiled for their nation.[7] Women changed the focus of their daily activities to make certain their soldiers had the necessary supplies. Subsequently, as historian Jim Cullen notes, their wartime activities "do not constitute an abrogation of Southern ladyhood; rather, they fall under the dicta of a new ladyhood whereby duty and sacrifice are enlisted in the service of the Confederate war effort."[8] Women often considered their activities during the Civil War as adaptations of their antebellum roles that included a wider conception of their prewar identities.[9] Working for Southern independence did not require a suppression of femininity but rather demonstrated a development of Confederate womanhood.[10]

The Civil War led many white women, as it did men, to subsume their personal interests in favor of a national cause. Wartime "true" womanhood subsequently encompassed the work done by white women in support of the troops. Through work in aid societies, factories, and farms, white women became major suppliers of food, uniforms, and other goods. Within weeks of the war's outset, white women had established at least one thousand aid societies throughout the Confederacy. In the areas that Sherman would later invade, organizations such as the Ladies' Association of Columbia for the Relief and Comfort of the Families of Absent Soldiers in This City & Its Vicinity, the Greenville Ladies' Association in Aid of the Volunteers of the Confederate Army, the Soldiers' Relief Association of Charleston, and the Ladies' Relief Association of Spartanburg, South Carolina, raised money, gathered supplies, and rallied morale throughout the war.[11] Most Southern towns had their own female aid societies that provided soldiers countless socks, undergarments, shirts, gloves, blankets, shoes, comforters, handkerchiefs, scarves, bandages, and food.[12] Southern poet Caroline Howard Gilman gloried that women's "useful, homely knitting work" had become "doubly dear" because "the Soldier needs thy busy love."[13] Some women did not stop at sewing, cooking, nursing, or fundraising for their nation. A few served as spies, using their status as women—as well as their clothing and looks—to smuggle information and supplies across enemy lines.[14]

To ensure that the Confederacy had troops for its civilian population to support, many white Southern women served as unofficial enlistment officers. They fervently encouraged the men of their families and communities to join the Confederate army and destroy the enemy. In this way, they further made the Civil War their war and put their imprint on the course of action that the South would take.[15] Their vocal roles at the outbreak of war later developed into material and moral support for the soldiers on the battlefield. White women, some of whom would later face Sherman's troops, often used the power of the pen to bolster the Confederate army. In the midst of the war, for example, Mary E. Tucker wrote a poem to stimulate enlistment, support her nation, and show confidence in the South's military leaders. She wanted her fellow "gallant Georgians" to "unfurl your proud banners, [and] beat loudly the drum" as they headed to the battlefield. Tucker urged action because "upon our fair borders the ruthless foe stands, / Already has wasted our homes, and our lands." Consequently, she bid "sons of Georgia to arms! Let no stain of dishonor / Attaint her fair name."[16] Other elite women used similar measures to urge the men of their communities to pursue what they considered the honorable course—fighting for their nation. In some cases, newspapers published the patriotic poetry. A poem published in the *Charleston Mercury* by a woman known only as C. M. C. alerted the readers that "the writer has a husband, three sons, two nephews, other relatives and friends . . . to whom these lines are most respectfully inscribed." C. M. C. hoped to invigorate the troops. "March, march on brave 'Palmetto' boys," she exhorted, "all the base Yankees are crossing the *border*." The South Carolina men should redouble their efforts for the Confederacy, especially because "young wives and sisters have buckled your armor on, / Maidens ye love bid ye *go* to the battlefield." The love and confidence of the women at home should inspire them to "let fear and unmanliness vanish before ye" and secure battlefield victories.[17] Although most antebellum white women rarely wrote their poetry for public consumption, they realized that the Civil War required them to think beyond their individual homes and families and to take public action. Consequently, to protect their identities yet make sure that their countrymen got the message, many Southern women writers used pseudonyms for their published work.[18]

In addition to becoming wordsmiths for the Confederacy, white Southern women became fundraisers for their nation, planning and attending countless bazaars, fairs, concerts, raffles, and dances to raise money for army supplies.[19] They supplied their kinsmen and other loved ones with clothes, medical supplies, and food, and they also sent these items to unknown Confederate soldiers as a way of supporting the nation as a whole.[20] In this manner, Confederate women successfully subsumed their personal loyalties and obligations to the greater good of their nation. In some instances, women used the deaths of their loved ones in Confederate service as an impetus to increased sacrifice for their nation. For example, after her brother died on the battlefield in the "noble cause," Maria L. Garlington of Laurens, South Carolina, hoped to organize a fundraising drive with the support of her school friends: "We should all send money to the hospitals. . . . I think we might deprive ourselves to help the poor soldiers."[21] Garlington realized that the support of other unknown Confederate women had most likely aided her brother and the other soldiers in his unit. She wanted to do the same for others. In addition, for Garlington, the only appropriate memorial to her brother would be an independent Confederacy.

Although the South had no overarching medical organizations, like the Union's Women's Central Relief Association and the United States Sanitary Commission, thousands of Confederate women nursed the wounded and dying in their homes as well as in makeshift hospitals around the South.[22] Soldiers and civilians alike applauded white women's work for the Confederacy. Confederate volunteer Rufus Cater revealed to his cousin in 1861 his "glowing admiration [of] the patriotism manifested by the Ladies of the South." He proudly recorded that "everywhere they have been engaged heart and hand in providing for the necessities of the volunteers and in inspiring them with heroic courage." Cater also commended Confederate women for "hav[ing] sent forth their husbands[,] their sons[, and] their brothers to the tented field with their blessings and their prayers admonishing them to deeds of valor and telling them if they must die to die the *soldier's* death."[23] Cater recognized elite women's importance in both recruiting and sustaining Confederate troops.

In addition to new roles, war brought other problems to the Southern home front. The Union blockade, government impressment, unstable currencies, and haphazard supply lines all contributed to dwindling supplies and inflation long before Sherman and his troops demolished the Georgia and Carolina countryside. Women around the Confederacy struggled to feed their families throughout the war. In 1863, women in North Carolina and Georgia, as well as some in Alabama and Virginia, instigated and participated in bread riots. During the Richmond bread riot, over one thousand women looted shops for bacon, flour, sugar, coffee, candles, cloth, and shoes, among other things. They, and their sisters across the South, used these actions to voice their displeasure with the lack of government assistance.[24] The riots in North Carolina made quite an impression on one woman there, who told of a *"raid* made on Jonesville" by "a band of *women,* armed with axes." The protesters "came down on the place, to press the tithe corn &c. brought wagons along to carry it off." As she noted, "women generally want to carry their point." In addition, she described "a similar attack . . . on Hamptonville a few days ago . . . with more success." The women who participated in that riot, she reported, "took as much as they wanted without meeting with any resistance."[25]

By actively participating in protests, white Southern women visibly stepped outside the boundaries of the home and took their traditional focus on family and household into the public arena. The bread riots demonstrate how white women adapted their conceptions of gender to deal with wartime problems. As they ransacked local stores and demanded to be heard by local officials, the female participants asserted a traditional view of gender roles—that they had a right to protection by virtue of their femininity. However, the bread riots also revealed Southern women's willingness to move outside the traditional confines of womanhood during times of crisis to look after their own interests.[26] Unwilling to credit women for their definitive stand and fearful of class uprisings, however, many wealthy Southerners comforted themselves with the notion that the female rioters were merely prostitutes and thieves, not those truly in need of food or help.[27]

In contrast to those who participated in the 1863 bread riots, later in the war many other women, especially wealthy ones, gave up portions of their family's food to send to the soldiers on the battlefield. For example, as Sherman and his troops headed her way, Catherine Edmondston described a community food drive for the soldiers. Together, rioting and sacrifice both revealed ways in which Confederate women deftly adapted to the realities of wartime life through what were, in some ways, traditionally feminine outlets. They manipulated preconceived notions about women's work and interests to serve their strengthening Confederate concerns. Their ability to survive a personal confrontation with the enemy later in the war may have resulted from women's early experiences and sacrifices.

By 1864, the elite white women of Georgia and the Carolinas faced the likelihood of greater hardships and shortages. The approach of Union troops waging war on the home front forced Southern women to confront and adapt to an unanticipated reality of wartime. No longer protected by the men of their families or by communities, elite women personally faced a belligerent enemy who acknowledged few boundaries.[28] Confederate women recognized the dangers of approaching troops. They feared, sometimes with justification, that they would be "subjected to the cruelties, and insults of lawless raiding parties" who would ignore those constraints which were deemed the marks of civilized behavior.[29] Although still hoping that their bodies would remain inviolable, slaveholding women no longer had confidence that their domestic space would remain untouched by enemy hands. They realized that the household, a nineteenth-century haven for women, would not protect them from what female rebels were quick to label Sherman's "hellish crew."[30]

Initial reports of Sherman's wide swath of destruction from Atlanta to Savannah alerted elite women to the coming perils. Stories of the Union plunder of food stores, burning of houses, as well as destruction of clothes, housewares, personal papers, and furniture made clear the domestic ramifications of the march. Sherman, they realized, would not spare white women or households but had instead targeted them as he struck at the heart of Southern domesticity. In addition, slaveholding women of Georgia and the Carolinas understood that they would not emerge from the war unscathed. Grace Brown Elmore of South Carolina noted that "we feel almost as sure of Sherman's reaching Columbia before long as if he were already here." Consequently, "every one is preparing for his reception."[31] By "preparing," however, Elmore did not mean fleeing. Instead of retreating like the soldiers often did, many Confederate women responded to the Union attack on the domestic front by doing as much as possible to retaliate against the foe. This effort to fight for their nation in some ways forced a redefinition of Southern femininity.

In particular, Confederate women transferred their domestic routines to sites outside the customary household to deal with the crisis of war.[32] They also took on tasks once reserved for enslaved women, often working in groups with other like-minded women and therefore preserving the shared sense that their work for the Confederacy was women's work. Elite white women's roles as Confederate seamstresses, fundraisers, recruitment officers, and nurses merged the long-standing ideal of female sacrifice with a defiant, even warrior-like, defense of the homeland. Working within this new identity, many elite white women continued to support the Confederacy, even late in the war, through any means available. Their "public domesticity," reflected through their continued work in hospitals, ladies' aid societies, and fundraising efforts throughout 1864 and 1865, illuminates Southern women's intense Confederate patriotism despite increasing war depredations and shortages.[33]

Confederate women's efforts for the nation gained them high praise from contemporaries, who recognized the importance of that work. Soon after the fall of Atlanta, Confederate president Jefferson Davis toured several of the cities that he assumed Sherman would invade. In each one, he praised the elite women of the South for their active support of the Confederacy. He also complimented them on their ability to act as ladies in the performance of these vital duties. A "peculiar claim of gratitude," Davis asserted in South Carolina "is due to the fair country-wom[e]n of the Palmetto State" who "have gone to the hospital to watch by the side of the sick." Davis revealed the gender and class conventions of the time when he praised the women "who have nursed as if nursing was a profession—who have used their needle with the industry of sewing-women." In addition, these women "have borne privation without a murmur, and . . . have given up fathers, sons, and husbands with more than Spartan virtue."[34] Davis acknowledged and appreciated the fact that many elite women had stepped outside the boundaries of antebellum womanhood but successfully retained their femininity. Confederate womanhood gave them an avenue through which they could fulfill both needs.

As Sherman's men approached their towns, Confederate women continued to sew for their soldiers. More than three years of war, inflation, and the scarcity of raw materials made such tasks increasingly difficult but did not deter them. They produced and relied on homespun for their own clothes and those they made for their families and soldiers.[35] More concerned about the condition of Southern soldiers on the battlefield than about the presence of Union troops in her town in December 1864, one Georgia woman wrote, "We are all here at work, carding, spinning, and weaving. Denise and [Di] have . . . wove nearly seventy four yds, since the Yankees went out on their last foraging trip which was five weeks ago."[36] Firsthand experience of invasion did not stop the labors of these Georgia women. They continued in their efforts to supply Confederate troops with much-needed blankets, coats, shirts, socks, shoes, and other necessities.[37] As a result of this dedication to their soldiers, many elite Southern women prioritized saving needles and thread over other valuables when Union troops arrived in their areas. For example, Sarah Jane Sams hid her sewing supplies at the first hint of Union invasion. Underneath several layers of clothes, she hid "three small bags containing needles, cotton and flax thread, tape and buttons."[38]

Their continued participation in soldiers' aid societies also highlights slaveholding women's continued dedication to the Confederacy. Despite the approach of Union troops, the Soldiers' Relief Association of Charleston, as well as the Greenville Ladies' Association in Aid of the Volunteers of the Confederate Army, continued to hold meetings days before Sherman's arrival in February 1865. Even with home front shortages, the female membership continued to collect donations as well as make and distribute supplies to soldiers. One week in early February, with Sherman's men already in the Palmetto State, the Charleston association distributed shirts, socks, blankets, pants, drawers, and shoes to Confederate troops. Also in February, these women sent supplies to hospitals and brigades across South Carolina. The *Charleston Courier* recognized the group's contributions, noting that a hospital in Summerville received items from a dozen women including over eighty pairs of socks and $920.[39] As Sherman's troops feinted to the city, another Charleston aid society offered the Southern troops "519 shirts, 267 pairs of drawers, 189 pairs of socks, 179 pairs of pants, 23 pairs of shoes, 37 blankets and comforters, handkerchiefs and scarves."[40] Instead of convincing Confederate women that the South's bid for independence was over, a fear of invasion motivated women to continue, if not increase, their soldiers' aid efforts for a war that, for slaveholding women, had no end in sight.

Individual Confederate women, even as they anxiously awaited the approach of Union troops, also continued to work to provide for Southern soldiers. Many South Carolinians spent their time, often with family members, sewing and weaving for the Confederacy. With the knowledge that Sherman and his men would soon arrive, all of Mary Gayle Aiken's "alarm about Sherman has returned." She acknowledged that "we have much to fear. . . . The Yankees will not show much mercy to S. Carolinians." The actions of Union soldiers in Georgia, she accurately predicted, would pale in comparison to their treatment of women in the seedbed of secession. In spite of this fear, Aiken's loyalty to her nation and its soldiers remained strong. "My eyes trouble me much, but I continue to sew, from morning 'til night."[41] Aiken's willingness to ignore her personal discomfort as she sewed for the Confederacy demonstrated her intense dedication to her nation and the men fighting for its independence.

By 1864, it became more difficult for women to find their own cloth, thread, and other sewing materials. As a result, elite women, traditionally excluded from most money matters, canvassed for contributions for the soldiers. By drawing upon Southern society's ideas about sacrifice and honor, many of them effectively raised money and materials for the war effort without seeming to step outside the boundaries of femininity. For example, North Carolinian Mary "Mollie" Davis discussed how she and another woman "begged money enough to buy severel bolts of domestic . . . fifteen hundred dollars." They needed this large sum to fill and send a box to a Salisbury hospital. With an enormous and seemingly endless task in front of her, Mollie wished her friend was nearby to help sew shirts and other garments. "I will be very busy sewing for the Hospital this next week."[42] As long as women's forays into the public sphere seemed to conform to female activities and were for the common good of the Confederacy, they did not overturn society's notions about femininity. The necessities of the Civil War allowed elite white women to escape the confines of peacetime propriety for the good of their nation.

Elite women who later found themselves in the path of Sherman's March further demonstrated their dedication to the Confederacy through their work in hospitals. In antebellum years, women had cared for the sick within their own households, but public nursing was reserved for men. This exclusive reliance on male nurses was one of the first casualties of war. The loss of male nurses to the ranks of the military required women to assume the responsibilities of tending to the increasing numbers of sick and wounded soldiers.[43] As the war lengthened, elite women's roles as both nurses in and suppliers to hospitals became increasingly important. Southern men and women proudly acknowledged white women's roles in the hospitals. As Sherman and his troops fought to gain control of Atlanta, Confederate soldier Douglas J. Cater marveled at the dedication of the dislocated women in the area. Cater noted that "the ladies of Georgia and other states many of whom are denominated *refugees,* having been driven from their homes by the invaders, are doing all in their power to relieve the sufferings of the wounded." The women poured into the town, "having with them every thing that a wounded soldier could wish (even were he at home) on their way to the hospitals." As a result, "that poor boy separated from mother and sisters by the waters of the Mississippi, lacerating wounds almost depriving him of life, for a time forgets his sufferings by the presence of one of the ministering angels." The soldier especially appreciated the nurse "with her own fair hands bathing his fevered temples, brushing back the unshorn locks from his forehead and bidding him be of good cheer, that he will be cared for." Cater took such actions as a sign of ultimate Confederate success. "Can such acts of Kindness go unrewarded? Impossible[.] Peace, liberty and independence . . . will be given to the people of this Confederacy as a reward for their great sacrifices."[44] A Confederate soldier from Tennessee made similar observations. "Our wounded who write or have returned all speak in the most glowing terms of praise of the ladies of Georgia and Alabama as also the refugee ladies of Tenn. and other states." These women, he continued, "are unremitting in their attentions and ministrations to the wounded and sick at the Hospitals [and] take them to their homes when they can be moved and there nurse them." As a result of such dedication, "too much praise cannot be lavished upon the ladies of the South. They are devoted heart and soul to the cause and do much to cheer the spirits and keep up the determination of the troops."[45] Highlighting their feminine nurturing natures, elite women were able to serve their nation in a previously male field. Furthermore, through their nursing efforts Confederate women promoted and supported loyalty to their nation.

The Civil War forced many Confederate women unwittingly to become front-line nurses as the war moved through their homes and towns. Out of necessity, they set up hospitals where space was available—houses, churches, town halls, schools, train depots, and even streets. Women then served as nurses in these makeshift hospitals throughout the Confederacy.[46] In August 1864, Mary Boykin Chesnut began volunteering at Columbia, South Carolina's Wayside Hospital, "which was gotten up and is carried on by that good woman Jane Coles Fisher." The Columbia women at the hospital fed wounded men, helped dress their wounds, and did "not for any cause [miss] one day's attendance."[47] Women in Augusta proudly recorded their work for the Confederate soldiers. They attended to the soldiers there and brought them whatever supplies they had. The experience made quite an impression on Mary Jones, who one morning "observed a poor soldier . . . evidently near his end" and offered him some wine. When she returned later in the day, "only the narrow, naked pine bedstead remained," but she would "long remember the expression of his dying eyes."[48] Other women in Georgia and the Carolinas did what Frances Thomas Howard casually noted—they "went to the hospital as usual." Howard's actions seem remarkable, considering that Savannah was under Union control as she made her regular visit to the Confederate hospital.[49]

Their control over household matters allowed elite white women in Georgia and the Carolinas to allot their time and space as they saw fit. Consequently, when the occasion arose, many willingly turned their homes into hospitals and wayside homes. Although "expecting the Yankees here daily," one North Carolina woman was "almost constantly engaged at the hospitals attending to the wants of the sick & wounded . . . several hundred of them." She noted the soldiers' appreciation of women's efforts: "They seem very grateful to us for our attentions."[50] A month later she provided a description of a hospital established in Mrs. John Smith's house. Despite the lack of space, injured men were continually brought there and it was "full of wounded Confederate soldiers . . . lying on the bare floor." This daunting task did not demoralize the volunteers, but the lack of official support made it an unwinnable fight. "Some of our ladies have gone there as nurses" but still could not completely handle the increasing number of patients. "Mrs Smith wrote word yesterday if [more] assistance was not sent immediately they would all perish together."[51] Smith did not abandon her efforts as a result of this fear for her patients and herself, but instead continued to enlist the help of more Confederate women.

Southern soldiers recognized the importance of elite women's roles as nurses, cooks, and suppliers. While in North Carolina, one man described a meeting with Miss Brice, who, as Sherman made his way through South Carolina, "has cert[a]inly done a great deal for the solgiers, she commensed the plan in Wilmington of having a table set at the Depot for the solgiers passing through to eat at[;] the ladies attend themselves daily."[52] The soldier praised the Wilmington's Ladies' Soldiers' Aid Society for taking care of wounded soldiers who constantly passed by rail through the city. In addition to working as nurses, the community also provided "tables of food" for the soldiers. Letters of thanks praising female sacrifice poured in for the women of aid societies in Georgia and the Carolinas, especially as they worked through the conditions created by invading Union soldiers.[53]

In their efforts to relieve the sufferings of the soldiers, many Confederate women willingly moved outside the boundaries of appropriate peacetime behavior. North Carolinian Louise Medway appealed to President Jefferson Davis for assistance. Medway represented "a number of Ladies here [who] have established a Soldiers's Aid Society for the purpose of ministering to the wants of the sick & wounded *en route*" because the government provisions neglected this group of soldiers by only "providing for them when on duty or in Hospital." Since its inception the society had "been very successful & have fed & sometimes partially clothed from 6 to 8,000 per month besides having wounds dressed &c." The problem arose from the delivery of the donations sent to this particular soldiers' aid society. Medway wanted help from Davis because the Custom House would not release to her several packages of donations to the society because of her sex and lack of official appointment. "Today several parcels—solely for soldiers use—are detained because the collector cannot (in accordance with his instructions) give a permit unless signed by the Surgeon of the Hospital for which the articles are intended," Medway explained. Because these supplies were not for patients at a hospital, but rather "for the wounded & sick arriving at the depot, a difficulty presents itself." Medway did not want these impediments to interfere with her efforts, so she requested "a permit for all articles coming to me for use of our Soldiers." This permit, she hoped would allow those abroad with more means and opportunities to help the Confederacy, whose "means are so small & the wants of our soldiers so many."[54] Recognizing the importance of women's work in this regard, Davis approved Medway's request.

Elite women further expanded their domestic duties by cooking for and feeding soldiers. Women's roles as the preparers of food for the Confederacy began long before Sherman invaded the South. For example, from a Georgia hospital in 1863, one Confederate soldier bragged "we have plenty to eat at this hopitle and the cleverist ladyes round hear you ever saw[.] you can go to thare houess and get milk butter coffey buisquit potatoes pyes custards and all kinds of goo[d] meates that you can call for and surrups of ever[y] kind." He continued to praise Southern womanhood and generosity: "Ask one what thay charge a thare reply is that you must come back a gain and get more *oh* they are so very good to me I will hate very mutch to leave them for I dont know when I will meat with a nother chance like this for good eating."[55] "Good eating" did not continue throughout the war, however. In addition to the time and effort involved, women's responsibilities as food suppliers required Southern civilians to share their own meager foodstuffs. In early February 1865, with Sherman and his troops marching toward her state, one elite South Carolina woman spent her entire morning and most of her supplies feeding hundreds of Confederate soldiers near her town. "The Regt. arrived from Virginia this morning, we prepared breakfast for some of the officers, but only Maj Furgeson came, [so we] sent Noah with everything we could prepare in a hurry to the camp."[56] As Confederate soldiers moved through Southern cities and towns, women provided them with the necessary sustenance to continue their battlefield duties. Soldiers in Southern hospitals benefited from women's green thumbs. "From their gardens large quantities of vegetables are sent to us," John Peter Kendall, an officer in Cheatham's Brigade, wrote. He was particularly impressed because he thought it "quite a luxury to get vegetables."[57] Sherman's imminent approach did not deter women's culinary efforts for the troops.

Other Confederate women across Georgia and the Carolinas similarly used their own rations to feed the troops. In March 1865, as North Carolina prepared to face the brunt of invasion, Catherine Edmondston described a community food drive for the soldiers. In this instance, the governor asked all North Carolina civilians to save "meat, meal, & flour for the army." More specifically Edmondston noted, "These supplies are to be over and above every man's *surplus* that the Government already has. It must be from his own stock of provisions, *what he denies himself for the sake of the army.*" Despite women's numerical dominance in the white home front population, Edmondston tellingly referred to the sacrifice of food as a "man's" duty. In using this language, she revealed a change in women's conception of their role on the home front. As the wartime heads of household, women had taken over male responsibilities and, in many ways, the male vocabulary. When discussing the shortages in more detail, she acknowledged her personal role in the voluntary deprivation. As a family, the Edmondstons "had determined last week to deprive ourselves of meat at one meal per diem & to give what we thus save to the army, but so pressing is the need that we go beyond that & give 500 lbs of meat which we had intended for our own table & will live on bread & vegetables instead." To make up for what would be donated to the troops, Catherine Edmondston vowed to "make every inch of my garden do its whole duty." Although she saw a long war ahead of her, she deemed the sacrifice necessary and deserved. She understood that "there will be many days this summer when we cannot taste meat," but the sacrifice was important. After all, it was worth it "if our army is fed."[58] Edmondston clearly spoke from a privileged condition. Unlike most of her fellow countrywomen, after four years of war she and her family had a large surplus of food to donate to the troops. Other white women struggled to produce and donate any surplus to Confederate soldiers while still supporting their own families. Even so, war and shortage did not destroy elite Confederate women's sense of charity.

In late 1864, the women of South Carolina extended their nationalistic work overseas, arranging and supporting a fundraising bazaar in Liverpool, England. They sent handmade items through the blockade to offer for sale. They fervently hoped that the work of British "friends of the Confederacy" would supplement their own efforts and that British generosity would help further supply Southern soldiers with food and clothing. One of the women of the Gregg family diligently collected items from her friends and family for the Liverpool bazaar. Outlining the contributions in a letter to the bazaar's South Carolina coordinator, Mary Snowden, Gregg praised the talents of various contributors. "I have had several articles promised me," she explained. "Amongst them a beautiful little Palmetto hat by a niece of mine. . . . Another niece, who makes all the *shoes* for herself & five children . . . has promised me a pair. and Mrs Chappell . . . a pair of home made silk gloves." As for her own contribution, Gregg had made "a *Confederate lady* dressed all in homespun, and made of homespun."[59] This "Confederate lady" demonstrated Gregg's pride in herself and her use of homespun. It also revealed her resourcefulness; Confederate women used various means to raise money for their soldiers.

The Columbia Bazaar, the most celebrated display of Southern women's patriotism, received sanction from the state's and the Confederacy's upper echelons. The Palmetto State's men and women supported this venture, as did Confederates around the South. In December 1864, as the women prepared for the fundraising effort, the state legislature passed a resolution "that the ladies engaged in preparation for a bazaar sale in aid of the hospitals and homes for soldiers, be permitted to use the Legislative Halls, and such other portions of the State House as may not be in use for the public service."[60] The motion passed "the Senate unanimously, & the House with only one dissenting voice have granted the use of the State House to the Bazaar."[61] Confederate women had successfully entered the political arena as they worked to raise funds for their nation in the State House.

Official sanction did not guarantee success for the bazaar, but Sherman's men may have unwittingly done so. Recognizing that "the enemy are knocking at our doors," Columbia's women still insisted on holding the large bazaar to raise money for their soldiers. They hoped that the close proximity of Union troops might inspire Confederate women, who "with hearts nerved by the necessity for prompt action . . . [would] be stimulated to redoubled efforts, and the sum realized [would] exceed [the committee's] most sanguine expectations."[62] Elite white women planned all aspects of the bazaar and, through various avenues, supplied all of the items sold there.[63] Despite shortages, many women found ways to contribute items for sale. A South Carolina woman who had diligently supported the Liverpool bazaar promised that "we will try to do *something* for the Fair—tho' I cannot promise *much,* for the lack of materials for fancy work."[64] Other women raised money from communities around the Confederacy to support their efforts. For example, South Carolinian Sallie White sent what she must have considered an appropriate amount—$1,865—that she had collected from "a few patriotic citizens of this place for the benefit of the Bazaar." In addition, White and her sisters sent "a box of fancy articles" to be sold. White's contribution joined those provided by other women in her state. Together they made "a nice contribution from *this* section of the State, for I hear that every body has been working for the Bazaar."[65] As a result of the active recruitment of donations, items for the bazaar poured in from men and women around South Carolina. One businessman sent a "R[ail]R[oad] reciept for a bale of Factory domestics, Shipped to your address, being a donation from the Batesville Manufacturing Co, to the Ladies Baazar in Columbia."[66]

The Columbia Bazaar attracted more than local attention. To ensure the event's success, its coordinators enlisted the help of their countrywomen throughout the Confederacy. The bazaar's planners, who had previously sent a broadside overseas to enlist the help of Confederate sympathizers, sent out an appeal to "the Friends of the Southern Cause at Home" to collect donations. They hoped the people of the South would respond with "that generous support to which [the bazaar] is so well entitled from every motive of humanity and patriotism."[67] In addition, Columbia's women sent personal pleas of help. In a letter to a friend outside of South Carolina one woman "*write[s] & beg[s]—Delia, Patti, yourself*—Mrs Brown & all interested in the soldiers to make some little fancy articles for our Table, & send them to me either by express, or some one coming to this place." The efforts of all of these women were necessary not only to raise money but also because the letter's writer "would be very much mortified if the table over which we preside, is anything but a success." In closing, the woman pleaded with her friends to "exert yourselves & comply with my request."[68]

To honor participants throughout the South, the organizers of the bazaar played up state and Confederate pride in the displays. The flags of each of the eleven Confederate States flew above tables highlighting the contributions from their respective states in the House and the Senate.[69] Grace Brown Elmore commented on the symbolism of the set-up. "The shield of each state that the table represents" hung in the room and allowed all to see that the states were "standing alone and entire but yet working for a common end."[70] S. C. Goodwyn described the bazaar in glowing terms. "The old State House presented a most magnificent appearance," she wrote and then described the scene. The bazaar's setup had been so impressive, she asserted to her husband, that "it really was worth seeing."⁷¹ Grace Brown Elmore also offered a description of the bazaar. "On each side of the hall he could have seen booths, draped in the gayest colors red and white or blue, garlanded with evergreens, and filled with all sorts of nick nacks."⁷² As a result, the bazaar presented a shared sense of Confederate identity both within Columbia and throughout the Confederacy.

The Columbia Bazaar offered attendees their choice of a wide variety of items. "The tables are loaded with fancy articles—brought through the blockade or manufactured by the ladies—Every thing to eat can be had if one can pay the prices—Cakes jellies creams candies—every kind of sweets abounds."⁷³ These delicacies did not come with a small price tag. As a result of wartime shortages, inflation, and the bazaar's purpose as a fundraiser, prices ran extremely high. "A small slice of cake is two dollars—a spoonful of Charlotte Russe [dessert] five dollars." Even at these prices, Emma LeConte reported, food was not the most expensive category of goods. "Some beautiful imported wax dolls not more than 12 inches high raffle for $500—and one very large doll I heard was to raffle for $2000." The high prices did not go unnoticed. In reference to the $2,000 doll, LeConte remarked, "One could buy a live negro baby for that!"⁷⁴ This comment revealed not only the ineffectiveness of Sherman's March as a tactic to demoralize and financially ruin Confederate civilians, but also the intensity with which Southerners clung to the ideals of the patriarchal antebellum slave system.⁷⁵

Enthusiasm for the bazaar belied the idea that Sherman's rapid approach dampened women's Confederate efforts. Instead of shocking Confederate women into submission, Sherman's proximity provoked them to an intense patriotism. Wealthy white Southerners flocked to the Columbia Bazaar. As she fled with her family from the path of Sherman's troops, one woman described the bazaar, which she had attended before her departure. "[You] ought to have seen the crowd, it was indeed a sight . . . you would never imagine there was a war in our land, could you have seen, the delicacies of every description." Prices were high, "but the people did not seem to regard the prices in the least, & they are coming thousands every day." The high attendance and seeming success comforted her. "I am glad to see they are making so much, for . . . the sick, & wounded soldiers."⁷⁶ The success of the bazaar led Mary Gayle

Aiken to celebrate that "the [world] & his wife [had] gone to Columbia to the Bazaar."⁷⁷

Even though it was not overshadowed by approaching Union troops, the bazaar had to adjust to the realities of impending Union invasion. Emma LeConte revealed that "the Bazaar will continue until Saturday." Although the organizers "had intended holding it for two weeks . . . Sherman's proximity forces them to hurry up." Rumors of the impending approach of Union troops circulated, including one that held that Sherman "had announced his intention of attending the Ladies Bazaar in person before it closes."⁷⁸ Despite the change in dates, many Confederate women reveled in the bazaar's success on behalf of the soldiers. For example, S. C. Goodwyn emphasized her relief that enemy soldiers had not arrived in time to destroy the bazaar. "I am truly glad Sherman did not interupt us. I have not yet heard the amount that has been made but I suppose at the lowest calculation 150 thousand if not $200,000." In any case, "it certainly has been a complete success."⁷⁹ The reported triumph of the Columbia Bazaar led Confederate women elsewhere to consider similar efforts on behalf of their beloved nation and soldiers.⁸⁰

The "complete success" of the Columbia Bazaar flew in the face of Union expectations of the frailty of elite Southern women's patriotism. In addition, it demonstrated to the invading soldiers that Confederate women remained committed to the Confederate cause and would not submit to the fears inspired by an invading army. Elite women in Georgia and the Carolinas may have faced difficulties obtaining resources for their troops and their fundraising efforts, but for many these problems did not dampen their continued support of their nation. Sherman's March gave Confederate women a sense of immediacy and inspired them to increase their efforts. Instead of surrendering to their fears about approaching troops, Confederate women redoubled their efforts to feed, nurse, and clothe Southern soldiers. Building on aid efforts begun at the outset of the war, many elite women effectively combined their Confederate loyalty with a distinctly Southern femininity. This allowed them to support the war effort as the Union invasion threatened their homes and personal safety. Although Sherman's March was designed to crush the morale of

Southern women and "take some conceit out of them," its prospect led many Southern women to intensify their support of the Confederacy.[81]

Confederate women's patriotic zeal shaped the way in which they confronted Union troops. White women's defiance further intensified when they came face to face with Union troops who burned and plundered their homes while attempting to personally humiliate them. The assault on Southern domesticity introduced Confederate women to a firsthand understanding of "hard war." Union soldiers, unfettered by the boundaries of polite society, destroyed Southern homes and the domestic accouterments they contained. As a result, Confederate women reasserted their Southern identities as they simultaneously demanded the protections guaranteed to ladies during peacetime.

CHAPTER 4

CONFRONTING THE ENEMY

On February 10, 1865, the Union army spread across the farming communities that surrounded Aiken, South Carolina. For the next few days, Pauline DeCaradeuc directly faced Union soldiers in a military campaign that turned her domestic sphere upside down. DeCaradeuc lived with her parents and four siblings on a 437-acre estate that contained twenty-one enslaved African Americans. When the soldiers arrived at her homestead, the war had already transformed DeCaradeuc's privileged life. Two of her brothers had died in service to the Confederate cause, and the war had eliminated many of the luxuries that had defined her prewar life. The arrival of Yankee soldiers brought new concerns, but DeCaradeuc never had to confront what terrified her most. She escaped physically unharmed and her house remained intact, even as she came face-to-face with "hundreds of [soldiers], in the house, upstairs, in the garret, in every chamber, under the house, in the yard, garden, &c., &c."[1] Her losses, in the eyes of formal bookkeepers, amounted to little more that the theft and destruction of material goods—mostly food, clothing, and various luxury goods.

Yet the perception of the devastation cut much deeper. In her confrontations with Sherman's soldiers, DeCaradeuc felt violated by the indignities that Union soldiers forced her to endure. Union soldiers acknowledged few of the boundaries of polite antebellum society and instead skillfully assaulted the accouterments of her femininity and the domestic sphere. The breaking of social mores and the invasions of feminine spaces also increased the sexual anxieties of many Confederate women. Although sexual assaults on white women were rarely reported along the march, the threat remained. After hearing that enemy soldiers asked about the young women of the house and where their rooms were, DeCaradeuc feared the worst. She protected herself by wearing "blue spectacles" and hiding her face in a scarf.[2] Even without a physical sexual assault, enemy soldiers violated feminine space. DeCaradeuc fumed that Union soldiers tore up some of her undergarments to use as handkerchiefs. The male enemy's destruction of her lingerie, items never shown by unmarried or respectable women to strange men, epitomized the desecration of women's private sphere. To add further insult, the soldiers refashioned these private items into something to use for blowing their noses and wiping their sweat. DeCaradeuc's sense of violation continued until the soldiers finally left the community. The destruction that seemed to be of little monetary value struck DeCaradeuc and other women as particularly infuriating. The ruining of private journals and personal papers seemed senseless and personal, as did the looting of clothing, china, trinkets, sheet music, and other items that would eventually be left in their wake, strewn on the paths that Sherman's men took out of town.[3] Just as DeCaradeuc asserted her political and social status as a Southern woman and adjusted her expectations to the realities of wartime, Yankee soldiers attempted to erase the gendered protections usually afforded to her and other white women.

Beginning in late 1864, thousands of slaveholding women in Georgia and the Carolinas experienced the personal humiliation that DeCaradeuc described. The invasion by sixty thousand Union men revealed to these women a harsher, more intense, and more personal war than they had experienced up to this point. They thought that they understood what sacrifices civilians necessarily made during war, but four years of hunger, shortages, and death could not prepare Confederate women for the Union's assault on domesticity. To elite women's chagrin, Northern soldiers willingly pillaged homes, taking clothing, china, trinkets, personal letters, and journals. As a result, Confederate women discovered that many of their fears in anticipation of the invasion had not been unfounded. General William T. Sherman and his men, denounced throughout the campaign as "savages," "fiends," and "devils," further infuriated Confederates as they ravaged Southern towns, homes, and bedrooms.

During the campaign, elite white women objected most vehemently to Northern soldiers' violation of the traditional norms that gave white women a protected status. Despite their own classification of Confederate women as enemies, Union soldiers assumed the female civilians would act as "ladies" when their homes were attacked. Much to the soldiers' surprise, however, their attack on Southern domesticity forced elite white women to redefine their femininity in ways that encompassed both regional and gender identities. Instead of surrendering, as their enemies expected them to do, Confederate women used the assault on the home front as an impetus to defend their nation, as well as their homes and loved ones, in specifically feminine ways. Elite women's realization that nothing was safe from the prying hands and eyes of Union troops provoked them to assert their Southern loyalty and patriotism in direct confrontations with enemy soldiers. Successfully adapting their femininity to one that included a verbal and physical defense of their homes and their nation, Confederate women made clear their belief that Sherman and his troops were inhuman, uncivilized, and capable of anything.

Most scholars of Sherman's March mistakenly trivialize these interactions within households and instead emphasize the troop maneuvers and destruction of traditional military sites. Women, and civilians in general, are largely hidden in plain sight. Scholars describe the burning of homes and other domestic property, but they tend to do so as tangential anecdotes rather than as illustrative moments; elite women and children are included because they were there, but there is no discussion of why the soldiers chose that route or attacked specific families and homes along the way. Although subtitled "The Story of Soldiers and Civilians during Sherman's Campaign," Lee Kennett's *Marching through Georgia,* for example, follows the entire march for thirteen chapters without discussing the women in a meaningful way. Their experiences appear in "The Victims," a separate chapter whose title accurately reflects the largely passive role that women had in this account of the campaign.[4] This segregation is especially peculiar considering the general lack of military engagements during the march. Indeed, scholars routinely repeat the assertion that Sherman marched "unimpeded" by the Confederate army.[5] Although they spent much of their time tearing up railroad tracks, heating them, and twisting them around trees to create "Sherman neckties," the soldiers also worked to destroy elite Southern women's sense of well-being. Sherman designed the march to demonstrate Union power over everything as well as to bring about a conclusion to the war.[6] He relied on home front confrontations, rather than on battlefield engagement, to defeat the enemy.

THE CIVILIAN WAR

Even as Union soldiers ignored traditional gender norms, they expected Confederate women to adhere to them. They assumed that elite Southern women would act as ladies even in the face of a home front attack. If women complied with these expectations, the home front campaign would come to a quick and successful end. When slaveholding women did not respond as expected, but instead behaved like "she-devils," they gave Union soldiers further justification for the attack on the Southern home front. If these women would not behave as ladies, they certainly did not deserve to be treated as such. During the home front campaign Union soldiers' opinions about elite Southern women would be affected by their confrontations with female enemies. As a result of their preconceived ideas about Southern ladies, Northern soldiers expressed surprise when "secesh" women virulently proclaimed their Confederate loyalty in the face of the enemy. Much to the shock of the Northern invaders, elite Southern women turned to what nineteenth-century Americans generally considered masculine qualities, such as anger and defiance, to protect their homes and nation. Consequently, as Union men (and women) often interpreted it, Southern women were no longer ladies. They had abandoned femininity, and thus given up their right to be treated as ladies.[7]

The behavior of elite women startled many Northern soldiers, who disdained their female enemies' use of "unladylike" language in reference to the "sneaking Yankee." Elite women's behavior toward their male enemies seemed, at least in the minds of many soldiers, to justify the Union attack on the Southern home front. Union officer James Edmonds, for example, contemptuously observed that the ladies at the Sparks home, Shady Dale, in Georgia "insulted both the Gen'l and myself by language which no well bred ladies would use."[8] Other women startled Union men by calling them "Lincoln's hirelings, Yankee scum, and bluebellied sons of b——s," among other things.[9] Such use of profane language, as well as women's willingness to stand up to the invaders, surprised and appalled Union soldiers. Not knowing how to interpret Confederate women's defiant words within their understanding of gender, Northern men determined that this behavior was unfeminine and that these white Southern women were, in fact, not ladies.[10]

As Sherman's men traveled through the South, a small number of Confederate women confronted the enemy troops with more than words. These physically combative exchanges with Sherman's soldiers demonstrated both the changing nature of female behavior in the final years of the Confederacy, as well as the lengths to which elite women would go to protect themselves, their families, and their domestic domain.[11] In rare cases, female Confederates physically retaliated against the enemy. One soldier reported that when the troops marched through Rome, Georgia, "women on the balcony of 'a young lady's seminary' poured kitchen slops and 'the contents of chamber pots' on their heads." Comparable confrontations occurred elsewhere. In Milledgeville, Georgia, a woman threw a large stone out of her second-story window at the Union troops below. In South Carolina, another tried to deter Union foragers by throwing scalding water in their faces.[12] In all of these incidents, ardent female Confederates attacked the soldiers personally, often hoping that nineteenth-century gender ideals would prevent the men from responding in the same way. As a whole, however, slaveholding women knew that they could not take up arms and join their men on the battlefield.[13] These women understood that to do so was to move toward unrestrained warfare that would have consequences far greater than domestic invasion and destruction.

Although Union soldiers disdained what they saw as unfeminine behavior by slaveholding women, Southern men gloried in the actions of their countrywomen. Confederate president Jefferson Davis, for one, recognized and celebrated elite female behavior. "Their gallantry is only different from that of her sons in this, that they deem it unfeminine to strike." Even without the regular use of physical violence, Southern ladies showed their dedication to honor: "yet such is the heroism displayed—such the noble demeanor they have exhibited—that at the last moment when trampled upon and it became a necessity, they would not hesitate to strike the invader a corpse at their feet."[14] In the eyes of Confederate soldiers and officials, white Southern women, like the men of their nation, demonstrated their adherence to the tenets of Southern honor and their loyalty to the Confederacy through opposition to the invaders.

Through words and actions, Confederate women defiantly asserted their nationalism to the invaders in ways that white Southerners accepted as both feminine and necessary. As a result, Sherman, who had designed his campaign to "take some conceit out of [Southerners]," found this to be no easy task. In Savannah, he noted, "Although I have come right through the heart of Georgia [the women] talk as defiantly as ever." The Union general expressed astonishment that Savannah's female citizens "remain, bright and haughty and proud as ever. There seems no end but utter annihilation that will satisfy their hate of the 'sneaking Yankee' and 'ruthless invader.'"[15] Much to his surprise, even in a city that surrendered rather than face the indignity of an invasion, Sherman faced intensely nationalistic Confederate women who hated the enemy and refused to submit. Despite his efforts to convince them that surrender was both necessary and better than rebellion, Savannah's elite white women continued to assert their loyalty to the Confederacy and their persistent hatred of Union ideals, tactics, and people.

Slaveholding women's anger resulted from the soldiers' disregard for the rules of peacetime propriety. Union soldiers, one outraged woman fumed, were "a hellish crew . . . no place, no person is sacred from their profanation."[16] In particular, Confederate women resented the soldiers' entrance into their bedrooms, their personal sanctuary. This behavior, unacceptable during peacetime, became routine during Sherman's March. "They are so low down," Loula of North Carolina raged, "and had no respect whatever for a lady's private room."[17] Another complained that "there was no place, no chamber, trunk, drawer, desk, garret, closet, or cellar that was private to their unholy eyes."[18] To emphasize the men's lack of propriety, many Confederate women gave vivid descriptions of their mistreatment and proudly related their defiant responses to it. Furious over her treatment by the Union soldiers, a Columbia woman described the scene to her daughter. After her daughter mentioned that she "heard that the yanks were treating us kindly," S. McCain wanted to set her straight. The treatment could only be seen in that light "if going in to houses and holding loaded pistols to ladies heads to make them tell where there gold and silver was and pouring turpentine over the flour and over the beds and put[t]ing a match to them and not letting them have so much as a change of clothes" could be considered kind.[19] Another South Carolina woman indignantly described her bedrooms after the Union soldiers left. "In one of the bed-rooms the mattress was gone, the feather-bed cut open and the feathers left piled on the floor, the mirror smashed and the door broken from its hinges." The soldiers continued their rampage in other rooms, too. "In another the bedstead was destroyed, and some of the furniture cut into by axes, completely ruining it, of course."[20] After the enemy ransacked areas seen as inviolable prior to the march, Confederate women felt violated.[21] As Union soldiers' actions demonstrated that they had little respect for the sanctity of private feminine space, the invasion of women's private chambers infuriated elite Southern women.

Written missives, recorded immediately after and sometimes during the invasion, described what slaveholding women saw as uncivilized and unwarranted Union behavior, warned others in Sherman's path, stimulated Southern anger against the Northern troops, and highlighted women's roles as protectors of Southern honor. For example, wealthy North Carolinian Eliza Tillinghast hoped a letter detailing her hardships would motivate her brother in his fight against the Union. She urged him to "think of having 500 men running wild over your defenceless sisters— taking the last crumb—. . . of meat, flour,—in fact every-thing needful." In addition, he should remember that enemy soldiers "cut up the carriage—carried off the wagon." As a result, their neighbors "suffered hunger while the *fiends* were here." She was spared from that fate because of her ingenuity: "we saved about 20 lbs of flour by putting in . . . a bucket and sitting upon it all the time. [A]nd *three* families subsisted for *two* days on that." Tillinghast not only emphasized the outrage of having strange men in her Fayetteville home, but also the hardships the enemy forced her and other women to deal with. In her letter, she emphasized her fortitude, sacrifices, and resourcefulness.[22]

Similarly, when Sherman and his men reached her family's home in Aiken, South Carolina, Pauline DeCaradeuc recorded the assault on her domestic sphere in great detail. The first group of soldiers arrived at their gate in early February taunting them: "Here come the Yankees, look out now you d——d rebels." Many others soon joined this dozen, and together they swarmed "in the house, upstairs, in the garret, in every chamber, under the house, in the yard, garden, &c., &c." They made their presence known by "singing, shouting, whistling, and Oh, my God, *such cursing.* Both pianos were going at the same time." The soldiers' noise and use of profanity proved to be their least intrusive acts. They began to physically wreck the house, even using "axes [to break] open every door, drawer, trunk that was locked." They smashed mirrors and furniture and "flung every piece of clothing that they didn't carry off" onto the floors.[23]

As the soldiers continued their destruction, they ruined many personal items. DeCaradeuc especially resented the soldiers' defacement of the particularly feminine domestic trappings of her household. Not only did the men take blankets and linens, but they also "made the servants get our chemises & tear them up into pocket handkerchiefs." The male enemy's destruction of her lingerie, items never shown by respectable women to strange men, epitomized the violation of women's private sphere. Adding to her sense of horror, the soldiers also wantonly damaged household valuables. They "got some of Fa[ther]'s prettiest paintings and broke bottles of catsup over them." Furthermore, "they carried off every piece of silver, every knife, jewel, & particle of possessions in the house & negro houses." Yet, even DeCaradeuc observed that they took little of great monetary value but focused instead on leaving her belongings in ruins. "Every paper, letter, receipt, &c., they flung to the winds, all the roads are strewn with them."[24]

When raids resumed the next day, the soldiers asserted that the DeCaradeuc home "was the root of the rebellion & burn it they would." Although stopping short of torching the house, the Northern men continued to threaten its inhabitants, proclaiming "that they had to arrest and shoot every influential citizen in S.C., every mover of secession." The household, which held the possessions of five other families and plenty of supplies, lost a great amount. Out of the "7 barrels of fine flour, 300 bushels of corn, 1 barrel & 1 box of nice sugar, &c., &c." that they began with, they were left with only "15 bushels corn, 1 bag flour, 3 hams." The soldiers left with "all the wine & brandy." Each day the "Yankees came here in a body & dispersed over the house & place, carrying off everything they could." When Sherman's men finally departed, some carrying her valuable or personal possessions, DeCaradeuc angrily recounted the numerous violations she had endured.[25]

Confederate women drew sharp distinctions between the everyday hardships of war that they accepted as part of wartime necessity, and those they saw as an unpardonable violation—the invasion of their homes and bedrooms. As a result, their hostility became particularly pointed when Union soldiers ravaged Southern domestic spaces. When looking back on Sherman's March, Union soldier Robert Hale Strong observed that "some [women] were rabid rebels and took no pains to conceal it, but all were polite to us except when we were searching their houses."[26] The reaction to the invasion of homes demonstrated women's view of the invasion of domestic space as both unprovoked and unforgivable. Furthermore, Southern women's responses to the invasion of domestic space demonstrate the nineteenth-century belief in the home as women's domain. They fought fiercely to protect this realm when confronted by the enemy.

The enemies' breach of civility made Union soldiers seem hardly human to the Confederate women who faced them. From Georgia, Dolly Lunt Burge described her chaotic experiences in terms similar to those found throughout women's letters and diaries. "Like Demons they rush in. My yards are full. To my smoke house, my Dairy, Pantry, kitchen & cellar like famished wolves they come, breaking locks & whatever is in their way."[27] Other women came to similar assessments. North Carolinian Eliza Tillinghast summed up her reactions to the Union invasion of her home by noting that "a visit from the Yankee Army is not calculated to make us love the hated race any more." She focused her anger on the soldiers' crossing of gendered lines. She asserted that "to have our private apartments at the mercy of rabble soldiery is not particularly pleasant." After all, "Every box, drawer, trunk, closet, . . . and cranny in this house was turned inside out and thoroughly searc[h]ed by Sherman's men."[28] The inhumanity of the invading soldiers, portrayed by many as vicious animals, "demons," "devils," "fiends incarnate," "Vandals," and "Goths," confirmed Confederate women's belief that the two regions were irreconcilable and magnified slaveholding women's desire for vengeance.

Confederate women's reactions to the enemy were not for show. These female slaveholders assumed that their actions would affect the behavior of the enemy. Rumors that Union soldiers found their fiery resistance appealing and even arousing infuriated elite women. From Georgia, Dorrie Davis fumed at the tales spread by departing Union soldiers. "We have heard since the yankees left that they were very much pleased with their treatment up here, they say the ladies treated them very kind, and made their brags that they intended to come back here where the women were so spunky and get Wives." The idea of marrying a Union soldier appeared ludicrous to her, not only because of her hatred of and interactions with the men, but also because it revealed what she considered the ignorance of the Northern soldiers. "If they call the treatment they recieved while here kind treatment it is very evident they dont know what kind treatment is." In addition, she did not want anyone to get the mistaken idea that Confederate women had treated the enemy with any type of kindness. She continued, "They have said the very thing we would not have them say for the world, that is they were treated kindly, we ladies are so mad because the yanks say they were kindly treated that if they ever show their old blue backs here again they will fair badly."[29] Davis angrily insisted that others recognize her hostility toward the enemy. After all, the Yankees' belittling of their treatment at the hands of white Southern women demeaned the passionate sentiments of female Confederates and made their threats, verbal or otherwise, innocuous.

The unprecedented destruction visited on the home front not only invigorated the Confederate patriotism of those who experienced it, but also brought them a sense of camaraderie with other white women in Sherman's path. The resulting shared experience allowed them to create a community united against such outrages and promoted a heightened sense of Confederate identity.[30] After all, those who had lived through a Union raid knew the toll its horrors could take. Dolly Lunt Burge, for example, could not sleep after Sherman and his troops ransacked her Georgia home but instead "sat up all night watching every moment for the flames to burst out from some of my buildings." Burge's fear grew from her experiences with the enemy earlier in the day. "All day as its sad moments rolled on were they passing, not only in front of my house, but they came up behind tore down my garden palings, made a road through my back yard & lot field, driving their Stock & riding through, tearing down my fences & desolating my home." Burge interpreted the enemy's behavior as intentional. As for their destruction of her home, she wrote, they were "wantonly doing it when there was no necessity for it." She hoped that "such a day if I live to the age of Methuselah may God spare me from ever seeing again—Such were some of the scenes of this sad day & as night drew its sable curtains around us, the heavens from every point were lit up with flames from burning buildings!" As a result of what she had witnessed during the day, Burge expressed that she "could not close my eyes but kept walking to & fro watching the fires in the distance & dreading the approaching day which I feared as they had not all passed would be a continuation of horrors."[31] The scenes continued to haunt her and color her view of the war and the world around her.

Similar scenes of destruction and fear recurred throughout the campaign. As a result, Georgian Minerva Leah Rowles McClatchey sympathized with those in her situation. "Oh how my heart goes after Sherman's host—of unfeeling soldiers—I know terror and dismay [that] destruction will follow—and accompany their march—and pity the luckless citizens they may meet & pass on their route." Acknowledging the power and vindictiveness of Union troops, McClatchey continued: "They have made great threats of what they will do and their hands seldom hesitate to execute the wicked thoughts of their hearts."[32] Although these women realized that Sherman's March was directed at them, they refused to renounce their nation. In many instances, Sherman's March also inspired white Southern women to help each other as best they could. For example, in March 1865 the Greenville Ladies Association in South Carolina, not out of danger itself, raised over one thousand dollars to aid the people in Columbia after Sherman and his troops had destroyed the city and much personal property.[33]

Not all elite women responded to enemy invasion with physical or verbal assaults on the soldiers. Many Confederate women resolved to hide their fury from enemy eyes and appear to fit the mold of a reserved Southern lady. Others showed their strength through stoic acceptance of the events around them. They tried to remain calm and avoid further harassment by the invading soldiers. Some elite Southern women proudly described their calm demeanor as Union soldiers ransacked their property. Mary Sharpe Jones refused to budge even though "every trunk, Bureau, Box, room, [and] closet has been opened or broken open . . . & whatever was wanted of provisions, clothing, jewelry, Knives, forks, spoons, cups, Kettles, cooking utensils, towels, bags, &c, &c, from this taken." As a result, "the whole house [was] turned topsey-turvey." She and the white women of her household remained composed and unruffled as they faced the vandals. "God alone has enabled us to speak with the enemy in the Gates, and calmly without a tear to see my house broken open, entered with false keys, threatened to be burned to ashes, refused food & ordered to be starved to death." Perhaps the Yankees' verbal assaults were the worst she had to face. She angrily reported how she was "told that I had no right even to wood or water, that I should be 'humbled in the very dust I walked upon,' a pistol and carbine presented to my breast, cursed & reviled as a Rebel, a hypocrite, a devil."[34] In the streets of Milledgeville, Georgia, one woman "passed ten thousand [Yankees]" as she headed to the capitol building. Even in this circumstance, she exclaimed, "as for feeling afraid it was not there in me. I closed my lips & clenched my fists, & boiling over to give them a piece of my mind." Although she remained quiet, this woman clearly made her dislike of the enemy known by her refusal to walk on the same side of the street with them.[35] South Carolinian Emily Caroline Ellis had a similar experience. Ellis related that when "the 'vile wretches' arrived. . . . They commenced drinking, breaking the houses, stores, and robbing generally." Throughout her confrontation, Ellis proudly "met all of them with independence on my countenance."[36]

Confederate women had good reason to avoid contact and verbal confrontations with the invading soldiers. A fear of sexual assault haunted many, and they did whatever they could to protect themselves. For example, before Sherman and his troops reached her area, Grace Brown Elmore contemplated what she would do in the event of rape. She "thought long and intently upon the righteousness of suicide should that worst of all horrors happen." Caught between her religious beliefs and her sense of virtue, Elmore reasoned "that God would justify the self destroying hand, when life had become a burden and a shame through the wickedness of man." At the same time, she recognized rape as a deliberate strategy. The soldiers, she believed, "well . . . know how to avenge themselves, on woman, what she values more than all things, the loss of which would be living death." Elmore reconciled her conflicts concluding "if I had to choose between death and dishonor, I could not live—Life is sweet, but it would have lost it's savor. That which was taken could never be restored. God will, God must justify the deed." To her relief, Elmore never had to make this decision.[37]

Other Confederate women took active precautions against sexual assault. A Georgian described to her brother her attempts to avoid harassment by invading Union men. As the enemy approached, one of the slaves "tried to get me not to show myself, for she [said] many were asking her if there [were any] young ladies in the house." She found what she considered a simple solution. "I tried to look as ugly as possible" so that "none were they to see me would take me for any thing but an old married woman."[38] Appearing ugly and old, she assumed, would shield her from the leering eyes of enemy men. Other women drew upon traditional notions of sexual attraction, and took similar precautions. Pauline DeCaradeuc heard that the soldiers had "asked the servants if there were any young ladies in the house, how old they were & where they slept." Although frightened by these inquiries, DeCaradeuc felt that she and her friend had some protection because "during all this I had on blue spectacles & my face muffled up. Carrie too." Despite her assumed safety, the hint of a sexual assault made her realize "that burning the house was nothing." For the rest of the night, she remained "almost frantic [and] sat up in a corner, without moving or closing my eyes once the whole night." Although DeCaradeuc "suffered agony [and] trembled *unceasingly* till morning," the experience put the physical destruction around her into perspective. Some things were more valuable than property.[39]

Fear of rape by the enemy was not restricted to the South's elite women. Slave women took similar precautions to avoid molestation by Union troops. For example, Mary Jones Mallard described how her cook hid herself during a Union raid on the house. "From being a young girl she had assumed the attitude and appearance of a sick old woman with a blanket thrown over her head & shoulders & scarcely able to move."[40] The presence of enemy men on the Southern home front affected all female civilians. Nobody knew exactly what type of behavior to expect from the soldiers, especially soldiers that brazenly invaded women's private chambers.

Other white women had less success avoiding physical contact with Yankee soldiers. Louise Caroline Reese Cornwell described how Union soldiers entered one woman's house and "they compelled her to unfasten her dress and they examined her person until they were satisfied." This horrified Cornwell, who realized the implications of this type of attack on similarly privileged women. "How humiliating."[41] Mary Maxcy Leverett wrote in shock about events that occurred in Columbia. Although Leverett penned an extensive list and full description of the process by which the soldiers stole and destroyed her silver, jewelry, clothes, food, bags, and sewing supplies, among other things, she insisted that the destruction of her property was "a trifle to what was done in Col[umbia] on some houses." In these horrible instances, "ladies had their dresses violently torn open and were searched for their gold [and the] ladies rushed frantically away from these insults." Even though "as far as [she] could learn, no actual personal insult was inflicted on any lady," she considered these "rude & violent attempts to search them for gold" to be unforgivable. "Can meanness go farther?" she asked.[42] For Leverett, the personal affronts in ladies' households committed by Union soldiers struck a deeper chord than the general destruction of the countryside along the march. These domestic invasions were not wartime necessities, she and others believed, but instead they were the actions of cruel and depraved men. In both of these instances, ideals of white womanhood held strong and prevented the soldiers from raping these particular white women. Although in their attack of the home front Union soldiers pushed aside some of their preconceived ideas that white women deserved to be treated as a protected group, they usually held onto ideas that prohibited sexual assault of elite white women. This allowed some protection from the invaders for slaveholding women, but was not necessarily a guarantee.

African American women in Sherman's path did not enjoy the same safety from sexual violation as elite women. Racial stereotypes that categorized black women as hypersexual combined with their status as Southern property often led to the rape of slave and free black women by invading soldiers. Slaveholder Dolly Lunt Burge acknowledged the threat that Union soldiers posed to the slave women of her household and the fear that they had of rape. During a raid, her "room was full nearly with the bedding of & with the negroes. They were afraid to go out for my women could not step outside of the door without an insult from [the Union soldiers]."[43] Mary Jones Mallard reported a similar situation on her plantation. Because "squads of Yankees came all day," she reported that "the [slave] women finding it entirely unsafe . . . to be out of the house at all, would run in & conceal themselves in our dwelling." The fears of African American women were not unfounded. "These [Yankee] men were so outrageous at the Negro houses, that the negro men were obliged to slap at their horses for the protection of their wives, and in some instances they rescued them from the hands of these infamous creatures."[44] Both slaveholding Southerners and Union soldiers believed African American women occupied a separate place in society from their white counterparts. Elite women, like the invading soldiers, did not consider that African American women had the same morals as themselves. When Union soldiers approached her about a ball, a Confederate woman made the distinction clear. When "some of the miserable creatures" arrived to invite local women to a ball, "one lady told an officer she did not suppose a white lady would go. that maybe some of the negroe wenches would grase the occasion, but she felt sure no white one would."[45] In addition, because of their race and status, slave women were not protected by the same social mores as were elite white women. Enemy soldiers felt little need to protect the African American women they encountered along the campaign.[46] In fact, the rape and attempted rape of slave women frequently occurred during Sherman's March. For example, from South Carolina, one woman described this phenomenon. Young African American women were "obliged to take to the woods, so save themselves from being ravished" when the soldiers arrived each night.[47] Another woman described a similar incident to her daughter. As she told it, during a raid "one [Yankee] wretch had a mulatto wench in Elizas room."[48] News of the rape of any woman, black or white, further increased the anxiety of Confederate women as the enemy approached.

Despite social taboos against the violation of elite white women, a few Union soldiers crossed the line. Although some scholars have painted the Civil War and Sherman's March as "low-rape" experiences for white women, incidences of sexual assault did occur.[49] In Chester, South Carolina, Julia Gott revealed her shock that "they stripped old Mrs. R., Kate's mother, and whipped her."[50] However, the rumors were not always unfounded and worse violations happened. In a letter between two women, the writer revealed one instance of rape of which she knew. "The most horrible thing the Yankees did in our neighborhood . . . was to dishonor a young lady up about the Rock." The writer would not reveal the girl's identity except to say that "she was very respectable & well off." As a result of the attack, the fifteen-year-old girl "has been dangerously ill since."[51] In Milledgeville, "the incarnate devils ravished some of the nicest ladies."[52] As one woman reported, "the enemy . . . committed outrages on ladies, tho' I only know of Mrs. James Nickels." Although other sexual assaults occurred in Milledgeville, the soldiers' rape of Kate Latimer Nichols, wife of a Confederate captain, became well publicized around Georgia.[53] Anna Maria Green's reaction to the incident reflected that of her countrywomen. "The worst of their acts was committed to poor Mrs. Nichols." Green assumed that the "violence done, and atrocity committed" would "make her husband an enemy unto death."[54] This nightmarish experience surely sickened women other than the direct victim, who ended up in an asylum. The possibility of rape by the "fiends incarnate" haunted many Confederate women.[55]

The pillage and destruction of slaveholders' property that formed the backbone of Sherman's campaign was carefully defined to exclude the rape of white women. The Union army never sanctioned coerced sexual attacks on white women and always punished the perpetrators of such crimes when they were uncovered. Commanding officers immediately court-martialed the few men caught attempting to rape or raping white Southern women. The offenders faced hanging, public humiliation, or dishonorable discharges.[56] For example, Union soldier Charles Brown Tomkins discussed the consequences and occurrences of rape. "There was an execution in the 14th A. C. . . . of a soldier for committing a rape on an 'old lady.'" Later in the day, in Tomkins's division another soldier "'drummed out'" a fellow soldier "for attempting to commit a rape on a young woman."[57] Similarly, Union chaplain John J. Hight wrote that while in Conyers, Georgia, "our men helped themselves to anything they desired to eat. No effort was made by the officers to restrain them." However, some took the raiding further. "Rumor says that one of the soldiers was shot by a woman, whom he was attempting to outrage."[58] In another case, a Confederate woman threatened to use a revolver to keep an aggressive soldier away.[59] In protecting themselves from rape, these women likely saved the soldiers' companies from executing these men.

The Union's discipline of suspected rapists did little to allay the fears of Confederate women. With dread of physical attack governing her actions, South Carolinian Charlotte St. Julien Ravenel described her interaction with Union troops as one that would, she hoped, maintain peace and distance. As the enemy soldiers filled her house, she remained "in the hall to see what they would take from there and to keep a watch," but she did not try to stop the pillaging. Despite her initial intention to remain quiet, the soldiers soon forced her to engage them in conversation. They bombarded her with questions that she hesitantly, yet often defiantly, answered. "The first one that come into the room asked for fire arms, I told him they had all been taken," she wrote. "The next one asked for silver, I had no idea of showing him, so said I was not the lady of the house, he made no reply but went on looking." The soldiers ultimately found and took the silver as well as the food, horses, and other valuables. As they left, Ravenel comforted herself with the satisfaction that at least she had not made it easy for the vandals.[60]

In the interest of personal safety, other slaveholding women similarly held their tongues in the presence of the enemy. Mary Sharpe Jones of Georgia noted that "in all my intercourse with the enemy, I have avoided conversation or any aggravating remarks." Remaining quiet became difficult, but she tried to do so "even when I felt a sword pierced through my soul." The soldiers especially tried her patience when they "taunted me with the want of courage on the part of my Countrymen—Charges, which I knew to be bare & false as the lips that uttered them." Jones, the head of a household that she shared with her pregnant daughter, knew that silence offered her some protection from the vengeance of the soldiers. She believed that if she did not blatantly cross the lines of propriety, the soldiers might not either. Despite her outward composure and civil behavior, however, Jones asserted that "every development of the enemy but confirms my desire for a separate and distinct nationality."[61] Her interactions with Union soldiers allowed her to further crystallize her identity as a Confederate.

In Columbia, Mary Maxcy Leverett demonstrated her continued loyalty to the Confederacy through a similar show of stoicism. She spoke to Union soldiers, and although she "trembled from head to foot," she "was so determined that they should see no sight of fear that to stop the tremor and prevent a tear being seen or a sob escaping I had sometimes to compress my lips & bite them in the midst of a sentence, until I shrugged off the emotion." Leverett willingly "shrugged off the emotion" because she "hated so to let an enemy see he had it in his power to make me shed a tear." Her sense of Confederate womanhood required her to present a facade of fearlessness in the face of what she saw as an unforgiving enemy. Despite her cool demeanor, she hoped "that some one could write with a pen of fire and tell the world, the history of the sufferings & agonies of those three days of Yankee rule." She resented the horrors of Union occupation which "was like *'hell let loose'* in some parts of Columbia."[62] Union soldiers noted the fearlessness of Confederate women throughout the campaign. For example, Major Henry Hitchcock wrote that he was "sorry enough . . . for the women here and their anxiety and terror—though I must say they show very little *fear* of us."[63] Confederate women's outward acceptance of Union power often hid deep-seated hatred of the enemy and patriotism for the Southern nation.

Other women chose to be more daring in their quiet defiance of the enemy. When Union soldiers invaded her home and demanded her liquor, gold, and silver, Pauline DeCaradeuc worried because she "had a belt on under my dress, with my revolver, and a bag of bullets, caps & powder in my pocket." This ammunition both offered protection and invited danger. When the soldiers demanded all the weapons in the house, DeCaradeuc defiantly went upstairs and "threw the revolver between [the bed] sheets," hoping that it would be safe there and that she would not be punished for concealing it. After disposing of her weapon, she still worried that the soldiers would find it, and they almost did. "Hardly I had finished [hiding the revolver] when the door burst open & the room was filled with them, they pulled the bed to pieces, of course." A few moments later, when "a horrid looking ruffian came into the parlor, [and] seeing only women there . . . entered [and] shut both doors," DeCaradeuc again feared for her safety. The "ruffian . . . said in an undertone, 'You cursed rebels, now empty your pockets.'" During this incident, DeCaradeuc was concerned, not for her vulnerability as a woman, but instead for the contents of her pocket—she still had the bag of ammunition on her person. While the Yankee focused his attention on the purse of another woman in the room, DeCaradeuc "dropped [her] bag in a corner & flung an old bonnet over it." She became overtly hostile only after the "ruffian" found her watch and tried to get more from her. When "the villain put his hand on my shoulder, I rose & stood before him, with all possible dignity & he turned away."[64] Her affront at the soldier's physical contact led her to a show of defiance that demonstrated to the male invader her lack of fear and ultimately protected her from any further harassment. She successfully saved herself and her weaponry. To her relief, after the enemy had left for the day DeCaradeuc found her revolver tangled in the stripped bed sheets.

The women in DeCaradeuc's household made other efforts to thwart the ambitions of the Union soldiers. As the soldiers ransacked the house, she recorded, "Mother and G[rand]M[a] went among them like brave women, trying to save some few things in vain." The soldier who pressed DeCaradeuc's mother for gold and silver could not get her to reveal anything, despite his threats. Although he warned, "I'll burn your house this minute, if you don't tell me," she refused to speak. Frustrated with the woman's resolve, the soldier "walked up & down the room cursing, swearing, threatening, & spitting on every side," but he did not set the house on fire. Union soldiers ultimately uncovered the silver and other valuables hidden on the property by "sticking the ground with their swords and . . . wherever the ground was soft they dug."[65] In spite of the final result, the women of the house proudly recounted their role in defying the enemy and making things difficult for raiding Union soldiers.

Despite assertions by Union soldiers about the unfeminine behavior and attitudes of Southern women, many rebel women held that their strong Confederate patriotism and their ability to withstand the enemy invasion evidenced their "true Southern womanhood." This belief that they had maintained their status as defenders of the home and were therefore authorized to give directives led some elite women to demand that intruding Union soldiers follow their wishes. In Georgia, as one woman reported, a female Confederate successfully forced a Northern soldier to remove a Union flag from her house. He "had the impudence to hang out with his colors at her window but she soon made him take it down."[66] These Confederate women also considered Union disdain for strong Southern sentiments as an impetus to further declarations of pride. In a confrontation with a soldier who "tried to make me say if I was a 'Secesh,'" one Milledgeville, Georgia, resident proudly responded, "I am a southern woman." She maintained this position because he "said so impertinently, say 'are you Secesh' that [she] determined not to answer him" directly and instead reasserted her Southernness. Even while defiantly dodging the question, this woman's answer demonstrated her belief that all Southern women were "secesh" who proudly supported their region's values. This woman also rejoiced in the response of another woman to the same question. "One [of the soldiers] asked Sal & she said yes, to the hearts core." Although the Union soldiers disdained these women's impertinence and continued disloyalty, they did not punish either woman for her answer.[67]

Throughout the campaign, white Southern women delighted in their defiance to Northern soldiers, especially when their undying loyalty to the Confederacy garnished respect from Union men. In February, Emma LeConte proudly remarked that "the Yankee officers . . . paid the tribute to the women of this state" by calling them "the most firm, obstinate and ultra rebel set of women they had encountered."[68] LeConte saw the branding of South Carolina women as "firm, obstinate and ultra rebel" as a compliment of the highest order.[69] In a letter to a female friend, a North Carolina woman named Loula proudly described her bravery after the Yankees "tore up the whole house and stole whatever they wanted." The destruction of her home infuriated Loula, especially because the "impudent scamps" raided her house eight times. Loula detailed the items stolen by the enemy, including horses, mules, silver, jewelry, cloth, and "even . . . the baby's *napkins*." At first, she obediently complied with requests for her property, giving her "beautiful ring" and other jewelry to "a great drunken fellow" because she feared "he might attempt to take them by force." She had her limits, and as the visits increased she refused to part with her diamond ring, which, she proclaimed, she "would have swallowed . . . before a Yankee should have it." In the end, the enemy found and stole other valuables as well as burnt both her gin house and her cotton. Loula found this seemingly endless experience heart-wrenching. "You don['t] know how awful we felt when the wretches were prying into every sacred thing in the house, even into . . . relics of the dead we never dreamed of concealing." Despite, and perhaps as a result of, the attack on her sentimental items, Loula "talked to them all pretty plainly, & let them know at once I was not afraid of them, nor afraid to reveal my real sentiments & contempt for their Government." She refused to be intimidated and bragged about the soldiers' response to her defiance. When "one of them told me I was a brave little woman." she declared "yes I would always acknowledge with pride that I was a rebel and gloried in being a secessionist long before the war commenced."[70] Even with the enemy still in her home, Loula focused her anger on those responsible for the assault on her domestic space.

The attack on her family's "relics of the dead" proved particularly painful to Loula, as it certainly did to other white Southern women. Mourning rituals were considered an important part of domestic responsibilities, especially during wartime. Union soldiers defiled the memory of lost loved ones throughout the campaign. In addition to destroying the property of the dead held in Southern homes, the troops also despoiled Southern cemeteries along the path of Sherman's March. The behavior made deep impressions on Southern women. For example, Frances Thomas Howard described one instance where the "cemetery is desecrated with their fortifications. The Yankees have broken open the doors of vaults, and in one instance that I know of, the coffin of a lady was opened and a cross and chain stolen from her body." These actions proved to her that "such men are not human."[71] This behavior confirmed Southern women's beliefs that the enemy belonged to a separate and uncivilized race.

Across Sherman's path, elite women connected their Confederate patriotism with their self-importance as Southern ladies. After initially restraining herself to a quiet opposition to the Union soldiers in her home, Georgian Mary Sharpe Jones eventually displayed her pride in her Southern nation and Confederate identity. The invaders, she exulted, "always redressed me as an uncompromising rebel," and she proudly concurred. "I never failed to let them know that before High Heaven, I believed our cause was just & right."[72] Other Confederate women also made their love of their nation and hatred for the enemy clear to the invading troops. George Ward Nichols, a Union soldier on Sherman's March, recounted a conversation with a "rebel lady" who told him that she and the other women of Atlanta "would much rather give up our homes than live near the Yankees" because "we hate you."[73] Frances Thomas Howard recorded an incident in which a Miss Moodie insulted Sherman while he was within earshot. When visiting the owner of the home that housed Sherman's headquarters in Savannah, she let it be known that she "wish[ed] a thousand papers of pins were stuck in [Sherman's] bed and he was strapped down on them."[74] From South Carolina, Emma Holmes proudly recounted her confrontation with a Union soldier. "I hurled so many keen sarcasms, such home thrusts, that [he] said 'I was the best rebel he had met.'" The soldier also acknowledged the powerful role that Confederate women played in their region's bid for independence, explaining "that it was such women as I who kept up this war by urging on our brothers and friends." Holmes responded, telling "him I considered it a high compliment, that I was delighted to find I was able to do so much for my country."[75] Harriott Middleton received a similar compliment. In her description of the destruction of Columbia, she recorded a comment by the Union soldiers. "As for the women, [the Union soldiers] said the women in Carolina were the pluckiest, the bravest, the most outspoken they had met in the South and they said, 'We admire it so much.'"[76]

Although some of his soldiers praised Confederate women for their dedication to their nation, Sherman was not so complimentary. In his mind, their patriotism had led to no good. Ellen Devereux Hinsdale related a story of one woman's confrontation with Sherman. According to the story, "he cursed the women called us d——d rebels, & the cause of the trouble in the country." The outrage continued as she relayed that Sherman threatened "that the next time he comes here he will treat us as the Indians would."[77] Sherman's declaration that Southern women and Indians deserved to be treated with the same rules of war defined the growing distance between the Confederacy and the Union. After all, if the Union equated the Confederacy with savages, the only solution was to conquer and control the "savage" population.

Union major Henry Hitchcock also judged Southern women's role in the rebellion as both vital and worthy of punishment. He confronted one young woman about her war role. "'You have or had influence with [Southern men]—did you ever use it to keep them at home?' She admitted she had not, and that if they hadn't gone to the war, women would have called them cowards, etc., etc." As a result, Hitchcock blamed her, in part, for the start and continuation of the war: "You have done all you could to help the war, and have not done what you could to prevent it."[78] The woman's pride in her patriotism, as well as Hitchcock's recognition of her vital role in the war, allowed him and other Union soldiers to justify their attack on the feminized Confederate home front.

Despite such "compliments" and complaints about women's power in the continuation of the Confederate war effort, Union soldiers assumed that Confederate women would eventually grow tired of war and call for a return to traditional gender relations. When a Union soldier confidently asserted that "the war would soon be over, and, in a few months, we would all be in the Union," Emma Holmes challenged him. She refused to give up on Southern independence even when things looked bleak. In response to the soldier, she asserted, "Never [will the South surrender], the war may last three or four years longer, & we would then stand equal with the United States."[79] Harriott Middleton and the women of her household likewise challenged the soldiers' assumptions that the war would end with a Union victory and peaceful reunification. When one soldier "said that they meant to kill out all our men and then, the war being over . . . that the Southern women would then have to marry them," the women laughed. They made their contempt of the ridiculous idea clear to the soldier, who "looked angry, or rather fiery when informed that no South Carolina woman would demean herself by marrying a Northern man." Refusing to believe that Southern women could survive on their own, he taunted, "What will become of you then?" In defense of her region and family, one woman defiantly retorted, "We will die . . . or form an army of women."[80] The Middleton women would not surrender to Union power. Even after Union soldiers had wreaked their vengeance on South Carolina, and their family estate in particular, they threatened to continue the fight and protect their nation.

Not only did Confederate women revel in their strong opposition to the Union troops and the United States, but they also ridiculed the terrorizing tactics of the invading armies. As the campaign continued, elite white women concluded that the Union strategy clearly demonstrated the cultural depravity of the North and the moral superiority of the South. As Sherman's troops acted in ways that violated traditional notions of white womanhood, Confederate women often appealed to these notions of feminine dependence and helplessness as they denounced the "powerful" North for resorting to a war on traditionally unprotected groups such as women, children, and African Americans. To elite Southern women, such tactics revealed the ultimate weakness of the Union and its doctrine of free labor. Still supporting the paternalistic logic of slavery, Dolly Lunt Burge criticized the North for making "the poor cowardly negro fight," especially considering that "the all powerful Yankee Nation [had] the whole world to back them. Their ports open, their armies filled with soldiers from all nations." Why, she questioned, should they "take the poor negro to help them out, against this 'little Confederacy' which was," she laughed, "to be brought back into the Union in sixty days time?"[81] From these actions, Burge concluded that the "little Confederacy" must have proved far more powerful than the North had expected. In addition, these measures proved to her that the Union was not as strong as it had boasted. This realization gave her even more confidence in her nation's ability to ultimately secure success and independence.

The criticism of Union war tactics also extended to the treatment of slaves during the March. These criticisms revealed elite Southern women's continued adherence to the paternalistic ethos as well as their inability to see their own disregard for enslaved women's femininity. Burge, like many others, particularly condemned the Union for claiming to fight for the slaves, while at the same time letting its soldiers ransack slaves' meager homes and property. "Their [slave] cabins are rifled of every valuable." This pillage made the slaves fear the Yankees, Burge observed. As a result, "they all, poor things, huddled together in my room fearing every moment that the house would be burned."[82] Union soldiers treated the slaves at the Jones home in Georgia in a similar manner. Although an enslaved woman named Sue "had hid away a few potatoes for the little children . . . [and] entreated for them," the soldiers "took every one & tore a breadth from her new woolen dress which she was making & had sewing in her hands, to make strings to tie up their bags of plunder." Furthermore, Mary Sharpe Jones reported, Union soldiers "have stolen even the drawers & petticoats of the women for that purpose & sometimes they have taken their other garments & put them on, leaving in their stead their filthy crawling shirts."[83] In these situations, Burge and other slaveholding women saw themselves as the protectors of their slave "families," a role normally accorded to family patriarchs. Burge overestimated her slaves' loyalty to her, but she rightly noted the damage done to African American property. After the war, many former slaves appealed to the United States government for restitution for property destroyed and stolen by Union troops on Sherman's March.[84] Once again, elite Southern women believed that Union soldiers crossed the line in their willingness to abuse women of all colors by looting and destroying their personal items.

Although she verbally stood up to the invaders, staunch and vocal Confederate Emma LeConte decried the Union's attack on civilians and appealed to antebellum ideals about womanhood. Playing on society's preconceived notions about femininity, she painted white Southern women as targeted because of their gender. Women, she deduced, were unfairly treated as helpless victims because of their perceived vulnerability. In addition, as far as she could tell, the Union had no tactical reasons for such an assault but pursued this course to torment the civilians. "From what I hear their chief aim while taunting helpless women has been to 'humble their pride'—'Southern pride.'" To this end, she noted, soldiers would ridicule the women: "'Where now' they would hiss—'is all your pride' . . . 'this is what you get for setting you selves up as better than other folks.'" Despite such taunts, LeConte reported, "the women acted with quiet dignity and refused to lower themselves by any retort."

However, LeConte recognized that not everyone remained silent in the face of ridicule; some women challenged the enemy and refused to be threatened into submission. While "soldiers were pillaging the house of a lady—One asked her if they had not humbled her pride *now*. 'No indeed' she said 'nor can you ever.' 'You *fear* us any way'—'No' she said. 'By G—— but you *shall* fear me.'" The soldier then "cocked his pistol and put it to her head," asking "Are you afraid now?" LeConte proudly reported that when the woman "folded her arms and looking him steadily in the eye, said contemptuously, 'No.' He dropped his pistol and with an exclamation of admiration left her."[85] This anecdote not only shows women's disdain for the enemy, but also highlights one way in which Confederate women fought for their nation and their homes.[86]

Like the woman LeConte described, Mary Maxcy Leverett refused to back down from her confidence in herself and her nation. Leverett not only showed no fear, but she also scorned Union tactics directly to the soldiers. In Columbia, she challenged the Yankee men who came to ransack her home. Leverett "pointed to the ruined town . . . and asked if this was what they styled 'civilized warfare'?" She took her criticism a step further, telling "them not a nation in Europe in the nineteenth century would be guilty of such an outrage." Despite this verbal challenge, and although her family was "considered such notorious rebels that there was no end to the officers who came to argue, to persuade or to *literally* ask 'if we had had enough?'" Leverett remained unharmed and seemingly unperturbed. She maintained her Confederate loyalty, despite numerous raids and taunting from the soldiers. As the "great army of ruffians" left town on the road by her house, they "[fired] a parting shot at the house." Instead of revealing her fear, Leverett "went quickly out into the piazza and showed myself to them, to let them see I did not flinch, and stood some minutes looking at them." Even though she "expected every moment to have a ball put thro' me," Leverett remained outside until she saw the "last stragglers" leave.[87]

Leverett's confrontation with the enemy in this situation was not her first. In a letter to her son, Leverett described an earlier verbal altercation with Union soldiers. After the invading soldiers "asked . . . whether we had not been beaten enough to want peace, see their force how immense, see how they had destroyed our resources, railroads &c.," Leverett replied, "we . . . would agree to none but an honorable peace." The soldiers seemed surprised by her answer. "Their countenances fell." When the soldiers pointed out "the wholesale destruction going on over the State, & asked if we were not ready to give up," she made her dedication to the Southern nation clear. "I said 'No! It would make us more determined & drive every man into the field with feelings more embittered & intense than ever. It was a *good thing* for us.'" The enemy soldiers refused to believe Leverett's answer and "again they were disconcerted." They assumed that "the men would have to come home to take care of their families," but Leverett asserted that the women "would take care of ourselves, that I had suffered (pointing to our sacked house) but was willing to suffer. I could bear calamity." When the soldiers tried to discourage Leverett with the larger picture of destruction, they failed again. "They referred to Georgia, how they had ruined her! 'I said Georgia was recovering already, like an India rubber ball, and so would we.'"[88]

Many elite women who confronted Sherman in North Carolina also remained steadfast in their support for the Confederacy. One woman acknowledged the horrors of Union invasion while reasserting her Confederate patriotism. "Terrible has been the storm that has swept over us," she wrote, listing her losses and the horrors of the invasion. The Union's demonstration of its power, however, did not dampen her spirit. In fact, their taunts after ransacking her home made her even more determined to remain a steadfast Confederate. "After destroying everything we had . . . one of these barbarians had to add insult to injury by asking me 'what I would live upon now?'" Undaunted by events, she quickly responded, "Upon patriotism: I will exist upon the love of my country as long as it will last, and then I will die as firm in that love as the everlasting hills." The soldier did not agree: "We shall soon subjugate the rebellion, and you will then have no country to love." The woman refused to budge: "Never! . . . never! you and your blood-handed countrymen may make the whole of this beautiful land one vast graveyard but its people will never be subjugated. Every man, woman and child of us will keep quietly in honourable graves, but we will never live dishonourable lives."[89]

Although Sherman had hoped to subdue and eliminate elite women's efforts in support of the Southern war effort, his march through Georgia and the Carolinas served for many as a motivator to increase Confederate patriotism. Shocked by the lengths to which the Northern enemy would go during wartime, Southern women adapted their behavior to fight for the Confederacy. They refused to surrender to an enemy that would stoop to the level of making war on women, an enemy that they considered inhuman, savage, and heartless. Instead, the attack on the home front further confirmed to Southern women that North and South were irreconcilable. These assessments allowed them to defiantly assert themselves as Confederate women who would do anything to protect their homes, families, and nation. By successfully adapting their behavior to deal with a direct attack on their homes and personal belongings, many Confederate women found ways to support their nation ardently while retaining their femininity. Elite Southern women's resolute support for their nation demonstrated that their regional identity and concern for the Confederacy played as large a role in their lives as did their gender and that they could successfully combine the interests of both.

Despite women's continued support of the Confederacy, the South's bid for independence did not prove successful. Nevertheless, after Sherman's men left their towns, and even after General Robert E. Lee surrendered at Appomattox, many Confederate women remained dedicated to their defeated and now-defunct nation. Sherman's campaign on domesticity left behind a female population who refused to submit. The destruction of Southern homes, property, and countryside, combined with a direct attack on femininity, inspired elite women to a continued and heightened support of the Confederacy and all it represented. Sherman had mistakenly assumed that he could make white Southern women "howl" and, therefore, eliminate their loyalty to the war and the Confederate nation.

CHAPTER 5

ASSERTING CONFEDERATE WOMANHOOD

In November 1864, as Sherman's troops approached her family's plantation in Upson County, Georgia, Loula Kendall Rogers prepared for the imminent invasion of her personal space. As part of her preparation, she turned her private journal into a form of defiance and a way to vocalize her anger to the Yankees directly. In a journal designed for her eyes only, she inserted an explicit statement of her feelings so that any thieving Union soldiers would "know that *I hate, loathe and abhor the very scent, sight & name* of a *Yankee* with all my *heart, soul, mind, and body.*"[1] If any Yankee dared to read her journal, he would at least be subjected to her insults. Her decision to write her journal for enemy eyes served other purposes. If an invading soldier read it, Rogers wanted to make it clear to him that she and other Confederate women would not easily be subdued. Her pointed entry also served to remind the hated Northerners of the various violations of feminine space committed by Sherman's men.

The Union's intentional violation of gendered boundaries hardened Rogers's hatred of the enemy. She had been a devoted supporter of the Confederacy from the beginning of the war, and she paid a heavy cost for it. By February 1864 she had lost one brother to the war, and she mourned the loss of another at the Battle of Nashville in December 1864. Yet Rogers, like many other Confederate women, focused on the personal insults and domestic destruction unleashed by the Yankee enemy. In her eyes, these brutish tactics against privileged slaveholding ladies confirmed her beliefs that the Yankees were dishonorable and not worthy of respect. "There is no word in the English language strong enough to express our hatred and contempt for an enemy so degraded—if they were *gentlemen* we could bear it better."[2]

The crossing of gender boundaries by Union soldiers strengthened Rogers's Confederate pride. It did not subdue her. She was disgusted that "they always search every where, even in ladies' private rooms, a thing our Southern boys have never thought of doing."[3] When Yankee soldiers came to her house, she was appalled. "It was dreadful to see such great rough men prying into every secret drawer in our house, and we helpless women along with no means of defiance among those who had no more respect for woman than a cow."[4] An enemy who violated feminine space proved to her and other Confederate women that the North and the South belonged to completely separate cultures that could never be united. Frustrated with what had happened to women's private sanctuaries along Sherman's path, she wished that Northerners would similarly have "every depredation they have committed here be measured out to them in *their own coin*." Even so, she did not want Southern men to behave in such ungentlemanly ways. She trusted "*our brothers, husbands and sons may never invade the holy sanctuaries of a private family, insult poor helpless women, and so degrade themselves by every revolting crime that could come under the head of sin, as did the barbarous soldiers of the United States.*"[5] Rogers decried gendered tactics regardless of whom they would impact. Whether this was true or not, she insisted to herself that "*our soldiers have always as a general thing been respectful to ladies* whether they were friends or foes."[6]

When Northern soldiers left Southern communities, Confederate women like Rogers demonstrated that Union men had underestimated the women's powerful regional identity; Sherman had failed to break the will of elite Southern women and end their support for war. The bitterness, determination, and patriotism with which Confederate women responded to the attack on their home front, as well as their methods of defending themselves and their families, revealed that they valued their nation as much as they did their femininity. Instead of dissolving Confederate women's devotion to their new nation, Sherman's attack on domesticity intensified it as the march violated the gendered standards of wartime etiquette. The campaign also drove female rebels to draw even sharper distinctions between themselves and Yankees and to urge their husbands, brothers, and sons to continue the fight. Despite white Southern women's passion and rhetoric, however, Sherman's March had shattered the material basis of Confederate support in Georgia and the Carolinas by destroying homes, farms, food supplies, agricultural products, railroads, and raw materials. As a result, many Confederate women reluctantly recognized the probability of Southern defeat, but they vowed not to abandon their nation. Although the South was ultimately "obliged to submit" to the Union as a result of military defeats, Confederate women vehemently vowed that "never could [the Union] *subdue* us."⁷

The invasion of the domestic sphere during Sherman's campaign not only failed to bring Southern women to their knees but also magnified their patriotism and increased their hostility toward the Yankees after the soldiers departed. Sherman's March ultimately strengthened elite women's long-standing connections to kin and place, as well as their identification with Southern values, by giving them a common enemy and experiences around which they could unite.⁸ After years of sacrifice and dedication to regional concerns, most of the white women who directly faced the home front campaign emerged with a reinvigorated sense that irreconcilable differences separated Confederates and Northerners.⁹ Confederate women could not forgive the assault on domesticity, or Sherman's pursuit of it. As a result, in the months and years after Sherman's March, the elite women targeted in the campaign proved "the best patriots among us."¹⁰

The responses of Confederate women in the path of Sherman's March complicate the conventional wisdom about Southern white women during the war. Led by Drew Gilpin Faust, and repeated by many others, modern scholars have argued that the Confederate defeat occurred because women lost the will to fight. They contend that Southern women were naturally prone to oppose the war because it was antithetical to their nature, and from the onset of fighting they needed to be convinced to support it. The war, in this interpretation, threatened the femininity of white Southern women, who logically withdrew their support when their sacrifices proved too much to bear. In Faust's words, by the end of the war white women "undermined both objective and ideological foundations for the Confederate effort; they directly subverted the South's military and economic effectiveness as well as civilian morale." For Faust, and others, the military defeats and home front shortages resulted in a plummeting decline in home front morale. As a result, "it may well have been because of its women that the South lost the Civil War." Similarly, George C. Rable asserts that "by the end of the war, many women wavered in their support for the Southern cause" and demanded an end to the hostilities that had taken the lives of so many of their men."[11] In this view, the Confederacy failed, at least in part, because white Southern women from all walks of life chose to withdraw their support.

The experiences of the elite women in Sherman's path illuminate how Faust and others have overemphasized the essentialist gender ideals that require women to nurture and protect and deemphasize the privilege and interests that they had in the Confederate cause.[12] The war became increasingly personal for those who directly faced the aggressive assaults of Union troops and their violation of gender conventions.[13] As one Confederate soldier asserted in March 1865, "the people who have suffered are very patriotic, but those who were not molested are badly whipt."[14] As he observed, most of the elite white women who faced Union troops emerged from their confrontations reinvigorated with a patriotic virulence recognized by Union soldiers and glorified by Southerners in the postwar era. For example, as Union troops surrounded and fought to gain control of Atlanta in the summer of 1864, Mary Ann Cobb relayed her observations to her husband: "Those who have suffered the most in blood and treasure are the best patriots among us."[15] Cobb could not realize how prophetic her words were. Throughout the South, women who confronted Union troops confirmed this assessment. The targets of the Union's assault on domesticity rededicated their energy and resources to fighting the enemy, both during and after the Civil War. Sherman's March and, in particular, its attack on elite domesticity revealed to Confederate women the cultural gulf between themselves and the enemy as it further fueled their commitment to Southern independence.[16]

The assault on the Confederate home front by Union soldiers appalled the white women of the region, many of whom immediately filled letters and journals with descriptions of their experiences and expressions of their outrage. Through this outlet, elite women confirmed their disdain for the enemy's tactics and employed a tone that some may have viewed as masculine. Their vivid accounts of Union soldiers and their behavior on the Southern home front allowed the women to air their disdain of the "fiends" and to fuel further the anti-Northern hatred of other Confederates—male and female. For example, after enemy troops left her home, North Carolinian Ellen Devereux Hinsdale described the encounter. "The fiends have killed every hog, chicken, taken all the cattle they could & killed the rest," she lamented. "With few exceptions they have burnt the dwellings in the country, taken all the provisions every where, torn to pieces all the clothing of women & children they could find." As if the destruction of property was not enough, the enemy also actively worked to demean and otherwise humiliate the residents. "Some of our girls . . . they compelled to play all night on the Piano." By forcing the women to entertain them, the Union men demonstrated their masculine power and the reality of an absence of Confederate men as protectors. The invasion terrified the civilians, so as Union troops burned the local arsenal, Hinsdale's "house was filled with the women & children of the neighborhood children screaming & everyone frightened almost to death" of "the devils." Instead of surrendering or bemoaning her fate, Hinsdale wished that she could take a more active role in the ongoing struggle against the Union. "If I was a man I should go in the army at once."[17] Despite the rampant destruction, loss of property, and degrading insults, Hinsdale was not ready to give up on Southern independence, but instead looked for new ways to support her nation.

Sherman's earlier visit to Savannah had similarly galvanized white Southern women and unintentionally intensified their hatred for him and Yankees in general. His decision to hold court at his headquarters in order to demonstrate his good intentions toward the "rebels" that he expected would be acquiescent did not sit well with most of Savannah's white women.[18] The housing of Sherman's officers in Confederate homes in Savannah, and elsewhere along the campaign, equally fostered animosity toward the enemy. Fanny Yates Cohen, for example, became enraged when she was forced to provide lodging for one of Sherman's officers. She categorically refused to welcome the man into her house, entertain him, or befriend him. "If we are conquered I see no reason why we should receive our enemies as our friends and I *never shall do it, as long as I live*." Like many others in the same situation, she voiced her displeasure about the decision to surrender Savannah without a fight. Cohen's father feared that Fanny would "compromise him by [her] too open avowal of hatred," but that did not change her view of the enemy.

She tried to remain civil to the occupiers but could not mask her disgust; surrender did not mean peaceful reunification. Many other Confederate women in occupied Savannah shared Cohen's "open avowal of hatred" and proudly voiced their resentment of Northern troops.[19] One woman walking in Savannah "notic[ed] the United States flag stretched above the sidewalk, [and] she stepped down into the sand to avoid passing under it." When reprimanded by the guard "to walk under the flag, she refused to obey him." For this insolence, the woman was taken to Sherman, who asserted that he would "make [her] walk under it." The woman remained defiant: "You *cannot* make me. . . . You may have me carried under it, but then it will be your act—not mine."[20] Sherman and others discovered that women's Confederate loyalties were not as easily broken as they had assumed.

Those in the state targeted by Sherman as the "hotbed of secession," in particular, demonstrated that they could not easily be subdued by destruction. Instead, South Carolina's women used the march's attack on domesticity as a stimulus to intensify their Confederate loyalty. After hearing of an explosion near the river, Emma LeConte of Columbia "[rejoiced] to think of any [Union soldiers] being killed" and mourned that the explosion had not been more deadly: "If only the whole [United States] army could have been roasted alive." In addition, she resented "their horrid old gridiron of a flag . . . flaunting its bars in our faces all day" and hated the results of the Yankee invasion. She could not "picture [Columbia] . . . as it now is." Instead, she imagined it as it had been before the invasion because it seemed inconceivable to her that "the ruins and ashes" were her beloved hometown. This unwelcome change provoked her to pass judgment on the Union. "*How* I *hate* the people who have done this!"[21] To this end, LeConte also resented "the U.S. flag run up over the State House." She saw it as "a degradation—to see it over the capital of South Carolina" especially "after four long years of bitter bloodshed and hatred." She considered the Stars and Stripes as an emblem of the enemy and a "hateful symbol of despotism!"[22] This spite toward the Union and its flag did not come from her personal experiences and losses alone; LeConte and others like her focused on the larger troubles facing their nation. Ellen Mordecai, for example, agreed with a friend who asserted "it is the *country,* not the individual adversity that she mourns."[23]

The havoc that invading Union soldiers wreaked upon the home front in Georgia and the Carolinas served, for many, as an impetus to increased loathing of the Union and a subsequent rededication to the Southern Cause. Dolly Lunt Burge, for example, directly connected Sherman's March with her continued devotion to her nation. Writing from Madison, Georgia, a town relatively untouched by the full wrath of Union soldiers, Burge recorded "the passing of Sherman's army by my place," which left her "poorer by thirty thousand dollars than I was yesterday morning. And a much stronger rebel."[24] After seeing the "Blue Coats" for the first time, Georgian Margaret Dailey exclaimed, "I do not admire nor love them much." The Union men's presence in her town seemed particularly distasteful to Dailey because "our country is over-run by the impudent race, going where they please and doing as they please."[25] Because of the seemingly unrestrained actions of the Yankee soldiers, some Confederate women regretted their composure during the invasion. "When I think of those insolent wretches," one woman wrote, and "how they threatened to burn us out & how they took every thing they could lay hands on[,] I wonder [how] I did not jump upon one & tear him to pieces."[26] The crossing of gendered social boundaries by Northern troops as they invaded the domestic sphere incensed many Confederate women.[27]

Like other elite women in Sherman's path, Emma LeConte especially resented the invasion of her domestic sphere and found that it increased her animosity toward the enemy. LeConte recorded her shift in attitudes, noting that "before they came here, I thought I hated [the Yankees] as much as was possible—now I know there are no limits to the feeling of hatred."[28] Grace Brown Elmore agreed: "Wicked as we knew the Yankee to be, we never could realize the extent of their malice until their occupying of Columbia."[29] The incidents surrounding the destruction and burning of Columbia provoked LeConte to conclude that "the more we suffer, the more we should be willing to undergo rather than submit. Somehow I can not feel we can be conquered." Echoing the sentiments of other Confederate women, LeConte continued: "We have lost everything," but "if everything . . . could be given back a hundred fold I would not be willing to go back to them." Instead she "would rather endure any poverty than live under Yankee rule. . . . Anything but live as one nation with *Yankees*—that word in my mind is a synonym with *all* that is *mean despicable and abhorrent*."[30] Elmore's experience in Columbia resulted in a similar hostility toward the enemy. "The very devils from hell could not rouse greater feelings of disgust and abhorrence than those cowardly wretches did in us."³¹ LeConte confidently asserted that despite the destruction and horrors of invasion, "the people are undemoralized and more determined than ever."³² LeConte could not imagine other white Southern women responding to the assault on domesticity any differently.

After her prominent slaveholding South Carolina family lost most of its property to the Union campaign, Harriott Middleton offered views similar in meaning and intensity to LeConte's. Middleton's face-to-face confrontations with Union soldiers left her no option but to consider them wholly undeserving of sympathy or decorum. "Never hesitate again in using bad language about the Yankies. Nothing can be bad enough." In Middleton's mind, as well as that of other Confederate women, the attack on the feminine sphere excluded Union troops from civilized society. Middleton fumed that "this defenseless town was given up to the soldiery all that first long night." The result was so horrifying that "the sights and Sounds beggar description." Even so, she and others struggled to describe the events to friends and relatives across the Confederacy.³³ Likewise, Georgian Eliza Frances Andrews wondered in April 1865 "what is it . . . that makes [Yankees] so different from us." Although she "used to have some Christian feeling towards Yankees," her experience as a refugee, who returned home to find all of her possessions destroyed, changed her opinion. "Now that they have invaded our country and killed so many of our men and desecrated so many homes, I can't believe that when Christ said 'Love your enemies,' he meant Yankees."³⁴ She was not alone in this conviction. From South Carolina, Harriott Middleton echoed these sentiments after Sherman's troops vacated her home. "I know now what it is to hate! . . . I would like to *see* the Yankees lying in their blood."³⁵ Similarly, after Union troops left her North Carolina home, Nellie Worth proclaimed, "Oh how I do hate the very name of Yankie!"³⁶ Rather than forcing their surrender, Sherman's March provoked Confederate patriotism from many of the white women it targeted.

Some white Southern women took their desire for vengeance even further, demanding that Confederate soldiers fight fire with fire. If Confederate women had to suffer, Yankee women, too, should have to endure the indignations and terror of invasion. Grace Brown Elmore, for example, described her reaction to Union soldiers who were passing through

Columbia after destroying it the night before: "How my whole soul rose against them as they passed, a band of highway robbers, the slayers of women and children," she wrote. She acknowledged how the march had affected her psychologically. "My whole nature is changed, I feel so hard so pitiless, gladly would I witness the death of each of those wretches." She demanded vengeance on all who supported the Union, regardless of age or sex. "God hear the curses poured upon their heads, God grant they may suffer in their homes, their wives their children as they have made us suffer."[37] Justice, Elmore asserted, required that traditionally protected groups in the North experience the same horrors that she had. She doubted that the North could withstand such an assault. Other elite women made similar statements. Janie Smith expressed her hope that "when our army invade[s] the north, [the soldiers will] carry the torch in one hand and the sword in the other." She further asserted, "I want dissolution carried to the heart of their country, the widows and orphans left naked and starving just as ours were left." When making these statements, Smith realized that she stepped outside the peacetime boundaries of "polite" behavior, but she felt it necessary. She acknowledged that her friend Janie Robeson might think she was not acting like a lady: "I know you will think this is a very unbecoming sentiment, but I believe it is our only policy now."[38]

In many cases, elite Southern women's sacrifices required their undying support for their nation. They could not abandon a cause to which they had dedicated so much time, energy, and emotion and so many lives. Catherine Rowland, whose Augusta, Georgia, plantation had been destroyed by Union soldiers, and whose brother had died on the battlefield, affirmed that Confederate women had "suffered too much to think of giving up now & it is a sacrilege to the dead to speak of such a thing." In addition, "reunion with such a foe can never be, there is a great gulf between us; the blood of our noble dead & my noble brother cries out for vengeance & we ought to fight on as long as we have a man left."[39] Eliza Frances Andrews asserted "I am more of a rebel to-day than ever I was when things looked brightest for the Confederacy."[40] Similarly, after the Union soldiers ransacked her Georgia plantation home, burned her outhouses, and stole most of her valuables and food, another white woman pronounced, "I thought my hatred was deep enough before, but now I am a hotter rebel than ever, and *never will* be resigned to going back into the Union with such a corrupt people." One Georgia woman's May 1865 letter decried Union tactics, especially those that targeted the trappings of domesticity. After the enemy repeatedly "[pried] into every sacred thing in the house," she vowed to never forgive. "If I live a thousand years I shall never forget the enemies of our country." She would never "[regard] them as brothers & friends." Furthermore, she considered "it a contamination to be compelled to breathe the same air, much less tolerate their society among us."[41]

The animosity towards Union troops and recognition of their military successes and actions did not preclude women's unflagging confidence in the Southern soldiers in the months that preceded the Confederacy's official surrender. From Indian Springs, a town east of Milledgeville, Joe Varner recorded her impressions of and reactions to the March to the Sea. In late November 1864, she expressed her surprise that "the Yankees have made rather more progress through our dear old State than we ever dreamed they would," but she maintained "we are hopeful & have no idea of being subjugated." Taking this a step further, Varner vowed that "they may burn, destroy & do every other h——ish deed (such only as they can do) yet thee noble spirit of our brave Southern people can never be fettered."[42] Elizabeth Allston agreed. "I had rather do anything, suffer anything, than submit. But to think of the noble, glorious men we lose by the hands of such wretches! Though everything looks black around I feel that we must succeed."[43] Similarly, Annie Fuller of Greenville, South Carolina, regretted that her state, "the pride of our hearts, 'the land (we thought) of the brave' & chivalrous," seemed to have "cower[ed] before the threats of the despised Yankees." Nevertheless, she remained steadfast in her belief that "men women and children [would] rise equal to any emergency, determined amid any endurance, and prove to our enemies, that never! never! never! can we be subdued."[44] Although the confidence of these white women may have been misplaced, they and many others refused to see Sherman's March and the destruction that it caused as signifiers of Confederate defeat.

In Georgia's state capital, Milledgeville, invading Union soldiers could not destroy the Confederate loyalties of many of its white women. Writing on November 19, 1864, Anna Maria Green Cook acknowledged that when Sherman's troops first captured the town, "we were despondent our heads bowed and our hearts crushed." Despite the discouraging turn of events, and although "our degradation was bitter," she continued, "we knew it could not be long, and we never desponded, our trust was still strong." Cook further proclaimed her Confederate patriotism and taunted the Union ignorance of such loyalty. "How can they hope to subjugate the South. The people are firmer than ever before." To prove their confidence, perhaps to themselves, she and her family "went through the house singing, 'We live and die with [Jefferson] Davis'" to the tune of "Dixie."[45] Even after four long years of loss and sacrifice, Cook and other Confederate women believed in the Southern Cause and people. Grace Brown Elmore of Columbia, South Carolina, had a similar reaction to the Union soldiers. "They think we are subdued, they think we are done! So long as life lasts, so long we must struggle." After all, she concluded, "there are many high hearts who will strike till freedom comes."[46] After Columbia burned, Mary Maxcy Leverett stressed the importance of the continuation of the fight. She wanted all Southern men to stay on the battlefield and refused to accept anything else from them. "If our men never fought before, tell them I say they must do it now: if they give up, or their knees shake, I won't count them as men, but as dogs who deserve to, deserve to die."[47] Another woman refused to accept capitulation to the Union troops. "We don't and won't believe it," she wrote. We "pray that our brave men will hold out even til the bitter end, rather than submit to such a race, who feel so impudently, that all our's is theirs, and we have no rights."[48]

For some women, confidence in the Confederacy came from a belief in divine retribution for what they saw as the inhumane acts performed by Union soldiers on the campaign through Georgia and the Carolinas. After describing the scene of destruction to her brother, a woman on the outskirts of Atlanta affirmed that she and the rest of the household were "doing as well we can—better than we expected we could do, after having been foraged to death by the *Blue Devils*." The Union troops had taken the family's food, clothing, and valuables, but she still remained strong in her support for the Confederacy and hatred for the "Yankee Devils." After having "been tried in a fiery furnace" near Atlanta, this woman maintained hope that providence would lead to a Confederate victory. "I think I can confidently say that a Just God will never permit such a vile, wicked nation, as the Yankees are ever to conquer a nation that is so far superior to them in every thing except lying and stealing." This ultimate divine retribution had been unquestionably earned because "I do not think the Demons from the bottomless pit could act much worse than the Yankees."⁴⁹ Many of the slaveholding women along Sherman's path maintained their faith in divine intervention on their behalf. Some women in North Carolina, for example, remained strong because "the general feeling here is that the time is not far off when they will be punished for what they have done & are doing, to us."⁵⁰ Nellie Worth had similar confidence that her nation was the one supported by the divine. In her eyes, the Yankees had proven themselves devils. "May the chilling blight of heaven fall on their dark and doomed souls. May all the powers of earth and heaven combine to destroy them, may their land be one vast scene of ruin and desolation as ours is. This is the blessing of the innocent and injured one, I forgive them? May heaven never."⁵¹ With their confidence in divine retribution for the actions of the enemy, elite Confederate women could continue to believe that their nation would ultimately achieve its quest for independence.

Women's dedication to and confidence in their nation required that they continue to support the armies and the Confederacy at times when defeat seemed inevitable. Even after Sherman and his destructive troops had passed through their homes and towns, many elite white women insisted that their male relatives continue in the service of their nation. Although "sad indeed are the great victories of the Yankees the past week," especially in her home state of South Carolina, Sue Montgomery continued to support the troops. "Think not my dear," she reassured her cousin, "[that] I would for one moment by *word* or *deed* try to tempt you away from your *post* of *honour & duty*—No, far from it."⁵² Mrs. Alston Pringle agreed. "Our son (and friends in the Army) are just where they ought to be. I would not for worlds have my child any where else but with our brave Generals, casting in his all for our freedom & rights."⁵³ Confederate women continued to criticize deserters and those not in the Confederate military. In the same fashion, after "days of pain and anxiety, and oh, nights of terror," Lily Logan remained steadfast. Writing to her brother, Confederate general Thomas M. Logan, she worked to bolster the soldiers' morale by revealing her willingness to continue the fight. "I am sure we will be victorious soon, and are ready to bear even more for our glorious cause. . . . Keep up your spirits and let us whip Sherman soon."⁵⁴

Even in April 1865, after Robert E. Lee surrendered his Army of Northern Virginia to Ulysses S. Grant, many Confederate women in Georgia and the Carolinas refused to accept defeat.[55] Their personal trials during the war seemed to them justifications to continue the bloody fight, not reasons to surrender. One woman told a Union chaplain that even if the Confederate soldiers were "whipped," the women at home were "not subdued in spirit."[56] White women's continued defense of the Confederacy grew not only out of their strong identity to their region, but also from their sense of Southern honor and their fear of having made wartime sacrifices in vain. These women did not want to acknowledge that the men of their worlds had died for a failed cause, so they refused to accept that their fight for Southern independence had failed. Emma LeConte typified the reactions of many of her countrywomen who "*cannot* believe we are conquered."[57] Like other South Carolina women, Charlestonian Emma Holmes "could not, [and] would not believe it."[58] A woman from Sommerville, South Carolina, living in England, offered similar sentiments to her husband serving in the Confederate army. Charlotte Burckmyer asserted her confidence in ultimate Confederate success. "Of one thing . . . I feel sure, the Yankees are crowing too soon and too loudly—the end is not yet. I believe the curtain has fallen upon one phase of the war only to arise upon another." She trusted that the South would make another stand to defeat the Union and could not "believe as the Yankee press and government are giving out that my countrymen who have fought so gallantly, endured so nobly and sacrificed so freely, will be content to lie down and be bound hand and foot by the dirty, dastardly nation who are over-running our homes."[59] Despite news to the contrary, Confederate women refused to believe that the South's bid for independence had ended so unsatisfactorily.[60]

After describing to her brother the horrors visited upon her and her North Carolina neighbors by Sherman's troops, Eliza Tillinghast reasserted her dedication to the Confederacy in May 1865. "And now I tell you as *upon oath,* 'the *truth* the whole truth, and nothing but the truth'—The South is *not whipped* it is overwhelmed and by *brute* force."[61] With a rationale that would quickly be invoked in the creation of the Lost Cause, she blamed "uncivilized" Union tactics for the defeat of Confederate armies and resented the enemy's warfare. Elizabeth Collier agreed, using the same language. Confederate troops had been "overpowered—

outnumbered, but thank God we have not been whipped."[62] Tillinghast further believed, as did other elite white women, that "had the Yankees carried on the war by the rules of warfare, we would have been successful our men have *never* been whipped on a *fair field*." However, the unorthodox Union assault on the home front and the feminine world led to an unfair advantage. "Our armies were reduced to starvation by the destruction of mills, the burning of farming utensils, . . . burning commissary depo[t]s all over our country." Despite this turn of events, Tillinghast reaffirmed her faith in the Confederate nation and Southern troops. "We are not *humiliated* that our army of N[orthern] V[irginia] had to surrender" because this "little handful" of men "had been suffering the pangs of hunger and [had] killed thousands of the hated foe ere they laid down their arms completely overwhelmed by an immense army of well fed well equipped men." These Southern soldiers deserved high praise, she continued, for "resisting to the bitter end the aggression of the tyrant." As a result of this, Tillinghast asserted, "we are as *proudly defiant* as ever, we can *hate* them and we will hate them forever." Her unfailing belief in the South's right to secede and form an independent nation provoked Tillinghast to an intense Confederate patriotism and a refusal to submit to Union rule after the surrender.[63]

Georgian Mollie Cunningham, like many other Confederate women, shared Tillinghast's and Collier's frustrations at Union soldiers for not waging a "fair" fight. She played upon antebellum ideals about womanhood as she criticized Union war tactics in the late campaigns. "I know our brave men could whip any fair fight but they are overwhelming us with numbers and waging war upon the defenceless women and children, by marching through our unprotected country destroying and taking every means of subsistence from the defenceless women and Innocent Children."[64] She highlighted assumptions about elite white women as "defenceless" instead of pointing to their open defiance of enemy soldiers in their homes during the invasion. Blaming Union military victory on "uncivilized" tactics allowed elite Southern women to reaffirm the noble nature of their own soldiers, who had failed in protecting their women on the home front, while criticizing the enemy's victory. It further created an explanation for Confederate defeat that would live on in regional memory as a central component of the Lost Cause.[65]

Disbelief at Lee's surrender and at the end of the Confederacy grew out of the frustrations that resulted from having made so many sacrifices for the Confederate cause. Too much effort and too many lives had been invested in the success of Southern independence for white Southern women to accept anything but victory. Emma LeConte, perhaps more eloquently than many other Confederate women, questioned the war's outcome: "Have we suffered all—have our brave men fought so desperately and died so nobly for *this*?" Despite Union assumptions to the contrary, this Confederate woman noted that because the four years of war had brought them "little else than the anguish of anxiety—the misery of sorrow over dear ones sacrificed," the South could not give up. LeConte stressed her frustration as she continued. "Is all this blood spilled in vain—will it not cry from the ground on the day we yield to these Yankees! *We* give up to the *Yankees*! How *can* it be? How can they talk about it?"[66] Military surrender seemed impossible to her after her personal confrontations with the enemy.

As word spread through Georgia and the Carolinas of the surrender, Confederate women expressed disdain for such a future. Emma Holmes, for example, scorned the very notion of a peace with the North. "To go back into the Union!!! No words can describe all the horrors contained in those few words. Our souls recoiled shuddering at the bare idea." Reconciliation, she continued, was impossible because nothing could "ever bridge over that fearful abyss of blood, suffering, affliction, desolation, and unsummed anguish stretching through these past four years. The blood of our slain heroes cried aloud against such an end—as if end it could be." Holmes also acknowledged the reinvigoration in the Confederate spirit as a result of Yankee tactics and victories. Upon news of Lee's surrender "our Southern blood rose in stronger rebellion than ever and we all determined that, if obliged to submit, never could they *subdue* us." Holmes also predicted a difficult reunion with the United States as a result of the bitterness felt by the South. "Peace on such terms, is war for the rising generation."[67] Similar declarations of confidence in the Confederate nation occurred throughout the South. In May 1865, Georgian Loula Kendall Rogers proclaimed that the South was *"overpowered but not conquered!* No not whipped yet, for in spite of this miserable ending of all our brilliant hopes, I believe our enemies may yet be scattered and by some divine interpositions [our soldiers will be] delivered from their hands."[68] In North Carolina, Catherine Edmondston refused to accept surrender, instead noting that "what . . . sustains me . . . is faith in the *country*. Faith in the *Cause*, an earnest beleif that eventually we will yet conquer! We cannot be defeated. This is which I beleive sustains."[69]

Peace with the Union horrified a great many Confederate women, especially those who had personally faced enemy soldiers in their homes. North Carolinian Eliza Tillinghast assured her brother that "if [he] knew what we have suffered in the cause of our Precious country [he] would not wonder" at her bitterness toward the enemy. As she portrayed it, "We have lost every thing but our honor." In addition, because of the "many precious lives . . . which our family has laid upon the altar of our country," she explained, "there is a wall of bones, and a River of blood and it will flow forever between the foe and us, and until they cut a canal to the waters of Oblivion and deluge our land with Forgetfulness we can never consider a yankee any thing but an oppressor and an enemy." She did not stop there, but continued to detail her attitudes toward an enemy that had invaded her feminine sphere. "While I have no personal feeling towards any one of them I hate the nation from the bottom of my soul, Even as I hate Satan, and all things low, mean and hateful."[70] She blamed the Union as a whole for violating her home and instituting an assault on Southern domesticity. Although she could forgive Northern soldiers' actions on the battlefield, she could not do the same for the policies that allowed their desecration of Southern homes and bedrooms.

In part, Confederate women's refusal to come to grips with surrender resulted from their disdain for an enemy that had invaded the domestic sphere and employed other similarly gendered and improper methods such as dancing on pianos, stealing personal papers, and rustling through women's undergarments. "How humiliating it is to think of our being given up to such a people," Loula Kendall Rogers lamented. She doubted that a word "strong enough to express our hatred and contempt for an enemy so degraded" even existed. Union soldiers' worst failure, however was the fact that they had trespassed into women's worlds. She asserted that "if they were *gentlemen* we could bear it better."[71] The behavior of enemy soldiers made surrender unbearable for many. After four years of struggling and hoping for peace, Emma LeConte agreed. She wanted to continue the fight for the Confederacy because peace with the Union "is cruel—it is *unjust*." Furthermore, "this is worse than war—What is such peace to us!" Despite the horrors she had experienced in wartime South Carolina, LeConte affirmed, "I never loved my country as I do now—I feel I could sacrifice *everything* to it—and when I think of the future—oh God! it is too horrible."[72] Sherman's March had not dampened her patriotism and it further convinced her that Yankees were members of an incompatible race.

Other white Southern women similarly refused to conceive of a future without an independent Confederacy. The idea of reunification with the Union sickened them. For example, Eliza Tillinghast revealed her hopes and her willingness to sacrifice further for her battered nation. "We still look forward to the welfare of the Confederacy." This confidence, in spite of the surrender, kept her spirits high and her patriotism strong. "Were it not for hope in the future I would rather that the last brother I have in the world was in his grave." Although death seemed drastic, she "would far prefer seeing the last one buried than to be sure that they were to live victims of Yankee tyranny." Tillinghast also resented the idea of paying taxes to the United States because she saw it as making her "pay the debt contracted by Yankeedom in paying men to desolate their country, murder their kindred[,] insult their sisters[,] and exult over them all their lives."[73] She did not want to reimburse or honor the men who had, as she understood it, defiled her homeland and her home. Military defeat did not insure surrender of the populace.

Even weeks after Sherman's March had ended and Confederate generals had surrendered, the perceived wrongs by enemy soldiers inspired many elite Southern women to hope for continued acts of retaliation. Loula Kendall Rogers wrote that she could not "help to save my life from wishing that the North may feel all the horrors of war as we have done." She hoped for vengeance—that Northerners too would have "their homes desolated, their private property stolen and every depredation they have committed here be measured out to them in *their own coin*." Despite her desire for revenge, Rogers realized that she could "*never wish* that our *Southern sons* should be guilty of such wickedness." Instead, she "hope[d] and pray[ed] that *our* brothers, husbands and sons may never invade the holy sanctuaries of a private family, insult poor helpless women, and so degrade themselves by every revolting crime that could come under the head of sin, as did the barbarous soldiers of the United States."[74] Rogers, like many other Confederate women in Georgia and the Carolinas, defiantly maintained her belief in the inviolability of the domestic sphere. These elite women hoped for retribution on the Yankee enemy, but they could not fully sanction a retaliatory assault on the Northern domestic sphere.

Anna Maria Green Cook wanted Southern men to continue their battle against the Union. She, too, hoped "that [our soldiers] would never yield while a man lives to fight . . . if need be until our children's children may hail the glad day of deliverance."[75] Willing to do anything in her power to secure Confederate victory after the invasion of the domestic sphere, Emma LeConte thought that women should be given the opportunity to chase Union men out of the area if Southern men could not do the job. Despite losses on the battlefront, the women of the Confederacy, she asserted, had not been defeated and would gladly mount an attack against the Northern enemy. "Why does not the President call out the women if there are not enough men[?]" she asked. "We would go and *fight*, too—we would better all die together.—Let us suffer still more—give up yet more—*anything* anything that will help the cause." Further, LeConte vowed to do "anything that will give us freedom and not force us to live with such people—to be ruled by such horrible and contemptible creatures—to submit to them when we hate them so bitterly."[76] Although not willing to enter the traditional battlefield herself, Eliza Tillinghast also vowed to do all in her power to continue the fight against the Union. "I want to live if for no other reason than to cheer these little ones in my care on to liberate their country from the thralldom of Sarrisons and Yankeedom." Eventually, though, she hoped that the fight would be won. "God is punishing us now, but as there is justice in Heaven the Yankees will get theirs in due time." In closing, this "unhappy but hopeful Sister" urged her brother to "come to us as soon as you can . . . with a heart full of love to your country—your country that your mother's last efforts, last thoughts and last prayers were for—your country that your father loved honored, and hoped for. Your country! that your kindred have laid down so many lives for; that your sisters have worked and prayed for."[77] Confederate military defeats and Lee's surrender had not discouraged Tillinghast, and she assumed the soldiers had the same convictions in the nation's ultimate success. If not, she eagerly offered her brother reasons to continue believing in the Southern cause. Anna Maria Green Cook wrote that "our hearts no longer beat lightly in joy and pride for our armies have surrendered and our state is under yankee dominion."

However, she vowed, "we would give up Luxury, if even in homespun garments and with coarse fare we might be free—Our people might be free."[78] Elite Southern women who had personally faced domestic warfare refused to give up their Confederate identity.

Despite the war's official outcome, Elizabeth Collier refused to relinquish her Confederate identity and quietly reunite with the North. The idea repulsed her. "Can we ever live in peace with the desecrators of our homes & the murderers of our Fathers, Brothers & Sons—*Never*—We are bound to rise again."[79] After experiencing the horror of war firsthand, Collier's intense Confederate womanhood would not allow her to respect Northern leaders or acknowledge a complete end to Southern independence. As a result of the Union's gendered tactics, many elite women scoffed at those in the United States who assumed a quick and easy reunification. "What do they expect? They invade our country, murder our people, desolate our homes, conquer us, subject us to every indignity and humiliation."[80] North Carolinian Eliza Tillinghast further berated the Union for its postsurrender portrayal of the South, an activity that further incensed her and aroused her patriotism for the South. "They are daily telling scores of falsehoods on us . . . [which] are enough to make Satan grin with delight." While decrying the descriptions of Confederate president Jefferson Davis as a woman fleeing in a dress and United States President Abraham Lincoln as a hero, she was especially outraged at the Union glorification of Sherman. She could hardly believe that the Union was lionizing "Sherman the foul fiend who *cursed the women* and *children* of *your* native place." She could not understand how Northerners could respect a man who said that "when he 'came again he would come with the fire brand and leave complete desolation and the third time he would leave the country as if the indians had passed over it, and the land would have to be *repeopled*.'"[81]

Although a tragedy in the North, news of Lincoln's assassination and false rumors of Seward's death were considered "very cheering" and "Providential" by many Confederate women in Georgia and the Carolinas.[82] Charlotte St. Julien Ravenel, for example, celebrated that "today's news is very cheering; it is that Lincoln and Seward have both been assassinated."[83] Another South Carolinian, Emma LeConte, also rejoiced: "Hurrah! Old Abe Lincoln has been assassinated! It may be abstractly wrong to be so jubilant but I just can't help it—After all the heaviness and gloom of yesterday this blow to our enemies comes like a gleam of light." Like other Confederate women, LeConte jubilantly understood Lincoln's assassination as a sign of better things to come and the materialization of the divine justice for which they had hoped. Confederate women exulted that their "hated enemy has met the just reward of his life.... Could there have been a fitter death for such a man!"[84] In addition, Loula Kendall Rogers saw "the tyrant Lincoln's death" as "retribution ... from the hand of an all powerful God." She praised Lincoln's assassin, John Wilkes Booth, at having performed "the boldest [deed] I ever heard of in fact or fiction."[85] Across the South, white men and women refused to consider Lincoln's assassin as a criminal. Kate Cumming noted that signs put up for the capture of Booth's accomplices "were immediately torn down by some of the citizens."[86] Emma LeConte recorded her reaction to the news of the assassination as "simply gratified revenge—the man we hated has met his proper fate." She also "thought with exultation of the howl it had by that time sent through the North and how it would cast a damper on their rejoicings over the fall of our noble Lee."[87] Lincoln's death became not only a rallying point for Confederate patriotism but also a blow against the hated Yankees.

Elite white Southern women often felt that their military loss to the Union was exacerbated by the "unworthy" leaders in Washington, D.C., who would once again rule over them. Just as they had carefully observed and commented on the political events surrounding the secession crisis, Confederate women in Georgia and the Carolinas voiced their displeasure over the rise of a disloyal Southerner to the White House. Their lack of respect for Lincoln was only exceeded by their opinion of the scalawag who succeeded him in office—Andrew Johnson. As one South Carolina woman disdainfully put it, "The rail-splitter will be succeeded by the drunken ass—such are the successors of Washington and Jefferson—Such are to rule the *South*!"[88] Emma Holmes thought "Andy Johnson ... far worse than Lincoln, fiercer and more blood thirsty as renegades always are."[89] They had little hope that Johnson would fill the office well. After all, as many elite white Southerners saw it, Johnson's desertion of his native Tennessee in favor of the United States during the secession crisis clearly revealed him as a disloyal and unethical character. Georgian Loula Kendall Rogers voiced her disdain for the United States government. "Lincoln is removed, but another unprincipled wretch occupies his seat. How can they respect him as they should a President? Just think of such men presiding where once pure and upright *Washington* sat!" The transition of power, as she saw it, was an insult to the Revolutionary traditions of the nation. "Who could have dreamed a few years ago that this Republic envied by all the world would ever come to this!" The United States, in her mind, bore no resemblance to the country for which her ancestors or her contemporaries had fought. "Anarchy and bloodshed every where, no justice, no law, freedom of the press abolished, and soon we shall be afraid to *breathe* our sentiments lest what we have may be taken from us."[90] For many others, as well, Johnson's inauguration added insult to injury. A Georgia woman raged against her circumstances. "It is so humiliating to be under Yankee dominion after all our hard fighting, and under such an unprincipled man as Andy Johnson." Her lack of respect for the new United States president as well as her dissatisfaction with submitting to the rule of a country that had wreaked havoc on her home, family, and country led her to a desire to leave her homeland. "I am nearly crazy to go to Europe, but am not able to get there."[91]

In the face of Union military victory, many Confederate women in 1865 remained "*so* bitter at our fate."[92] Catherine Edmondston noted that "no one is well, no one is happy! Anger, indignant anger, fills every heart." She further recognized the effect of taking the Iron-Clad Oath of Loyalty. This mandatory oath forced upon Southern men "a sense of personal humiliation." As a result, Edmondston asserted, the man who took it "resent[ed] it by infusing a double portion of hate in the sentiment with which he regard[ed] those who [had] degraded him."[93] Confederate women understood and shared in these feelings of bitterness. After four years of sacrifice for their nation and after facing the enemy in their parlors and other domestic spaces, they refused to reconcile with the North or accept the reality of defeat. Like Emma Mordecai, some asserted that "no words can ever paint the bitterness, the hatred I feel to our despicable conquerors—ungenerous, low-minded, pitiful wretches."[94] Others assumed that the surrender only marked the end of one phase in the war. The South, they confidently asserted, would ultimately emerge victorious. In many instances, women held firmly "the conviction that the South can *not* be conquered—that it can *never* be re-united with the North is so deeply rooted in my heart—[and] since the war began

ASSERTING CONFEDERATE WOMANHOOD

that conviction has never been shaken once."[95] One woman adamantly asserted that Yankee tactics had guaranteed that the South would ultimately overcome its conquerors. "I cannot think the good lord will allow such wickedness to go unpunished, and look forward to the time when our enemies will be scattered to the four winds."[96]

Disdain for the Union's ways of life and war continued in the hearts and minds of white Southern women long after surrender became finalized. Their attitudes toward the United States and its wartime tactics further advanced Confederate women's loyalty for the Southern nation. "The way I feel about Yankees," Eliza Frances Andrews asserted a month after the surrender, "I would rather be wrong with Lee and his glorious army than right with a group of fanatics that have come down here to plunder and oppress us in the name of liberty."[97] Loula Kendall Rogers resented that she had to live side by side with "those who have *always* been our enemies."[98] Eliza Middleton Huger Smith similarly expressed her willingness to continue her opposition to the United States. She acknowledged, "I will lose all we have here; but if I can give up the lives of my Sons in the cause, surely I can stand the rest."[99] Another woman also refused to accept the official end to the hostilities. Sue, a friend of Jane Ann Smythe, "thought our cause not so desperate but that we could still hold out & I still cried for 'no surrender.'" When her "father said I talked like a woman, & did not reason," she asserted that "I was, & am still determined, that under Yankee rule, I never will live." She did, in fact, talk "like a woman," a Confederate woman who valued her nation above all else. Much to her delight, Sue was not the only one in her presumably elite household to adhere to her Confederate womanhood. "Mother surprised me. I have always thought her so luke warm but she too now says 'never give up until our independance is achieved.'" In contrast, her father's defeatist attitude upset her. "Father really distressed me & I had to beg him for my sake not to talk before others so discoragingly."[100]

Months and years after the surrender, Confederate women continued to hope for a revival of their nation and its bid for independence.[101] Reflecting women's role in creating and carrying on the Lost Cause ideology, one North Carolina woman affirmed in September 1865 that "Southern spirit can never be entirely conquered—at least Southern women cannot."[102] Another detailed her loyalty and her efforts to ensure a continued love of the Confederacy. "I expect to be a rebel as long as I live & make my children & their children swear eternal enmity to the United States & its dishonoured Flag. I never can be a loyal citizen whatever means they may adopt to make me one."[103] In 1868, Grace Brown Elmore still harbored resentment for the Yankees who had invaded her home. She continued to believe that "death [and] anhihilation would be preferable to coalition with the North, and so every woman almost feels." Consequently, she felt that women should "endeavor to keep pure the fire of patriotism even under the temptations and humiliations inherent to a conquered people." Furthermore, Elmore could not understand why anyone would want to "tak[e] a seat in the Senate cham[b]ers with such compeers as Beast Butler, Sherman, and a host of scoundrels; that a Southern woman would not touch with the tip of her toe."[104]

White Southern women's persistent belief in the Confederacy and continued hatred of the enemy stemmed from their experiences as civilian targets during Sherman's March. The campaign against the trappings of Southern domesticity served to increase women's belief in the irreconcilable cultures of North and South. As a result of their confrontations with invading troops, Confederate women confidently asserted that the Yankee soldiers "know that every *true* born Southron hates them with a hatred that *knows no change,* and can *never forget* what they have done, even to the tenth generation."[105] Certainly, they assumed, any population would react in like fashion to an attack on domesticity and womanhood. As a result of surviving four years of shortages and wartime horrors as well as living through Sherman's destruction of the home front, Confederate women believed that they had been transformed into a new type of Confederate. Emma LeConte summed it up by noting "we have suffered till we feel savage."[106]

Although Sherman's March ultimately helped secure military Confederate defeat, it did not crush elite female civilians' support for the Southern nation or its ideals. Sherman expected his invasion of homes, pillage of feminine property, and humiliation of white women to weaken morale on the Confederate home front, but elite women in Georgia and the Carolinas refused to surrender their homes or hearts to the Union. The Union assault on domesticity brought the war too close to home for slaveholding women, and they refused to forgive the transgression. As a result, many white Southern women did not abandon their nation or urge an end to the fighting, but instead they used the Union assault on domesticity as further motivation to continue the Civil War at any cost. In the end, Sherman's March provoked Confederate women to become "much stronger rebel[s]."[107]

EPILOGUE

SHAMING SOUTHERN SOLDIERS

As Sherman's men left Atlanta and moved east in November 1864, Georgian Samuel Wiley considered himself to be in a "safe place, behind an army of invincible soldiers, a great part of my time with nothing to do, comfortably clad and enough to eat and a tent to sleep in." He was stationed just outside Richmond, Virginia, in service to the Quartermaster's Department when he heard reports about the destruction of Atlanta and Sherman's soldiers marching east. "There is scarce room or reason to hope that you all have escaped," he wrote to his mother. "It is most tantalizing, distressing, saddening." The rumors about what was happening in his hometown and elsewhere made "everyone here . . . painfully anxious to hear." The presumed attack on his parents' home and on his "dear wife and little innocent children" revealed that he was in a no-win situation. He could not simultaneously defend the honor of his family and fulfill his duty to his nation. "How I wish I could step in to your room this morning, if you yet have a room—if you yet have a home," he mused. Wiley spent most of the war serving "in the rear" as he recovered from various ailments, and his rage about Sherman's attack on the home front led him to lament his inability to be effective at home or in battle. "I feel impelled to rush to the front, regardless of my 'surgeon's certificate,'" he proclaimed and then asked, "what could I do to avenge your private wrongs and insults?" After all, for many white Southern men, no greater shame existed than not to be able to prevent or avenge the insult of one's mother.

By waging war on Wiley's wife and mother and the domestic front, Sherman may have found the best way to break the will of this Confederate soldier. Wiley, like other Southern soldiers, struggled to come to grips with the vision of "Sherman's raiders among you in your house, stealing, plundering, and destroying everything" and leaving his mother and wife dependent on "the charity of a district equally impoverished." He wished he could return home as a "defender of our dear and sacred rights" rather than "chide myself for occupying such a place of comparative ease."[1] Wiley's frustration at his inability to protect his family exemplified the experiences of thousands of men from Georgia, South Carolina, and North Carolina.

During Sherman's campaign, Wiley articulated the despair and self-loathing that it created within the Confederate ranks. He, like thousands of other Southern white men, had failed to live up to the ideals of manhood that drove many of them to the front lines in the first place. Their failures on the battlefield had allowed strange men to enter their communities, harass their loved ones, evict their families, and often burn their homes. "We all imagine the worst," he explained anxiously to his mother. "When I think of what may possibly be the situation of my dear, aged and infirm parents, and my dear wife and little innocent children, and other near and dear relatives and friends I chide myself for being a drone; for not doing something active, actual and practical." His chosen imagery—of a useless drone who lacks both a stinger and the ability to make honey—paralleled his own inability to protect or serve his family.[2]

Other soldiers from Georgia and the Carolinas shared Wiley's sense of distress. Although Sherman's March did not, as a whole, dishearten elite Confederate women, it contributed to the demoralization of Southern soldiers and the end of their will to fight. The ease with which "Sherman had marched through Georgia from one end to the other," and later through the Carolinas, demonstrated that Southern soldiers could not fulfill their obligations to rebel women. Over five months, Sherman's men continuously shamed those men who could offer little resistance to the domestic campaign. Sherman bragged about his success in terms of humiliating the Confederates: "I don't believe anything has tended more to break the pride of the South, than my steady persistent progress."[3] As one Confederate soldier explained, it was "gloomy times for all South Carolinians as Sherman is marching thro their state with weak opposition."[4] The cumulative effect of attacks on one community of women after another helped dishearten this man and many other Southern soldiers. They could not protect the white women of the South and they could not prevent the advance of the enemy on the home front. Newspaper editor Joseph Addison Turner publicly noted the humiliating reality early in

1865. "This should mantle with the blush of shame the cheek of every Georgian, and every Confederate. We, for one, feel deeply mortified—humbled, chagrined—even degraded. It is a bitter draught we have had to quaff."[5] In his statement, Turner revealed a key, and intended, component to Sherman's March. The Union's attack on Confederate women threatened the very essence of Southern masculinity by revealing the helplessness of the soldiers on the battlefield to protect the women of the region. Consequently, Sherman's troops shamed Confederate soldiers as they assaulted their homes, women, and way of life.

Elite white Southerners went to battle and supported the war in order to defend an independent Confederacy, their valuable slave interests, and their women, families, and honor. However, by 1864 a string of devastating military defeats and a national policy of emancipation left the defense of women, family, and honor as the sole surviving ambition. For some, this personal motivation was enough to continue the fight. After nearly four years of fighting and Sherman's devastating Georgia campaign, one soldier still asserted, "For [Southern ladies] I battle till the end, / To save [them] from shame and thrall."[6] For others, Sherman's tactical decision to have his men insult the women of the South left many Confederate men with a sense that they had nothing left to defend. Union troops' actions as they purposefully entered white women's bedrooms, tore apart elite women's wardrobes, and otherwise threatened Confederate women's virtue exposed Southern men's inability to protect their women. This reality created a crisis of manhood for Confederate soldiers, who, as W. J. Cash claimed in 1941, "went rolling into battle in the misty conviction that it was wholly for [the Southern woman] that they fought."[7] Much like their female counterparts on the home front, Confederate men viewed Sherman's campaign as an unforgivable violation.

Sherman's March revealed an unprotected flank in the Confederacy. When Confederate soldiers departed for the battlefield, they left their mothers, wives, daughters, and sisters vulnerable. They willingly left their families exposed, at least in part, because at the outset of the war they could not conceive of Union troops directly confronting elite white Southern women and placing them at the center of the conflict. When this domestic tactic became a reality, Sherman's men created a crisis of manhood in the Confederate ranks. The Union troops' burning of homes, confiscation of food, entering of bedrooms, and looting of material goods all threatened to emasculate Southern men, who were obligated to provide for their families and protect them from harm. Although all Confederate soldiers were shamed by Sherman's actions, the men from the invaded regions, who felt personally responsible for their own families' welfare, were hit especially hard. This reality made Confederate soldiers scramble for news about events on the home front. Soldiers from Georgia and the Carolinas nervously hoped for any news that might reveal the condition of their families and homes. "In agony of suspense," they anxiously fretted over the fates of their women.[8]

The experiences of Georgia soldier J. M. Sharp reveal the interconnectedness of soldier morale and Sherman's domestic battles. For starters, Sharp showed particular concern about his inability to fulfill his paternal obligation of helping his family through the invasion. From a distance and through the intermittent mail, he did his best to guide his family through the impending ordeal. In August, as Union troops moved closer to his family, he constantly worried about his wife and children. "I am very uneasy about you but I hope they will not hurt you nor take all you have to eat." If the Yankees reached their home, he did not want his wife to pretend he was not a Confederate soldier because that would besmirch his name. He urged her, when confronted by enemy troops, to be truthful: "Dont deny that I am in the war for they think more of a man that will fight for his country than one that wont."[9]

Distance from the home front made matters even worse for Sharp, who like many Confederate men felt responsible for running and protecting his household. As he heard rumors of the Yankees' behavior on the home front, he was desperate for news from home: "Eliza I want to hear from you the worst I ever did in my life."[10] During the Atlanta campaign, he revealed his exasperation. He had heard news that "the Yankees . . . had taken everything you had . . . that they had not hurt your person but had taken all you had Such as clothing house hold furniture etc," Although the possible reality of losing their household possessions was difficult to contemplate, Sharp put it into perspective. "If I could only know that you would not suffer for something to eat I would be satisfied but I surly cant stand it to know that you are suffering fore something to eat." Sharp, like other soldiers, repeatedly worried about the lack of food as it revealed his most basic failure as a father and husband.[11]

Sharp also feared that Sherman's men would cross lines that seemed dreadfully farfetched. Like many Southern fathers, he was terrified that Sherman would wage war on children. "Take good care of the children," he urged his wife, and "Dont let the Yankees take them off." The lack of news made everything worse as it allowed his imagination to run wild. "What would I give for a letter direct from you to [k]now exactly how you are Situated."[12] The following month, when he still had not had any news from his wife, the silence seemed unbearable. "I want to hear from you so bad it is nearly 2½ months since I have received a letter from you. Though I hear friteful tales about the way the Yankees treated you & I want you to try & contrive a letter to me some way & let me know how they did treat you & whether you are suffering or not." He was frantic for information and distressed that he had no way of knowing whether or not she had received his letters. "If you get a chance to write I want you to let me know exactly how they have treated you & if you cant live there all I can say is for you to come out to where you can live." Sharp felt helpless to aid his family. "I hope that you are not suffering for I could not stand it."[13] After five months of silence, his fears grew as he heard assorted reports about Sherman's troops pillaging their way across his home state. "I have wrote you so many letters & have got none from you." He had, however, heard from a friend "that the Yankees had taken every thing.... The boys could not tell me how you was making out but I know that it is bad but I trust you have not suffered much that is for something to eat."[14]

In the end, Sharp and other soldiers had to base their actions on a lack of knowledge. The conflicting pulls of national and familial duty weighed on him. He concluded that he was needed on the home front as much as, if not more than, he was needed on the battlefield. Still the competing sense of obligations pained him. "I will do all I can to get to go home my self & if they fool with me much I will go any how." He did not, however, intend to give up. "I am getting to think this war will not last much longer & I am getting so I do not care how quick it stops. well I have always wanted . . . it to stop still I am not ready to surrender to them vandals & I will fight them just as long as it will do any good & then I had rather go to another Nation than to give up to them."[15]

EPILOGUE

The lack of information from home led wealthy South Carolinian Harry Hammond to worry and assume the worst about the situation at home. When he heard "no news from Georgia," he began to "feel very anxious" especially because "I can hear nothing." Rather than imagining Sherman's men capturing children, he feared that the local newspapers were right and the women would try to attack "the enemy with clubs and pitch forks." Hammond pleaded with his wife to refrain from such action, because his experiences showed that such an uprising from female civilians would have no impact. "I have been with an invading enemy, and such a thing is impossible against an army that is moving forward." At the same time, though, he did not want to discourage his wife from protecting herself. After all, he knew that Sherman's men might soon make their way toward other parts of Georgia and toward South Carolina. "I ought not to write it to you who may need to be inspired with every bit of confidence in the means of resistance about you." If he could not fulfill his duty of protecting his wife, who sought safety with her family in Augusta, he hoped that the women would at least make an effort to protect themselves.[16]

The anxiety in the Confederate ranks about Sherman's March resulted from a combination of the lack of direct information from loved ones and the countless rumors of the home front campaign. Hammond, for example, had not heard from his family three months after the Union army approached their community. In February, Hammond still wondered if his wife and children in Augusta were safe from the Union army. "I have not heard from you and I can not hope to hear from you soon." His rough knowledge of Sherman's whereabouts did not give him any comfort because "I can not learn that Sherman has moved nearer to you than Blackville" and even that "information is very meager." Hammond continued to hope that the enemy soldiers would bypass Augusta, but he realized "how vain it is to reason upon what may happen in these times when so many accidents determine events which crowd into the hours and days more rapidly than the imagination can picture them."[17]

Countless other Confederate soldiers suffered from the uncertainty that Sherman's campaign created. Frank Coker agonized because "our news from Georgia is megre and entirely unsatisfactory." After all, he didn't "know whether Sherman is marching on Savannah or Columbus and then to Mobile." The lack of information made him "very uneasy" for his wife's fate. He let her know that he "hoped and still hope that if Sherman has determined to cut his way to the coast he has taken the nearest rout[e] to Savannah as that would take him away from our part of the state." Coker realized with anguish that "even now you may be a refugee with our houses and furniture in ashes. What a thought—my Wife and children wanderers and homeless."[18] Duncan Buie similarly worried specifically about his love, Kate. He had not heard from her or anyone else in their hometown and was especially "anxious to hear from home, and my little sweetheart." The sporadic news from the paper made him "afraid the Yankees frightened her out of her wits besides taking everything valuable from her." He did not doubt that the Union soldiers would do so because "they are cowardly an mean enough to do almost anything."[19] Many other Southern soldiers dreaded the fate of family members and loved ones who remained in the path of "the vile invader . . . with his vandel hordes."[20]

The lack of news from home, combined with intense worry about how women fared at the hands of enemy soldiers, led to a decline in morale. Such was the case for the 17th South Carolina Regiment. John Alfred Feister Coleman, like many who served in the regiment, lived "in great suspense" for several months because they had "no news from home." This dearth of information about South Carolina proved psychologically draining, especially as rumors spread that Sherman wanted to extract extra justice on the "seedbed of the Confederacy." Coleman "never wanted to hear so bad before since the war began," especially because he "fear[ed] that my all is destroyed, my wife and children without food or shelter." If he could not provide these most basic necessities, he had failed as a man and was needed elsewhere.[21] Although Coleman did not desert, others in his unit could not handle the unknown fates of their families who faced Sherman's domestic campaign. As Coleman reported, "A great many of our men have been deserting for the last three or four weeks." It was no coincidence that these desertions occurred as Sherman and his men made their way through the regiment's home state and into the soldiers' homes.[22]

Although many soldiers suffered from their distance from their loved one, those who served in close proximity may have had it worse. B. F. Mason found it especially aggravating to be nearby and yet helpless to act on his family's behalf. In a letter to his mother, he expressed his frustrations about being so close and yet so far. "I can tell you it is verry trying to me to be so near home and unable to hear from those who[se] interest is dearer to me than my own—I have not heard from home in two months of cours I am uneasy about you all Knowing as I do that Shermans Raid must have passed verry near you if it did not reach you."[23] For Mason, and other soldiers serving in the lower South, the pull to leave their post and protect their families must have been especially strong.

For soldiers who witnessed the Union treatment of white women, knowledge was certainly not power. Instead it made them feel powerless. They learned firsthand that female Confederates would not be left unmolested, and therefore they knew that they would be failing their duty as men when Sherman came to their "unprotected" homes. From Pocotaligo, South Carolina, John Jenkins worried about his family in Summerville as he reported that the Yankees "shell the trains, commonly crowded with Refugee Families women & children, furiously as they pass." He had reason for concern. After all, "as menay as twenty shots were fired at one train yesterday morning."[24] These images revealed an enemy that disregarded the ideal that all men protected white women and children and they also magnified the fears in the Confederate ranks. With this kind of knowledge, Felix Prior voiced his concerns in a letter to his wife, Nancy. Writing from the trenches around Atlanta, Prior let her know that he was "uneasy having heard the yanks have been in our county."[25] A few months later, his concerns about her fate had continued to grow. From camp in Macon, Prior stressed to her that "I am very uneasy about home as I fear the raiders may have paid a visit at home[.] I understand they passed through our county in large force."[26]

News from loved ones on the home front proved to be a spirit-breaking distraction for many Confederate soldiers. Although he suffered from uncertainty about the campaign, the reports of the damage inflicted by Union soldiers did little to soothe South Carolinian John Craig Evans. He was in the trenches at Petersburg, Virginia, in January, when he heard the news about "the calamity that has befallen so many in Georgia." The reports led him to panic for his own family because he predicted "Sherman will show very little favor to S.C."[27] As a result, he dreamed about all the possible horrors that "my dear ones at home" might have experienced. Even though few Confederate women expressed a fear that Union soldiers would kill them, this confidence apparently did not extend to Southern soldiers. After news that Sherman's men had destroyed homes and confronted women in South Carolina, Evans could not help but panic. "I pray," Evans wrote, "that your lives and persons are spared."²⁸ William Chunn also hoped that his mother had emerged from the trial unscathed. "Since the evacuation of Atlanta I have been very low spirited and my anxiety in relation to you has been intense. . . . The fall of Atlanta . . . has cast a deep gloom upon the people and the army."²⁹ Reverend John Jones of Georgia agreed. "The loss of Atlanta is the greatest blow of the war. Our prospects are exceedingly dark to me, and without special divine interposition we are a ruined people."³⁰

Not surprisingly, Sherman's campaign led many soldiers to feel a need to return to their families. The Confederate military was struggling, and many soldiers felt that their services could be better used at home. Reports about Sherman's campaign made this desire for home especially true. After seeing a "few letters from home which gave a distressing account of the yankey depradations in our county," Georgian H. T. Howard "hope[d] for the best." He apologized to his wife for failing in his manly duty to protect her and assumed that she had been "frightened nearly to death." He could not forgive himself for being away when she needed him. He tried to fulfill both his military and personal duties, but he and the other members of the local military company had their "application[s] for furlough to come home . . . disapproved and we were compelled to remain and leave you in the hands of your enemys."³¹ Howard, like other Confederate soldiers, shuddered at the thought of his wife confronting Union men on her own and he blamed his own personal failures for making that the case.

Many Confederate soldiers struggled with the sense of helplessness that Sherman's March engendered. Georgian Edgeworth Bird internalized his fears about his wife in light of what he had heard about Sherman's progress. "We are in the midst of very unpleasant rumours about Atlanta. . . . I won't believe it till I hear the official news of it, but I can't help being depressed."³² Although apparently he could not do the same, he continued to encourage his wife and family to keep up their spirits. The possibility of the Union advance weighed on Bird's emotional state, especially as his wife seemed "so positive . . . in your belief that we are soon to have the Yankees around our home." This knowledge, and his inability to help them because he was serving in Virginia, made Bird "look the more anxiously each day for letters from you that I may know the exact state of your own feelings" as he was "so very, very anxious about you and our dear children."³³ Bird also bemoaned his inability to protect other women in his family from the enemy's domestic tactics. After he "heard the news that our beloved Georgia was likely to be overrun," he especially fretted about his wife's "dear Grandmother" and other elderly family members. "So hard is it, that in the evening of her noble, well-spent life, she should be harassed by our insulting, brutal enemies."³⁴

The hopelessness affected some elite Confederate men differently than others. Family members proclaimed that South Carolinian and former senator James Henry Hammond died after the fall of Atlanta because "he apprehended a vandal march that would desolate everything on its line." The elder Hammond was particularly desolate about the potential of having enemy soldiers march through his beloved state where scores of women and children resided. After all, the congressman predicted "that in S.C. to annihilate or desecrate broadcast would be the order of the move." This reality, his son proclaimed, led Hammond to be "not simply desirous, but determined, not to be witness to what he was powerless to mitigate or prevent." As a result, Hammond had "sought and hastened his death, not by any act, but by force of will" because he had been so upset by Sherman's actions in Georgia and Confederate soldiers' inability to protect the women of their communities. James Henry Hammond died only days before Sherman and his troops left Atlanta to begin the March to the Sea.³⁵

The gendered tactics of Sherman's campaign struck Confederate soldiers as particularly offensive. Tom Hightower, a Georgian stationed in New Market, Virginia, had not heard about the fate of his wife but could hardly believe the other news he heard. From his fellow soldiers he learned that Sherman and his soldiers had "burned every house in town that was not occupied." That was not the worst, though. At least empty houses had no women or children in them. What troubled Hightower most was that the enemy soldiers had gone to "old Mrs. Battle's" and been in her bedrooms. As he wrote to his wife, at Mrs. Battle's house the Yankees "tore open all her feather beds and poured them out in the middle of the floor, poured three sacks of salt on them and a sack of wheat bran and a jug of vinegar and stirred them all up together."³⁶ John Coleman—a South Carolina soldier who heard that "Columbia has been entirely burned by Sherman" and that "his men robbed and burned all most every house on their march through S.C.—despaired at the treatment given to elite women. He fumed that "young ladies were forced to play on the piano while the enemies were dancing." He, too, noticed that age was no protection, either. "One old lady in Lancaster Dist. was kept tied two days before she would divulge where her valuables were hid."[37] Confederate men and women both took special umbrage at such pointedly gendered insults.

Southern soldiers also dealt with the emotional toll caused by the many sensationalized and exaggerated stories about Sherman's campaign and the treatment of civilians. As Sherman made his way through the lower South, Confederate soldiers heard rumors of rape, starvation, and murder, leaving them little choice but to fear the worst for their families. One soldier wondered on March 16, 1865, "what are my poor dear ones suffering now? I hear that Cheraw has been entirely destroyed." Loss of property did not concern him. Instead, he hoped his family had survived Union raids. "If I could only know that you are all alive and suffered no bodily harm, I would be so glad but here I am without one word from you since the 24 Feb."[38] Georgian Felix Prior had similar concerns. "I am very uneasy about home as I fear the raiders may have paid a visit at home[.] I understand they passed through our county in large force."[39] Feeling the shame of not protecting their families from domestic raids, Confederate soldiers desperately hoped that their loved ones had escaped with their lives and their virtue.

The fear that their loved ones would be raped or assaulted filled the minds of many Southern soldiers, and they agonized over the possibility that they had abandoned their women to face something worse than death. Harry Hammond noted "the barbarity of our enemies in burning down the houses of women and children" and hinted at worse.[40] In a later letter to his wife, he described the scene at one of his fellow soldier's houses during the Yankee invasion. "Maj Wardlaw has heard from home the Yankee stragglers were at his place for seven whole days and destroyed everything." Wardlaw, Hammond, and the other men in their company were more concerned about "poor mrs Wardlaw" who "did not have a change of clothes left for herself, or her child." Even worse, "for ten days she and the ladies and children were all huddled together in the parlor and never once undressed."[41] The women's refusal to undress hinted at their fears of rape by the enemy men.

EPILOGUE

In Augusta, Georgia, a newspaper proclaimed that the Confederacy and its soldiers could benefit from the uncertainty and concern over such possibilities. After reporting the rape of a Milledgeville woman at the hands of Sherman's soldiers, the *Register* hoped the incident would spur the troops on to victory. "To our armies we would say—Write on your battle flags, 'Avenge the Honor Of Our Women!'" Furthermore, the paper's editors felt sure that the soldiers would "then thunder it over the land until the rocks shall echo back the sound and the hills reverberate the echo and every heart be filled with vengeance."[42] South Carolina governor Andrew Gordon Magrath called for similar responses to the Union invasion of the home front. "The foe now upon the soil of the State is here for *rapine* and *lust:* let him meet resistance unto death. That foe devotes us to a doom worse than death: let him receive the fate he designs for us."[43] By playing on the honor of Confederate soldiers and using the language of rape when referring to the enemy invasion, Magrath assumed he could galvanize the troops and spur them to victory.

The tone of the *Register*'s and Magrath's calls for action reflected the feelings of many Georgia and Carolina soldiers. As Southern men, they viewed the assault on the home front, and on the women of their family, as a personal attack and an affront to their honor.[44] Consequently, the Union's attack on elite women shamed white Southern men on two accounts: not only had Southern women faced insults at the hands of the enemy, but also Confederate soldiers realized that they had done little to prevent such an attack. A Texas soldier wrote with disgust of the event and the local men's inability to do their duty to their women and stop the invasion. In his mind, "General Sherman ought to have been totally defeated and ruined, but the sad fact will be handed down to posterity that while Sherman's minions were devastating the country with fire and committing outrages upon defenseless women, the men of Georgia staid at home or at least a large portion of them, trying to save what they had."[45] Another soldier explained the consequences of men's failures, noting "the successful and . . . unopposed march of Sherman through Georgia . . . [has] changed the whole aspect of affairs."[46] After hearing news of recent events in Georgia, Alexander Couper acknowledged that "the fall of Savannah will distress our families." Despite the grim outlook, he "hoped it will arouse the dormant energies of the nation."[47] Iverson Dutton Graves understood the damage inflicted by Sherman's

March, but felt that "this is the time to put on a cheerful countenance and boldly and contemptuously spurn every advancement to a dishonorable peace."⁴⁸ Like many of the Confederate women whom he left behind on the home front, he saw no reunion with an enemy that would disregard white women's protected status. Furthermore, any reconciliation with such an enemy would only add to the shame of allowing the march. For many, the assault on Southern domesticity made repeated Confederate failures on the battlefield pale in comparison to their neglect on the home front.

The sense of humiliation that resulted from their failure to protect Confederate women from Union rapacity provoked in some Southern soldiers a desire for vengeance. H. L. Bebow, for example, proclaimed, "I am an advocate for the *last* child and the *last* man." Although "deeply humiliated and chagrined to think that my own *dear* Carolina, has been surrendered to an implacable and relentless foe without any *seeming* effort to defend her," Bebow could not surrender. "Should I survive this cruel war . . . I can return to Columbia and gaze with pride upon the blackened ruins of my *once* happy home with the proud consciousness, that I was victimized on account of my devotion to the cause of freedom and independence."⁴⁹ Bebow believed that the only honorable choice was to continue to fight for the virtue of white Southern womanhood and for Columbia, South Carolina.

The Union attack on "unprotected" white Southern women—especially on daughters, wives, and mothers—demanded "fierce retaliation" from the region's men.⁵⁰ However, by March and April 1865, most Southern soldiers glumly realized that physical retribution was out of their power. As battlefield losses mounted, Confederate soldier C. F. Holst recognized that "our prospect & afairs are getting darker & darker." He wryly laughed off the Confederacy's inability to carry out an appropriate response. Still, he dreamed up a plan. "As we cannot conquer the Yankees or drive them from our soil; our authorities intends to concentrate all our Armies & march them on northern soil to avenge the injury done to us." They would abandon the South, already "ransasked & ruined . . . to the Yankees," and go north to "ravage & burn their Towns & Cities in turn." This fantasy proved little comfort to Holst, who was "filled with anguish & dismay that the Yankees have full sway[.] Of course fire & faggit will be the order of the day, we will be houseles[s], ragged & starve."⁵¹ His dismay increased as he acknowledged the destruction that Confederate troops had allowed not only on the landscape but also on the domestic front.

Other Confederate soldiers could hardly face the dishonor of defeat. Georgian Raleigh Spinks Camp realized that "a visit to the old settlement would have been one of pain instead of pleasure." He knew that he would find his town "in heaps of ruin and piles of devastation, all which mark the path of despoilers and the hearts of the cruel invader." Camp felt particular outrage at the attack on private homes and citizens which "stamp[ed] our Enemy as the most cruel and heartless set of men."[52] As the march reached its conclusion and the Southern armies began to surrender, Georgia and Carolina soldiers had to face the reality that they could not militarily revenge the insults on their women. They would have to live with the shame of inadequacy and the unfulfilled desire for vengeance.

Military defeats combined with the awareness of their inability to protect their region or families struck at the heart of Southern soldiers' honor. They had failed both as soldiers and as Southern men; they had not fulfilled their obligations to either their nation or their families. At the news of Atlanta's fall, Harry Hammond bemoaned the behavior of Southern generals. "I have just seen the announcement of the Truce between Hood and Sherman. I regret it very much as an admission of weakness on our part."[53] Similarly, Henry Lea Graves reflected on the horrors of evacuating Savannah and leaving it unprotected. "I have no words to picture the gloomy bitterness that filled my breast." His shame had many facets, including the "feelings, of a soldier turning his back on an enemy, of a Georgian abandoning his native state, of a patriot witnessing a disaster to his country's cause." Graves felt most troubled by "thinking of the certain and terrible suffering entailed on thousands [of civilians] in that devoted city... about to be abandoned in their utter helplessness to the power of an Enemy."[54] Scenes similar to this one became all too common in the final months of the Confederacy. Recognizing this shame, G. Dunbar bemoaned his fate: "I feel very little inclined to call myself a Georgian any more."[55] W. A. Clarkson let his mother know of his frustration after "hearing of your treatment and unable to lend a helping hand." The news of the Yankees' focus on white women led him to describe how "every manly feeling would revolt against the actions of our enemy."[56]

THE CIVILIAN WAR

In June 1865, Emile Sternberg wrote about Southern defeat. It had been two months since General Lee had surrendered his Army of Northern Virginia, and since then various other Confederate armies had followed suit. The war, at least for all practical purposes, had come to a close. This soldier in North Carolina, though, had to face the woman and women that he had sworn to protect. "Perhaps you number me among the brave, who with laurel-wreaths on their brow have shed their blood upon the altar of liberty," he wrote. If so, "you have rather a too exalted opinion of your humble friend. No, my fair lady, the days of chivalry are over; and I have lost all taste for knight-errantry, since I have beheld so many of that gallant brotherhood with one arm or one leg." In his lengthy apology and explanation, he recognized that he had failed to live up to the presumed standards of a Southern gentleman. "I am very sorry that I have disappointed you in your high expectations, and that I can not afford you the pleasure of beholding my name enwreathed with laurel." The Confederate fight, he valiantly tried to explain, led him into a no-win situation. He either had to surrender his honor by returning home an invalid or he had to surrender it by returning home intact. Either way, he presumed that his love would have rejected his effort. "I doubt very much, my sweet charmer, whether you that professed 'thorough hero-worshipper,' who desires to see me battling like La-Fayette for the righteous principles of Liberty & Honor, you that beautiful princess who offers to give her hand & heart for Sherman's hated head.—I say, I doubt whether I would be accepted if I were to come and offer myself to you with an empty sleeve, or minus one of my walking-sticks." His defeated and somewhat confrontational attitude, like that of many Confederate soldiers, contrasted sharply with those of the women who faced Sherman's assault on the home front. "You say that if you were a man, you would die upon the battle-field, and that you would glory in perishing there. Well, my fair Amazon, I do not in the least dispute it; but, as far as I am concerned, I would rather live for my country than to die for it. Posthumous glory is a very poor inducement; I rather enjoy a moderate quantity of glory while I live, than to be elevated to the stars after my death." In essence, even though he had experienced "Sherman's villains"

in Fayetteville, he flipped the rhetoric of many Confederate women and chose dishonor over death.[57]

An Augusta newspaper commented on how helpless frustrations contrasted sharply with the inspired anger of Confederate women. As Sherman marched through the Carolinas, the paper reported that "one of the cheering signs of the times [is] that the women are unsubdued and hopeful. When the men of Georgia give up all as lost, when they cease to be really *men*, the women of the old State will still uphold the arms of the soldier in his struggle and hold the foe at distance."[58] The contrast between the continued anger of Confederate women and the resigned defeat of Confederate men likely resulted from the differing experiences of male soldiers and female civilians. They experienced different forms of warfare, as Union commanders chose tactics that were deemed appropriate to each enemy group's gender, race, and class. Confederate men and women all feared for their lives, but the casualty counts for each group were certainly not balanced. Domestic warfare, as this volume has demonstrated, meant different things for men and for women. However, the defeat and resignation felt by many Confederate soldiers also resulted from the gendered assault that Sherman levied against Confederate women. Even if Confederate soldiers did not proclaim that they were destined to die or return home permanently maimed, they too had to choose between dishonor and death. They had to choose between the dishonor that came from their inability to protect their mothers, sisters, aunts, wives, and loved ones and the dishonor that would follow surrender, desertion, or dereliction of duty.

By bringing the war front to the home front, Sherman and his soldiers demonstrated to their enemies that "war is cruelty."[59] During their assault on Southern civilians, Union soldiers disregarded many of the prescriptions that protected women and the domestic sphere from the onslaughts of war. Not only did they burn and pillage the Southern countryside to devastate the Confederacy's material resources, but they also struck a direct blow at Southern domesticity. Instead of only attacking war-related materials in their assault, Union soldiers ransacked bedrooms, tore up women's clothing, burned homes, and taunted white Southern women. As a result, the Georgia and Carolinas campaign struck not only at the physical manifestations of wartime and domestic life but also at the psyches of Southern soldiers and Confederate women as it demonstrated that nothing was safe from Union attack. The seemingly easy success of Sherman's March through Georgia and the Carolinas, and the wholesale destruction of so many households, both enraged and shamed Confederate soldiers. By attacking Southern women, Sherman had directly insulted Southern manhood. Although Confederate women refused to submit to Sherman's campaign, his inversion of traditional tactics did, in the end, make the Confederacy "howl."

NOTES

ABBREVIATIONS

AHC	Atlanta History Center Archives
Caroliniana	South Caroliniana Library, University of South Carolina, Columbia
Duke	Duke University Library, Rare Book, Manuscript, and Special Collections Library, Durham, North Carolina
Emory	Emory University, Special Collections Department, Atlanta, Georgia
GDAH	Georgia Department of Archives and History, Atlanta
GHS	Georgia Historical Society, Savannah
HEH	Henry E. Huntington Library and Art Gallery, San Marino, California
LC	Library of Congress, Washington, DC
NCDAH	North Carolina Department of Archives and History, Raleigh
OR	U.S. War Department, *The War of the Rebellion: A Compilation of the Official Records of the Union and Confederate Armies* (Washington, DC: GPO, 1880–1901)
SCHS	South Carolina Historical Society, Charleston
SHC	Southern Historical Collection, University of North Carolina, Chapel Hill
UGA	University of Georgia, Hargrett Rare Book and Manuscript Library, Athens

INTRODUCTION

1. Mary Maxcy Leverett to Milton Maxcy Leverett, 24 February [1865], *Leverett Letters*, 384–87.

2. From Savannah, Sherman himself estimated that he had caused over $100 million worth of damage in the State of Georgia on the March to the Sea. William T. Sherman to Henry Halleck, 1 January 1865, in *OR*, Ser. 1, Vol. 44: 6–16, esp. 13.

3. For the postwar vilification of Sherman and its connection to the Lost Cause, see Caudill and Ashdown, *Sherman's March in Myth and Memory*; Moody, *Demon of the Civil War*; Rubin, *Through the Heart of Dixie*.

4. For an interpretation of Sherman's pragmatic approach, see Brinsfield, "The Military Ethics of General William T. Sherman," 36–48. In 1864, Philip Sheridan launched a similar

home front campaign that engaged wealthy Confederate women in Virginia's Shenandoah Valley. Sheridan set out to destroy the landscape of the valley so that "crows flying over it . . . will have to carry their provender with them." Grant to Halleck, July 14, 1864, *OR*, Ser. 1, Vol. 37, pt. 2: 300–301. On the gendered nature of Sheridan's campaign, see Frank, "War Comes Home."

5. William T. Sherman to John Sherman, 22 September 1862, *Sherman Letters*, 162, emphasis added.

6. Bailey, *The Chessboard of War*; Ash, *When the Yankees Came*; Neely, *Civil War and the Limits of Destruction*; Kennett, *Marching through Georgia*. Recently, Lisa M. Brady's pathbreaking work on the environmental history of the Civil War discusses how Sherman and his troops transformed "gardens into wastelands" and how "Sherman attacked and destroyed the agroecological system on which the Confederacy and its citizens relied" without reflecting on the gendered nature of either gardens or citizens. See *War upon the Land*, 93–127, quotations on 93 and 95.

7. Campbell, *When Sherman Marched North from the Sea*, 4.

8. For example, see Lucas, *Sherman and the Burning of Columbia*.

9. See Grimsley, *Hard Hand of War*. See also Neely, *Civil War and the Limits of Destruction*; Glatthaar, *March to the Sea and Beyond*.

10. William T. Sherman to Ulysses S. Grant, 11 October 1864, *OR*, Ser. 1, Vol. 38, pt. 1: 28.

11. Grimsley, *Hard Hand of War*, 5.

12. Glatthaar, *March to the Sea and Beyond*, 72.

13. Glatthaar, *March to the Sea and Beyond*, 140, 146.

14. Neely, *Civil War and the Limits of Destruction*, 218. On the overstatement of damage in Atlanta, see Marszalek, *Sherman: A Soldier's Passion for Order*, 299–300.

15. Glatthaar, *March to the Sea and Beyond*, 148.

16. Hitchcock, 24 November 1864, *Marching with Sherman*, 89.

17. Lee B. Kennett explores the first stage of Sherman's March in *Marching through Georgia*. Kennett focuses primarily on the military aspects and actions of the campaign; only chap. 14 offers a close look at the interactions between soldiers and civilians. See also Walters, "General William T. Sherman and Total War," 447–80; Barrett, *Sherman's March through the Carolinas*; Walters, *Merchant of Terror*; Wheeler, *Sherman's March*; Davis, *Sherman's March*; McDonough and Jones, *War So Terrible*; Smith, "Sherman's Unexpected Companions," 1–24; Bailey, *Chessboard of War*. Some recent studies of Sherman delve beneath the political and military, but still focus more on military than on civilian targets during the march. For example, see Hirshson, *White Tecumseh*; Fellman, *Citizen Sherman*; Marszalek, *Sherman*; Kennett, *Sherman*; Trudeau, *Southern Storm*. For prominent exceptions, see Campbell, *When Sherman Marched North*; Nelson, *Ruin Nation*; Brady, *War upon the Land*. Jean V. Berlin briefly explored Sherman's recognition of women "as the powerful enemies they could be." Berlin, "Did Confederate Women Lose the War?" 174–78, quotation on 174.

18. Historian Mark Grimsley exemplifies this approach as he argues that Sherman's policy "suggests the continual working of political logic even in a circumstance as volatile as the unleashing of armed men against a hostile population." To Grimsley, as well as to others, political intentions define the march. Grimsley, *Hard Hand of War*, 2. See also Neely, *Limits of Destruction*; Kennett, *Marching through Georgia*, 1–14; Glatthaar, *March to the*

Sea and Beyond, 39–51. In his exploration of Sherman's destructive policy, Charles Royster asserts that the march was "[effective] in ending defiance." *Destructive War,* 347, also see 79–143, 321–404.

19. William T. Sherman to Ulysses S. Grant, 4 October 1862, *OR,* Ser. 1, Vol. 17, pt. 2: 261.
20. Sherman to Roswell M. Sawyer, 31 January 1864, *OR,* 32, pt. 2: 281.
21. William T. Sherman to Ulysses S. Grant, 6 November 1864, *OR,* Ser. 1, Vol. 39, pt. 3: 660. Samuel Augustus Duncan of New Hampshire made the issue of power clear in a letter to his future wife. "This inhuman war will not cease until the arrogant South is brought under the rod, and made to *feel* that the North is *a power,* to be *respected and feared.*" Samuel Augustus Duncan to Julia Jones, 15 March 1865, *Yankee Correspondence,* ed. Silber and Sievens, 51. An aide-de-camp of Sherman shared these sentiments. "If you are defeated," he told a woman, "you will have thoroughly learned what your people have never before the war, in the slightest degree understood—how to *respect* us." Nichols, 16 September 1864, *Story of the Great March,* 23.
22. Scholars' focus on Sherman's March and his stated military intentions, often overlooks the significance of the civilian consequences; they focus on political and military strategy and minimize the implications of the attack on the domestic sphere. On Northern ideas about masculinity, see Foote, *The Gentlemen and the Roughs,* esp. 3, 6, 19.
23. See Mitchell, *Vacant Chair,* 100–101; Ramold, *Across the Divide,* 10.
24. William T. Sherman to Reum, 16 October 1864, *OR,* Ser. 1, Vol. 39, pt. 3: 309.
25. William T. Sherman to Henry Halleck, 19 October 1864, *OR,* Ser. 1, Vol. 39, pt. 3: 357–58, emphasis added. Also see William T. Sherman to George H. Thomas, 2 October 1864, *OR,* Ser. 1, Vol. 39, pt. 3: 377–78.
26. William T. Sherman to George H. Thomas, 2 October 1864, *OR,* Ser. 1, Vol. 39, pt. 3: 377–78.
27. William T. Sherman to Ulysses S. Grant, 9 October 1864, *OR,* Ser. 1, Vol. 39, pt. 3: 162. (Emphasis added.)
28. For examples, see Hilde, *Worth a Dozen Men;* Varon, *Southern Lady, Yankee Spy;* Schultz, *Women at the Front;* Blanton and Cook, *They Fought Like Demons;* Leonard, *All the Daring of the Soldier;* Blanton, "Women Soldiers of the Civil War"; Sizer, "Acting Her Part," 114–33; Attie, *Patriotic Toil;* Giesberg, *Civil War Sisterhood;* Brown, *Dorothea Dix;* Maher, *To Bind Up Their Wounds;* Leonard, *Yankee Women;* Ginzberg, *Women and the Work of Benevolence,* 133–73.
29. See Witt, *Lincoln's Code;* Ayers, *Presence of Mine Enemies;* Griffith, *Battle Tactics of the Civil War;* Ash, *When the Yankees Came;* Weigley, *Great Civil War.*
30. See Durrill, *War of Another Kind;* Sutherland, *Seasons of War;* Sutherland, *Emergence of Total War;* Ash, *When the Yankees Came,* and *Middle Tennessee Society Transformed;* Kenzer, *Kinship and Neighborhood in a Southern Community.* Most studies of women emphasize how the war affected women rather than how they affected each other. Junker, "Behind Confederate Lines," 7–18; Sutherland, "Introduction to War," 120–37; Harris, "East Tennessee's Civil War Refugees," 3–19.
31. The raging debate over the course of the master narrative was explored at the 2013 Southern Historical Association's panel: "Should Military History be Central to the Study of the Civil War? A Roundtable Discussion," with Carol Reardon, Gary W. Gallagher, Lesley J.

Gordon, and James K. Hogue, Southern Historical Association Annual Meeting, St. Louis, MO, 1 November 2013.

32. See McCurry, *Confederate Reckoning*; Jones, *Saving Savannah*.

33. See Whites, *The Civil War as a Crisis in Gender*, 2.

34. For prominent examples, see Whites and Long, eds., *Occupied Women*; Berry, ed., *Weirding the War*; Quigley, *Shifting Grounds*; Nelson, *Ruin Nation*; Silber, *Gender and the Sectional Conflict*; Bynum, *Long Shadow of the Civil War*; Clampitt, *Confederate Heartland*; Clinton and Silber, eds., *Divided Houses* and *Battle Scars*; Whites, *Gender Matters*; Silber, *Daughters of the Union*; Manning, *What This Cruel War Was Over*; Faust, *Mothers of Invention*; Rable, *Civil Wars*; Frank, "War Comes Home"; Whites, "The Tale of Three Kates"; Fellman, *Inside War*; Sutherland, *A Savage Conflict*.

35. On Northern masculinity, see Foote, *The Gentlemen and the Roughs*; Frank, *Life with Father*. On Southern manhood, see Berry, *All That Makes a Man*, 163–226; Friend and Glover, *Southern Manhood*; Glover, *Southern Sons*, esp. 181–84; Wyatt-Brown, *Shaping of Southern Culture*, esp. 177–202; Wyatt-Brown, *Southern Honor*.

36. On nineteenth-century women's control of the home, see for example Fox-Genovese, *Within the Plantation Household*; Clinton, *Plantation Mistress*.

37. Rowe, 17 February 1865, "Southern Girl's Diary," 265. Several important works have found female loyalty to be lacking elsewhere in the Confederacy. See, Dyer, *Secret Yankees*; Inscoe, "Coping with Confederate Appalachia," 388–413; Pease and Pease, *Family of Women*; Faust, *Mothers of Invention*, esp. 234–47; Rable, *Civil Wars*, esp. 203–20; Edwards, *Scarlett Doesn't Live Here Anymore*, 85–99; Clinton, *Tara Revisited*, 132; Berlin, "Did Confederate Women Lose the War?" 185–88. Also see Crofts, *Reluctant Confederates*; Taylor, *The Divided Family in Civil War America*.

38. Faust, *Mothers of Invention*; Rable, *Civil Wars*. Gallagher, *The Confederate War*, provides a counterargument about morale.

39. For a detailed treatment of women's roles in creating and preserving the Lost Cause, see Cox, *Dixie's Daughters*; Janney, *Burying the Dead but Not the Past*; Janney, *Remembering the Civil War*.

40. Faust, "Altars of Sacrifice," 115. Clinton labels this "glorification and embellishment of women's role within wartime" as a "Cult of Sacrifice." See Clinton, *Tara Revisited*, 139–159, quotation on 139. For examples of postwar celebrations of Southern women, see Underwood, *Women of the Confederacy*; Simkins and Patton, *Women of the Confederacy*; Taylor et al., *South Carolina Women of the Confederacy*; Conner et al., *South Carolina Women: Confederate Women of Arkansas in the Civil War*; Sterkx, *Partners in Rebellion*; Charleston Weekly News and Courier, *"Our Women in the War."* See also the articles within *Confederate Veteran*, a monthly magazine which ran from January 1893 to December 1932. Jefferson Davis emphasized women's roles as well as their traditional femininity in 1864. "Among those to who we are indebted in South Carolina I have not yet alluded to that peculiar claim of gratitude which is due to the fair country-woman of the Palmetto State—they who have gone to the hospital to watch by the side of the sick—those who throng your wayside homes—who have nursed as if nursing was a profession—who have used their needle with the industry of sewing-women—who have borne privation without a murmur, and who

have given up fathers, sons, and husbands, with more than Spartan virtue, because they called no one to witness and record the deed. Silently, with all dignity and grandeur of patriotism, they have made their sacrifices—sacrifices which if written, would be surpassed by nothing in history." "Speech of President Davis in Columbia," 4 October 1864, Davis, *Jefferson Davis, Constitutionalist*, 6:354.

41. William T. Sherman to Ellen Sherman, 12 March 1865, *Home Letters*, 332.

42. Rogers, 11 May 1865, Rogers Papers, Emory.

43. William T. Sherman to Ellen Sherman, 23 March 1865, *Home Letters*, 334–35.

44. Thomas T. Taylor, 23 November 1864, Diary, Taylor Collection, Emory.

45. Caroline Gilman to Eliza, 25 December 1864, "Letters of a Confederate Mother: Charleston in the Sixties," 510, emphasis added.

46. Louisa Jane Harllee Pearce to Ameilia, [March 1865], Teague Papers, SCHS.

1. BECOMING CONFEDERATES

1. Edmondston, 6 October 1860, *"Journal of a Secesh Lady,"* 10.

2. Edmondston, 26 October 1860, *"Journal of a Secesh Lady,"* 11.

3. Edmondston, 18 February 1861, *"Journal of a Secesh Lady,"* 37.

4. Edmondston, 8 July 1861, *"Journal of a Secesh Lady,"* 84.

5. Edmondston, 22 May 1862, *"Journal of a Secesh Lady,"* 180–82.

6. Edmondston, 29 October 1864, *"Journal of a Secesh Lady,"* 627. Sheridan reported that he "destroyed over 2,000 barns filled with wheat, hay and farming implements; over 70 mills, filled with flour and wheat; [drove] in front of the army over 4,000 head of stock, and have killed and issued to the troops not less than 3,000 sheep." Philip Sheridan to Ulysses S. Grant, 7 October 1864, *OR*, Ser. 1, Vol. 43, pt. 2: 307–8.

7. Edmondston, 16 September 1864, *"Journal of a Secesh Lady,"* 615.

8. Edmondston, 12 March 1865, *"Journal of a Secesh Lady,"* 676.

9. Quotation from Whites and Long, *Occupied Women*, 2. Notable works on women and gender during the Civil War include Bynum, *Unruly Women*; Clinton, *Plantation Mistress*; Clinton and Silber, *Divided Houses*; Edwards, *Scarlett Doesn't Live Here Anymore*; Faust, *Mothers of Invention*; Giesberg, *Army at Home*; Rable, *Civil Wars*; Silber, *Daughters of the Union*; Varon, *Southern Lady, Yankee Spy*; Whites, *The Civil War as a Crisis in Gender*; Whites and Long, *Occupied Women*. These scholars join pathbreakers in Civil War women's history such as Anne Firor Scott and Mary Elizabeth Massey. See Scott, *The Southern Lady*; Massey, *Women in the Civil War*.

10. See Wyatt-Brown, *Southern Honor, Shaping of Southern Culture*, and *A Warring Nation*; Friend and Glover, *Southern Manhood*; Glover, *Southern Sons*; Jabour, *Scarlett's Sisters*; Roberts, *Confederate Belle*; Giesberg, *Army at Home*; Silber, *Daughters of the Union*; Mitchell, *Vacant Chair*; McPherson, *For Cause and Comrades*; Faust, *Republic of Suffering*; Manning, *What This Cruel War Was Over*.

11. Steven Cushman argues that there was no home front during the American Civil War in *Bloody Promenade*, chap. 3.

12. Wells, *Origins of the Southern Middle Class*; Wells and Green, eds. *Southern Middle Class*; Ryan, *Cradle of the Middle Class*; Cott, *Bonds of Womanhood*; Smith-Rosenberg, *Disorderly Conduct*; Kerber, "Separate Spheres," 9–39.

13. Welter, "Cult of True Womanhood," 21–41.

14. Southern women played an active role in public life prior to the Civil War. See Kelley, *Learning to Stand and Speak*; Varon, *We Mean to Be Counted* and "Tippecanoe and the Ladies, Too," 494–521; Wood, "'One Woman So Dangerous,'" 237–75; Kilbride, "Cultivation, Conservatism, and the Early National Gentry," 221–56; Kierner, "Hospitality, Sociability, and Gender," 449–80, and "Women's Piety within Patriarchy," 79–98; Bode "Common Sphere," 775–809.

15. For example, many white Southern women entered the public sphere as authors, keeping their sex private by using pseudonyms. See Fahs, *Imagined Civil War*; Baym, *Woman's Fiction*; Kelley, *Private Woman, Public Stage*; Whites, *Civil War as a Crisis in Gender*, 50.

16. Southern social relations were based on the status gained by race. White women had power in their households over their slaves and children. In her study of plantation women and their household relationships, Elizabeth Fox-Genovese showed that slaveholding women were not necessarily subjugated by the ideals of the Southern lady. Instead, they benefited from their roles as the heads of the domestic activities in the household. Fox-Genovese, *Within the Plantation Household*. Others also discuss white women's limited power in the Southern household. For examples, see Stevenson, *Life in Black and White*; Weiner, *Mistresses and Slaves*; McCurry, *Masters of Small Worlds*; Kierner, *Beyond the Household*; Edwards, *Scarlett Doesn't Live Here Anymore*, 15–31; Wood, *Masterful Women*.

17. Northern women, like their Southern counterparts, restructured their roles in society to mobilize for the Union war effort. See Giesberg, *Army at Home*; Sizer, *Political Work of Northern Women Writers*; Silber, *Daughters of the Union*; Attie, *Patriotic Toil*; Leonard, *All the Daring of the Soldier*; Leonard, *Yankee Women*; Ross, "Arranging a Doll's House," 97–113; Massey, *Women in the Civil War*; Giesberg, *Civil War Sisterhood*; Schultz, *Women at the Front*.

18. The most prominent example of women's role in the development of Confederate nationalism is Augusta Jane Evans's novel *Macaria; or, Altars of Sacrifice*. On Confederate nationalism, see Quigley, *Shifting Grounds*; Gallagher, *Becoming Confederates* and *Confederate War*; Blair, *Virginia's Private War*; Rubin, *A Shattered Nation*; Faust, *Creation of Confederate Nationalism*; Faust, "Race, Gender, and Confederate Nationalism"; Escott, "Failure of Confederate Nationalism"; Beringer et al., *Why the South Lost*, 64–81, 424–42.

19. Whites and Long, eds., *Occupied Women*, 6.

20. See Varon, *We Mean to Be Counted*, and "Tippecanoe and the Ladies, Too"; Olsen, "Respecting 'The Wise Allotment of Our Sphere'"; Wood, "'One Woman So Dangerous'"; Wood, *Masterful Women*; Kilbride, "Cultivation, Conservatism, and the Early National Gentry."

21. The most prominent diarist of the period is Chesnut, *Mary Chesnut's Civil War*. See also Holmes, *Diary*; Cook, *Journal of a Milledgeville Girl*. On female education in the South, see Farnham, *Education of the Southern Belle*.

22. Burge, 6 November 1860, *Diary*, 111.

23. Leora Sims to Harriet R. Palmer, 10 December 1860, *World Turned Upside Down*, 278.

24. Channing, *Crisis of Fear,* 178, 287. Genovese notes the influence and role of what he labels "extremist" women in antebellum and Civil War times. He stresses that in recognizing these Southern women, "the numbers do not matter"; the importance lies in the reality of their existence. Genovese, "Toward a Kinder and Gentler America," 133. Not all Southern women supported secession. For examples, see Dyer, *Secret Yankees;* Pease and Pease, *Family of Women,* esp. 1–6, 140–41.

25. Emma Holmes, 13 February 1861, *Diary,* 1.

26. Cook, 3 January 1861, *Journal of a Milledgeville Girl,* 9. For similar sentiments from Virginia, see McGuire, 21 May 1861, *Diary of a Southern Refugee,* 16; Emma Mordecai to Alfred Mordecai, 21 April 1861, Mordecai Papers, LC.

27. Thomas, 13 July 1861, *Secret Eye,* 184.

28. Chesnut, 18 February 1861, *Private Mary Chesnut,* 4.

29. Henry and Drucilla Wray to Sister, 17 April 1861, Wray Paper, GHS.

30. Mrs. Allen S. Izard to Mrs. William Mason Smith, 21 July 1864, *Mason Smith Family Letters,* 116.

31. A woman in Selma, Alabama, reportedly broke off her engagement to a man who did not enlist. She sent him a petticoat, a skirt, and a note reading "wear these, or volunteer." See Stevenson, *Thirteen Months in the Rebel Army,* 195. Emma Edmonds, a Union spy born in Canada, agreed with a soldier who told her that Southern women were "the best recruiting officers," refusing "to tolerate, or admit to their society any young man who refuses to enlist. See Edmonds, *Nurse and Spy in the Union Army,* 332, and *Unsexed;* Leonard, *All the Daring of the Soldier,* 170; Varon, *Southern Lady, Yankee Spy.*

32. J. Augustine Signaigo, "If You Love Me," reprinted in Simms, *War Poetry of the South,* 312.

33. See Evans, *Macaria.*

34. Branch, 1861, Sexton Collection, UGA. Women throughout the Confederacy had shared these sentiments. Virginian Judith McGuire confided to her journal that "we could not bear that one of [the men of the family] should hesitate to give his life's blood to his country." See McGuire, 18 June 1861, *Diary of a Southern Refugee,* 33.

35. Charlotte Branch continued to write to her surviving son throughout the war. See Joslyn, ed., *Charlotte's Boys.*

36. Holmes, 1 May 1861, *Diary,* 40.

37. Susan Middleton to Harriott Middleton, 13 April 1862, "Middleton Correspondence, 1861–1865," 63.

38. Neely, *Civil War and the Limits of Destruction;* Grimsley, *Hard Hand of War;* Royster, *Destructive War;* Mitchell, *Vacant Chair,* 100.

39. For studies on the occupied South, see Whites and Long, *Occupied Women;* Ash, *When the Yankees Came;* Hearn, *When the Devil Came Down to Dixie;* Capers, *Occupied City;* Rose, *Rehearsal for Reconstruction;* Wiley, "Southern Reaction to Federal Invasion," 491–510.

40. Historian Mary Elizabeth Massey notes that "Rose Greenhow's arrest was the first to attract widespread attention." Massey, *Women in the Civil War,* 90.

41. *Richmond Whig,* November 1861, Leila [Elliott] Habersham Paper, GHS. Also see Greenhow, *My Imprisonment.*

42. Eugenia Yates Levy Phillips, 28 August 1861, Journal of Mrs. Eugenia Phillips, LC.

43. Chesnut, 29 August 1861, *Mary Chesnut's Civil War,* 172. Also see Anna E. Kirtland to Harriet R. Palmer, 13 October 1861, in Towles, ed., *World Turned Upside Down,* 314.

44. Benjamin Butler issued General Order 28 on May 15, 1862. *OR,* Ser. 1, Vol. 15: 426. In issuing such an order, Butler clearly recognized the power and importance of women's roles as Confederates. On Butler's order, see Long, "(Mis)Remembering General Order No. 28"; Mitchell, *Vacant Chair,* 103; Campbell, "No Difference between a He and a She Adder"; Campbell, "'The Unmeaning Twaddle about Order 28.'"

45. White Southern women demonstrated their assumption of protection in their appeals to the enemy for personal guards for their homes during Sherman's March. For examples, see McClatchey, 3 November 1864, McClatchey Family Papers, GDAH; Burge, 19 November 1864, *Diary,* 159; Peggy Mira Cox Berry to Amanda Berry Markham and William Markham, 14 December 1864, Confederate Miscellany I, Emory; Sarah Jane Sams to Randolph Sams, 13 February 1865, Sams Letter, Caroliniana; E. V. Ravenel to Allan Macfarlan, 21 March 1865, Macfarlan Papers, Caroliniana; "Extract from an old Letter, Found Among the Papers of My Grandmother, Mrs. N. A. Bishop of Darlington, S.C.," UDC Edgefield Chapter Papers, Duke; Marrie to Sallie Lawton, 15 April 1865, Willingham and Lawton Families Papers, Caroliniana.

46. Chesnut, 21 May 1862, *Mary Chesnut's Civil War,* 343.

47. Chesnut, 12 June 1862, *Mary Chesnut's Civil War,* 379.

48. Edmondston, 22 May 1862, *"Journal of a Secesh Lady,"* 180–82. Still fuming a month later, Edmondston wrote, "The condition of N Orleans is terrible. No people ever were more oppressed or insulted. . . . Humanity sickens at the thought of the barbarity, the groveling cowardly cruelty of the wretch Butler!" Edmondston, 6 June 1862, *"Journal of a Secesh Lady,"* 188.

49. Thomas, 2 June 1862, *Secret Eye,* 206-7. In the same entry, Thomas voiced her personal outrage. "Ye Gods shall this man live. . . . Is there not spirit enough left to the men of New Orleans to strike the dastard 'to the vile dust from which he sprang?'"

50. General Orders No. 44, *OR,* Ser. 1, Vol. 10, pt. 2: 531.

51. Proclamation, 24 May 1862, *OR,* Ser. 1, Vol. 15: 743–44. See also Wiley, *Life of Johnny Reb,* 312.

52. Ulysses S. Grant to Philip Sheridan, 26 August 1864, *OR,* Ser. 1, Vol. 43, pt. 2: 202.

53. Ulysses S. Grant to Henry Halleck, *OR,* Ser. 1, Vol. 40, pt. 3: 223.

54. Philip Sheridan, as quoted in Morris, *Sheridan,* 179.

55. Grimsley, *Hard Hand of War,* 4–5; Fellman, *Citizen Sherman,* 225–26; Royster, *Destructive War;* Mountcastle, *Punitive War,* esp. 85–102.

56. Fellman notes that gender boundaries frequently blurred when the distinction between home front and war front became less clear. Fellman, "Women and Guerilla Warfare," 147–64.

57. Edmondston, 18 October 1864, *"Journal of a Secesh Lady,"* 624.

58. Edmondston, 18 October 1864, *"Journal of a Secesh Lady,"* 624.

59. Edmondston, 18 October 1864, *"Journal of a Secesh Lady,"* 624.

60. Edmondston, 29 October 1864, *"Journal of a Secesh Lady,"* 627. Sheridan reported that he "destroyed over 2,000 barns filled with wheat, hay and farming implements; over

70 mills, filled with flour and wheat; [drove] in front of the army over 4,000 head of stock, and have killed and issued to the troops not less than 3,000 sheep." Philip Sheridan to Ulysses S. Grant, 7 October 1864, *OR*, Ser. 1, Vol. 43, pt. 2: 307–8.

61. For descriptions of Sheridan's campaign, see Frank, "War Comes Home"; McPherson, *Battle Cry of Freedom*, 778–79, 784–815; Grimsley, *Hard Hand of War*, 167–68.

62. Sarah Elizabeth Wilson to J. H. Wilkes, 19 November 1864, Edward Marvin Steel Papers, Collection of Heiskell, McCampbell, Wilkes, and Steel Family Materials, Wilkes Family Correspondence, SHC.

63. Thomas, 23 September 1864, *Secret Eye*, 238.

64. Edmondston, 16 September 1864, *"Journal of a Secesh Lady,"* 615.

65. An interesting exception is the expulsion of women from four counties in Missouri by Sherman's brother-in-law and foster brother, Thomas Ewing, Jr., in August 1863. For an example of the relatively peaceful relationships between Union soldiers and Southerners in parts of the occupied South, see Ash, *When the Yankees Came*.

66. William T. Sherman to Ellen Sherman, 11 October 1864, *Home Letters*. Southerners continued to "ask for its citizens, the treatment accorded by the usages of civilized war," often with little success. Thomas Jefferson Goodwyn to William T. Sherman, 17 February 1865, Goodwyn Letter, Caroliniana.

67. William T. Sherman to James M. Calhoun, Mayor, E. E. Rawson, and S. C. Wells, representing the City Council of Atlanta, 12 September 1864, *Hero's Own Story*, 60. For a description of what the evacuation experience was like for white women, see Diary of Mary Rawson, Rawson-Collier-Harris Papers, AHC.

68. Julia Stanley to Marcellus Stanley, 1 August 1864, Stanley Letters (Reproductions), UGA.

69. Rogers, 13 September 1864, Rogers Papers, Emory. Also see Fletcher, 20 November 1864, Fletcher Journal, GDAH. Also see Mrs. E. A. Steele to Tody, 15 February 1865, in Jones, ed., *When Sherman Came*, 133; Sarah Lawton to Sister, 7 September 1864, in Boggs, ed., *Alexander Letters*, 269.

70. McClatchey, 19 September 1864, Diary of Minerva Leah Rowles McClatchey, 1864–1866, McClatchey Family Papers, GDAH.

71. Rowland, 24 August 1864 and 12 October 1864, as quoted in Whites, *Civil War as a Crisis in Gender*, 101.

72. Mary Bull Maxcy Leverett to Caroline Pinckney Seabrook, 18 March 1865, Leverett Letter, Caroliniana. Union soldiers acknowledged that they rarely burned occupied houses, but G. W. Hanger affirmed "where ever we came to a house where the people were gone they most always were burnt." G. W. Hanger to Parents and Sisters, 14 December 1864, "With Sherman in Georgia—A Letter from the Coast," 440. See also Nichols, 5 February 1865, *Story of the Great March*, 140. See also Ephraim L. Girdner to Mollie, 23 December 1864, Wiley Files, Emory; Palmer, 7 March 1865 and 19 March 1865, *World Turned Upside Down*, 436, 444. On Southern women as wartime refugees, see Massey, *Refugee Life*.

73. Evelyn Harden Jackson, 31 October 1864, Harden Family Papers, Duke.

74. See Sarah Elizabeth "Bessie" Wilson to J. H. Wilkes, 19 November 1864, Wilkes Family Correspondence, Steel, Edward Marvin Papers, Collection of Heiskell, McCampbell, Wilkes, and Steel Family Materials, SHC. Some women considered evacuating their children away

from the path of the invading army. For examples, see Liz LaRoche to Carrie Jenkins, 14 January 1865, Micah Jenkins Papers, Caroliniana; Ellen Devereux Hinsdale to Daughter, 6 March 1865, Hinsdale Family Papers, Duke; Louisa Warren Patch Fletcher, 20 November [1864], Fletcher Journal, GDAH; Mary Bull Maxcy Leverett to Caroline Pinckney Seabrook, 18 March 1865, Leverett Letter, Caroliniana.

75. M. A. Lark to Mother, 19 November 1864, Padgett Papers, Caroliniana.

76. For examples of white Southern women burying their clothes, see Sue to Jane Ann Smythe, 16 April 1865, Adger, Smythe, Flynn Family Papers, Caroliniana; Charlotte St. Julien Ravenel to Meta Heyward, 17 February [1865], Charlotte St. Julien Ravenel Diary, Ravenel Family Papers, SCHS; A. C. Cooper, [1864], in Wheeler, *Sherman's March*, 77.

77. See Mary Gayle Aiken, 5 January [1865] and 11 February [1865], Aiken Family Papers, Caroliniana; Ellen Devereux Hinsdale to Son, 25 February 1865, Hinsdale Family Papers, Duke; Fannie to Addie Worth, 25 February 1865, Jonathan Worth Papers, SHC; Lucy Capehart to [?], 23 March 1865, Capehart Family Papers, SHC; Amanda to Mrs. John Bryce, [20 February 1865], Bryce Family Papers, Caroliniana. Confederate women elsewhere came to similar conclusions. Morgan, 27 April 1862, *Diary*, 51.

78. Rogers, 17 November 1864, Rogers Papers, Emory.

79. Edmondston, 11 April 1865, "Journal of a Secesh Lady," 692.

80. Mary Lizzie to Friend, 8 February 1865, Smith Papers, Duke.

81. LeConte, 15 February 1865, LeConte Diary, SHC. Also see Charlotte St. Julien Ravenel to Meta Heyward, [16 February] 1865, Ravenel Diary, Ravenel Family Papers, SCHS.

82. Lawton Protectors Paper, 1864, GHS. Afraid of capture by approaching Union troops, the few men remaining on the Southern home front fled as Union troops approached. For examples, see Charlotte St. Julien Ravenel to Meta Heyward, [16 February] 1865, Ravenel Diary, Ravenel Family Papers, SCHS; LeConte, 14 February 1865 and 16 February 1865, LeConte Diary, SHC; Edmondston, 21 March 1865, "Journal of a Secesh Lady," 682; Sarah Jane Sams to Randolph Sams, 4 February 1865, Sams Letter, Caroliniana; Sarah Lawton to Sister, 7 September 1864, Alexander Letters, 269.

83. *Augusta Daily Constitutionalist*, 27 January 1865. Women elsewhere also volunteered to form female military corps. See Irene Bell, Annie Samuels, and others to Secretary of War James A. Seddon, 2 December 1864, as cited in Gallagher, *Confederate War*, 77.

84. Eliza Josephine Trescot to Eldred J. Simkins, 20 September 1864, Simkins Collection, HEH.

85. Heyward, 26 December 1864, *Confederate Lady Comes of Age*, 61.

86. Sarah to Hattie Taylor Tennent, 8 January 1865, Tennent Papers, Caroliniana. Also see Ellis, 11 February [1865], Ellis Diary, Caroliniana; E. B. Fuller to Mrs. W. H. Barnwell, 13 February 1864, Barnwell Family Papers, SCHS.

87. Sarah to Hattie Taylor Tennent, 9 January 1865, Tennent Papers, Caroliniana. Also see Edmondston, 31 March 1865, "Journal of a Secesh Lady," 386.

88. Louisa Jane Harllee Pearce to Amelia, [1865], Louisa Jane Harllee Pearce Letter, Teague Papers, SCHS. A Union officer on the march recorded a conversation with a Georgia woman who said something quite similar. "If you whip us . . . we will throw ourselves into the arms of France, which only waits the chance to embrace us." Nichols, 6 September 1864, *Story of the Great March*, 23.

NOTES TO PAGES 41-46

89. Kate Crosland to Bea and Nellie, 28 December 1864, McIntosh Papers, Duke.
90. S. C. Goodwyn to Husband, 23 December 1864, Goodwyn Papers, Caroliniana.
91. Elmore, 24 December 1864, *Heritage of Woe*, 83. Also see Esther Alden [Elizabeth Alston], 1 March 1865, in Jones, *When Sherman Came*, 251.
92. Elmore, 31 December 1864, *Heritage of Woe*, 87.
93. Perhaps Elmore realized that her presence might be some protection to her home. See also Nichols, 5 February 1865, *Story of the Great March*, 140; Ephraim L. Girdner to Mollie, 23 December 1864, Wiley Files, Emory; Palmer, 7 March 1865 and 19 March 1865, *World Turned Upside Down*, 436, 444. On Southern women as wartime refugees, see Massey, *Refugee Life*.
94. Mary Gayle Aiken, 20 January 1865, Aiken Family Papers, Caroliniana.
95. Holmes, 12 November 1864, *Diary*, 386. Also see Elmore, 4 January 1865, *Heritage of Woe*, 90.
96. Sarah [Tennent] to Hattie Taylor Tennent, 9 January 1865, Tennent Papers, Caroliniana.
97. "A South Carolinian" to Jefferson Davis, 22 December 1864, Davis Papers, Duke. Also see Rowland, ed., *Jefferson Davis*, 7:4; Murrell, "'Of Necessity and Public Benefit,'" 77-100.
98. "Many Wives and Mothers of Charleston to the Editor of the Charleston Mercury," 24 January 1865, in Conner et al., *South Carolina Women*, 85-86.
99. Edmondston, 12 March 1865, *"Journal of a Secesh Lady,"* 676.
100. Elmore, 26 November 1864, *Heritage of Woe*, 81-82. On women's use of the rape metaphor describing the march, see Price, "'Such Are the Changes of Life.'"
101. LeConte, 14 February 1865, LeConte Diary, SHC. The use of skirts as a hiding place was common during the Civil War. See also Cook, 25 November 1864, *Journal of a Milledgeville Girl*, 62; Mrs. W. K. Bachman to Kate Bachman, 27 March 1865, Bachman Papers, Caroliniana; Mrs. E. A. Steele to Tody, 15 February 1865, in Jones, *When Sherman Came*, 134; Mary Elinor Bouknight Poppenheim, 27 February 1965, in Jones, *When Sherman Came*, 245. Several female spies utilized this method for hiding money, communications, and weapons. See Boyd, *Belle Boyd in Camp and Prison*; Greenhow, *My Imprisonment*; Kinchen, *Women Who Spied for the Blue and the Gray*; Massey, *Women in the Civil War*.
102. Sarah Jane Sams to Randolph Sams, 5 February 1865, Sams Letter, Caroliniana. Also see Heyward, 18 February 1864, *Confederate Lady Comes of Age*, 97; Nancy Armstrong Furman to Mary Furman, 8 March 1865, in Jones, *When Sherman Came*, 218; Maria L. Haynsworth to Ma, 28 April 1865, Haynsworth Letter, SHC.
103. See Charlotte St. Julien Ravenel, 26 February 1865, Ravenel Diary, Ravenel Family Papers, SCHS; Burge, 19 November 1864, *Diary of Dolly Lunt Burge*, 159; Rowe, 17 February 1865, "Southern Girl's Diary," 264-65; DeCaradeuc, 18 February 1865, *Confederate Lady Comes of Age*, 69; LeConte, 19 February 1865, LeConte Diary, SHC; Caroline Lamar to Charles Augustus Lafayette Lamar, 23 December 1864, Lamar Family Papers, GDAH; Mrs. W. K. Bachman to Kate Bachman, 27 March 1865, Bachman Papers, Caroliniana.
104. Sarah Jane Sams to Randolph Sams, 4 February 1865, Sams Letter, Caroliniana.
105. Sarah Jane Sams to Randolph Sams, 5 February 1865, Sams Letter, Caroliniana.
106. Charlotte St. Julien Ravenel to Meta Heyward, 25 February 1865, Ravenel Diary, Ravenel Family Papers, SCHS. See also Charlotte St. Julien Ravenel to Meta Heyward,

26 February 1865, Ravenel Diary, Ravenel Family Papers, SCHS; Mary Maxcy Leverett to Milton Leverett, 24 February 1865, in Taylor et al., *Leverett Letters*, 385.

107. LeConte, 31 December 1864, LeConte Diary, SHC, emphasis added.

108. Matilda Montgomery Champion to Sidney S. Champion, 14 June 1864, Champion Papers, Emory.

2. PUNISHING SOUTHERN WOMEN

1. Sherman to Owen, 30 January 1864, *OR,* Ser. 1, Vol. 25: 725.

2. William T. Sherman to James M. Calhoun, Mayor, E. E. Rawson, and S. C. Wells, representing the City Council of Atlanta, 12 September 1864, *Hero's Own Story,* 59–61.

3. Reverend G. S. Bradley, 28 December 1864, in *Star Corps,* 225. For a discussion of Sherman's assault on elite Southerners, see Campbell, *When Sherman Marched North;* Dunkelman, *Marching with Sherman.*

4. See Whites and Long, eds., *Occupied Women,* esp. 3–9. On women and their centrality to the home in the nineteenth-century South, see Jabour, *Scarlett's Sisters;* Schweninger, *Families in Crisis;* Edwards, *People and Their Peace;* Scott, *Southern Lady,* 19, 28–44; Clinton, *Plantation Mistress,* 18–35; Friedman, *Enclosed Garden;* Burton, *In My Father's House,* 123–36; Fox-Genovese, *Within the Plantation Household,* 37–99, 192–241; Stevenson, *Life in Black and White,* 38–42; Weiner, *Mistresses and Slaves,* 53–71. Most scholarly work on the household focuses on the region's plantations. For notable exceptions, see Hagler, "Ideal Woman in the Antebellum South," 405–18; McCurry, *Masters of Small Worlds.*

5. William T. Sherman to R. M. Sawyer, 31 January 1864, *OR,* Ser. 1, Vol. 32, pt 2: 278–81.

6. William T. Sherman to Ulysses S. Grant, 6 November 1864, *OR,* Ser. 1, Vol. 39, pt. 3: 660; William T. Sherman to Ulysses S. Grant, 9 October 1864, *Sherman's Civil War,* 731. James Reston, Jr., recognized the gendered meaning of Sherman's use of the word "howl." "Sherman expressedly set out to make Georgia howl. But neither states nor soldiers howl; civilians do, particularly women. . . . His technique was to demoralize the women back home and let that have its effect on the soldiers at the front." Reston, *Sherman's March and Vietnam,* 93.

7. Michael Price, "Such Are the Changes of Life," 162–91.

8. William T. Sherman to Ellen Sherman, 12 March 1865, *Home Letters,* 332, emphasis added.

9. William T. Sherman, Special Field Orders No. 120, 9 November 1864, *OR,* Ser. 1, Vol. 39, pt. 3: 713.

10. William T. Sherman to R. M. Sawyer, 31 January 1864, *OR,* Ser. 1, Vol. 32, pt. 2: 279.

11. Benjamin Butler used a similar rationale for his "Woman Order." See Long, "(Mis) Remembering."

12. Welter, "Cult of True Womanhood," 21–41. Not all women subscribed to the "cult of true womanhood"—see Cogan, *All-American Girl;* William T. Sherman to Ellen Sherman, 23 March 1865, *Home Letters,* 335.

13. For discussions of Northern masculinity and ideas about womanhood, see Foote, *The Gentlemen and the Roughs,* 53–56; Ramold, *Across the Divide,* 7–54.

14. Hitchcock, 24 November 1864, *Marching with Sherman,* 89.

15. Henry Hitchcock to Francis Lieber, 15 January 1865, Lieber Papers, HEH.
16. Sherman to Henry W. Halleck, 4 September 1864, *Sherman's Civil War,* 697.
17. Special Field Orders No. 67, *OR,* Ser. 1, Vol. 38, pt. 5: 837–38.
18. William T. Sherman to James M. Calhoun, Mayor, E. E. Rawson, and S. C. Wells, representing the City Council of Atlanta, 12 September 1864, *Hero's Own Story,* 60.
19. William T. Sherman to Henry W. Halleck, 9 September 1864, *OR,* Ser. 1, Vol. 38, pt. 5: 839.
20. Sherman to Eugene Casserly, 17 September 1864, *Sherman's Civil War,* 713.
21. William T. Sherman to Ellen Sherman, 1 October 1864, *Sherman's Civil War,* 728.
22. Sherman to John Bell Hood, 10 September 1864, *Sherman's Civil War,* 706.
23. William T. Sherman to Ellen Sherman, 17 September 1864, *Home Letters,* 309.
24. J. Dexter Cotton to Wife, 17 September 1864, Cotton Papers, LC.
25. Chapman, 20 September 1864, *Civil War Diary,* 95.
26. Sherman to Thomas Ewing, Sr., 11 August 1864, *Sherman's Civil War,* 689.
27. Ellen Sherman to William T. Sherman, 17 September 1864, as cited in Marszalek, *Sherman,* 286.
28. William T. Sherman to Ellen Sherman, 21 October 1864, *Sherman's Civil War,* 738–39.
29. William T. Sherman to Ulysses S. Grant, 6 November 1864, *OR,* Ser. 1, Vol. 39, pt. 3: 660.
30. Burton, 15 November 1864, *Diary of E. P. Burton,* 41.
31. William J. Gibson, 14 November 1864, William J. Gibson Diary in Albion W. Tourgee, *The Story of a Thousand: Being a History of the Service of the 105th Ohio Volunteer Infantry, In the War for the Union from August 21, 1862 to June 6, 1865* (Buffalo: S. McGerald and Son, 1895), 334.
32. Vail, 15 November 1864, Vail Diary typescript, Wiley Files, Emory.
33. William T. Sherman to Henry Halleck, 1 January 1865, *OR,* Ser. 1, Vol. 34: 13. Andrews, 24 December 1864, *War-Time Journal of a Georgia Girl,* 32.
34. Edward W. Allen to Mollie, 17 December 1864, Allen Papers, SHC.
35. Sherman to Henry Slocum, 18 November 1864, *OR,* Ser. 1, Vol. 44, pt. 1: 489.
36. Edward W. Allen to Mollie, 17 December 1864, Allen Papers, SHC. For a thorough narrative description of the March to the Sea, see Bailey, *Chessboard of War.*
37. Rome, Georgia, was destroyed, E. P. Burton asserted, because "the soldiers want to see it burn." Burton, 10 November 1864, *Diary of E. P. Burton,* 39.
38. James Leath, 23 December 1864, Journal, HEH.
39. Edward W. Allen to James and Emily Allen, 25 September 1864, Allen Papers, SHC.
40. As quoted in Kennett, *Marching through Georgia,* 232.
41. Chapman, 19 November 1864, *Civil War Diary . . . of a Forty-Niner,* 100–101.
42. Delos Van Deusen to Henrietta Van Deusen, 28 December 1864, Van Deusen Papers, HEH.
43. Michael Dresbach to Wife, 14 December 1864, Wiley Files, Emory.
44. Jo to Linda McNeill, 24 December 1864, Lawrence Papers, GHS.
45. R. B. Hoadley to Cousin, 8 April 1865, Hoadley Papers, Duke.
46. Devine to Captain J. H. Everett, 19 December 1864, Everett Papers, GHS. Also see, Mrs. E. A. Steele to Tody, 15 February 1865, in Jones, *When Sherman Came,* 133; M. C. H. to Lou, 7 December 1864, in Boggs, ed., *Alexander Letters,* 282.

47. Nichols, 27 November 1864, *Story of the Great March*, 66. Another soldier called the March to Sea "one big picnick." Charles Ewing to Thomas Ewing, 15 December 1864, "Sherman's March through Georgia," 326. See also Osborn, 10 November 1864, *Fiery Trail*, 35.

48. Charles S. Brown to Mother and Etta, 16 December 1864, Brown Papers, Duke.

49. Jo to Linda McNeill, 24 December 1864, Lawrence Papers, GHS.

50. William T. Sherman to Ellen Sherman, 16 December 1864, *Home Letters*, 316.

51. Charles S. Brown to Mother and Etta, 16 December 1864, Brown Papers, Duke.

52. Orlando M. Poe to Nell, 16 December 1864, Lawrence Papers, GHS.

53. John C. Van Duzer, 22 November 1864, Van Duzer Diary, Duke; Bonner, "Sherman at Milledgeville," 41–54. Also see Gibson Diary, 23 November 1864, in Tourgee, *Story of a Thousand*, 337.

54. For a discussion of foraging and "bumming" during Sherman's March through Georgia, see Kennett, *Marching through Georgia*, 263–87. Also see Marszalek, *Sherman*, 301–2.

55. Jefferson C. Davis, Circular, Fourteenth Army Corps, 18 November 1864, *OR*, Ser. 1, Vol. 44, pt. 1: 489.

56. Kennett notes Union soldiers' fascination with women's "sweet little notes" and letters. Kennett, *Marching through Georgia*, 89.

57. Hight, 22 February 1865, *History of the Fifty-Eighth Regiment*, 487.

58. Michael Dresbach to Wife, 14 December 1864, Wiley Files, Emory.

59. Gibson, 27 November 1864, in Tourgee, *Story of a Thousand*, 338.

60. Edward W. Allen to James and Emily Allen, 17 February 1865, Allen Papers, SHC. Also see Sylvester Daniels, 17 February 1865, Daniels Diary, HEH. Thomas J. Myers described the division of the loot in a letter to his wife. See Myers to Wife, 26 February 1865, Myers Letter, NCDAH.

61. Edward W. Allen to James and Emily Allen, 17 February 1865, Allen Papers, SHC. Also see John H. Roberts to Brother, 7 January 1865, as quoted in Glatthaar, *March to the Sea and Beyond*, 149; Henry Orlando Marcy, 11 February 1865, Diary, Caroliniana.

62. Charles S. Brown to Mother and Etta, 16 December 1864, Brown Papers, Duke.

63. John Herr to Sister, 18 December 1864, Herr Papers, Duke. See also Noble to Mom, 14 March 1865, "Vett Noble of Ypsilanti," 35.

64. William T. Sherman to Abraham Lincoln, 22 December 1864, Sherman File, HEH.

65. Essington, 22 December 1864, Essington Diary, Lawrence Papers, GHS.

66. Special Field Orders No. 120, 9 November 1864, *OR*, Ser. 1, Vol. 39, pt. 3: 713.

67. William T. Sherman to R. M. Sawyer, 31 January 1864, *OR*, Ser. 1, Vol. 32, pt. 2: 279.

68. Hitchcock, 22 November 1864, *Marching with Sherman*, 84–85. As described by Hitchcock, Cobb's plantation was "about 6000 acres, and worked 100 hands. . . . No thrift or neatness about the place: sundry rude log cabins for storehouses, mean rail fences—everything shabby: old negroes wretchedly dressed."

69. Divine to J. H. Everett, 25 January 1865, Everett Papers, GHS.

70. Andrew Jay McBride to Fannie, 11 September 1864, McBride Papers, Duke University.

71. Michael Dresbach to Wife, 15 December 1864, as quoted in Glatthaar, *March to the Sea and Beyond*, 148.

72. Charles S. Brown to Etta, 26 April 1865, Brown Papers, Duke.

73. Women corroborated such stories. For examples, see Ellen Devereux Hinsdale to Child, 23 March 1865, Hinsdale Family Papers, Duke; Heyward, 18 February 1865, *Confederate Lady Comes of Age*, 65; Annie Jones to Cadwallader Jones, 6 March 1865, Jones Papers, SHC; Elmore, 21 February 1865, *Heritage of Woe*, 101.

74. William T. Sherman to Henry Halleck, 1 January 1865, *Hero's Own Story*, 83–84.

75. William T. Sherman to Ellen Sherman, 25 December 1864, *Home Letters*, 319–20.

76. William T. Sherman to George H. Thomas, 21 January 1865, *OR*, Ser. 1, Vol. 45, pt. 2: 621–622.

77. Henry Hitchcock to Mary Hitchcock, 4 November 1864, Hitchcock Collection, LC.

78. Bradley, 28 December 1864, in *Star Corps*, 225.

79. Hight, 19 January 1865, *History of the Fifty-Eighth Regiment*, 416. Not all Union soldiers agreed with Sherman's policy. See Thomas T. Taylor, 23 November 1864, Diary, Taylor Collection, Emory.

80. John M. Glidden to William H. Gardiner, 29 January 1865, "Yankee Views the Agony of Savannah," 429.

81. The impact of Sherman's March on slaves has been explored in Drago, "How Sherman's March through Georgia Affected the Slaves," 361–75; Rose, *Rehearsal for Reconstruction*; Schwalm, *Hard Fight for We*; Frankel, *Freedom's Women*; Penningroth, "Slavery, Freedom, and Social Claims," 405–35; Camp, *Closer to Freedom*; Campbell, *When Sherman Marched North*. For Field Order 15, see *OR*, Ser. 1, Vol. 47: 60–62.

82. William T. Sherman to Henry W. Halleck, 24 December 1864, *OR*, Ser. 1, Vol. 44: 798–800.

83. William T. Sherman to Henry W. Halleck, 13 December 1864, OR, I, 44:701–2.

84. William T. Sherman to Ulysses S. Grant, 18 December 1864, OR I, 44: 741–43.

85. John Herr to Katy Herr, 5 February 1865, Herr Papers, Duke.

86. O. M. Poe to Nell, 26 December 1864, Lawrence Papers, GHS. See also Samuel Mahon to Lizzie, 22 December 1864, "Civil War Letters of Samuel Mahon," 258.

87. Gibson, 12 December 1864, in Tourgee, *Story of a Thousand*, 343.

88. Edward W. Allen to James and Emily Allen, 4 February 1865, Allen Papers, SHC.

89. William T. Sherman to Henry W. Halleck, 24 December 1864, *Memoirs*, 558.

90. William T. Sherman to Mrs. Carolina Carson, 20 January 1865, Sherman Papers, Caroliniana.

91. As quoted in Hirshson, *White Tecumseh*, 275.

92. Hight, 19 January 1865, *History of the Fifty-Eighth Regiment*, 416.

93. Edward W. Allen to James and Emily Allen, 4 February 1865, Allen Papers, SHC. Some soldiers believed that destruction was in order while the army was still in Georgia. For example, Joseph Hoffhines reported that "this Government is now Entering upon a new policy. We are ordered to burn Cities and Barns and Houses where Ever we go and lay waste the Entire Country." Hoffhines to Wife, 11 November 1864, as quoted in Kennett, *Marching through Georgia*, 232.

94. Thomas E. Smith to Brother, 27 December 1864, as quoted in Royster, *Destructive War*, 344. Also see William Scofield to Father, 2 February 1865, Scofield Papers, Caroliniana.

95. Nichols, 30 January 1865, *Story of the Great March,* 131. Other soldiers also felt that justice had been served. "We bade the remains of the City of Columbia the Capitol of S.C. farewell which had recd her Just reward for the evil deeds she did in the great rebellion. The great City is Fallen." Jesse S. Bean, 20 February 1865, Bean Diary, SHC.

96. Sebastian Duncan to Mother, 1 February 1865, as cited in Glatthaar, *March to the Sea and Beyond,* 140.

97. Sylvester Daniels, 18 February 1865, Daniels Diary Typescript, HEH. The Union desire to wreak vengeance on South Carolina was not a new one. A full year before Sherman's March began, Isaac Jackson hoped for a chance to punish South Carolina soldiers on the field of battle. "No man ever looked forward to any event with more joy than did our boys to have a chance to meet the sons of the mothers of traitors, 'South Carolina.'" Isaac Jackson to Moses and Phebe Jackson, 13 July 1863, *Some of the Boys,* 111.

98. Sherman's men left countless descriptions of the destruction, especially in South Carolina, the home of secession's instigators. For examples, see Wills, *Army Life of an Illinois Soldier;* Platter Journal, UGA; Ward Diary, Caroliniana; Thomas Ford to Mr. William, 28 March 1865, Ford Letter, Caroliniana; Conyngham, *Sherman's March through the South;* Samuel Augustus Duncan to Julia Jones, 15 March 1865, in *Yankee Correspondence,* 51.

99. See Royster, *Destructive War,* 21. See also Burton, 27 October 1864, *Diary of E. P. Burton,* 37; Charles S. Brown to Mother and Etta, 16 December 1864, Brown Papers, Duke; Taylor, 23 November 1864, Diary, Taylor Collection, Emory; Bonner, "Sherman at Milledgeville," 281.

100. Charles Cox to Katie, 1 February 1865, "'Gone for a Soldier,'" 229.

101. Heyward, 18 February 1865, *Confederate Lady Comes of Age,* 67.

102. Other scholars similarly propose that Sherman designed his campaign with the intention of striking hardest at the Southern elite. For example, see Fellman, *Citizen Sherman,* 214–15.

103. John C. Gray to John C. Ropes, 24 February 1865, *War Letters,* 458; George M. Wise to John Wise, 13 March 1865, "Marching through South Carolina," 193. See also Sherlock, 15 February 1865, *Memorabilia of the Marches,* 195.

104. As quoted in Lewis, *Sherman,* 503.

105. E. H. King, 18 February 1865, as cited in Glatthaar, *March to the Sea and Beyond,* 146. According to some observers, even Union soldiers who were stationed outside of the city helped plunder it. Allen Morgan Geer was camped in the "suburbs of Columbia" the night Columbia burned. "The troops . . . break ranks and make for the city. the most for forage many for plunders, some for whiskey & excitement, a few to burn and destroy. & I & Capt. King for curiosity[.] As the flames spread from street to street, soldiers running wild noisy and intoxicated[.] Citizens hurrying to and fro[.] Women & children frightened and often weeping, the crash of falling buildings all presented a grand but sad seen of desolating ruin." Geer, 17 February 1865, *Civil War Diary,* 197.

106. Robert Stuart Finley to Mary A. Cabeen, 30 March 1865, Finley Papers, SHC.

107. Anthony J. Baurdick, 19 February 1865, Diary, Baurdick Papers, Emory.

108. William T. Sherman to Henry W. Halleck, 4 April 1865, *Hero's Own Story,* 96.

109. Jackson, February 18, 1865, *Colonel's Diary,* 184. Nearly a century and a half later, scholars continue to debate whether Union or Confederate troops initiated the blaze. The

details of this debate have not changed much since the controversy began immediately after the war. For a discussion of the controversy, see Lucas, *Sherman and the Burning of Columbia*. Also see Nelson, *Ruin Nation*.

110. Edwin Anson Bowen, 2 March 1865, Edwin A. Bowen Diary, Bowen Papers, HEH.

111. Charles S. Brown to Etta, 26 April 1865, Brown Papers, Duke.

112. Lieutenant Colonel Jeremiah W. Jenkins as cited in Royster, *Destructive War*, 20.

113. Lieutenant Colonel Jeremiah W. Jenkins as cited in Royster, *Destructive War*, 23. Also see William O. Wettleson to Father and Sisters, 27 November 1864, Wiley Files, Emory; Harvey Reid to Homefolk, 14 December 1864, Wiley Files, Emory; Samuel B. Crew to Brother and Sister, 15 December 1864, Wiley Files, Emory; Jones and Mallard, 16 December 1864, *Yankees a'Coming*; Mary Bull Maxcy Leverett to Caroline Pinckney Seabrook, 18 March 1865, Leverett Letter, Caroliniana.

114. On Union soldiers' adjusting conceptions of manhood and their behavior during wartime, see Foote, *The Gentlemen and the Roughs*, 41, 177–78; Ramold, *Across the Divide*, 10.

115. Hubert, 20 February 1865, *History of the Fiftieth Regiment*, 356. Also see William O. Wettleson to Parents and Sisters, 4 April 1865, Wiley Files, Emory; Thomas J. Myers to Wife, 26 February 1865, Myers Papers, SHC.

116. George M. Wise to John Wise, 13 March 1865, "Marching Through South Carolina," 193–94. Southern women agreed. For example, Mary Maxcy Leverett thought that "if Sherman chose to he could have stopped that, for he is a severe disciplinarian & they are afraid as death of him." Mary Maxcy Leverett to Caroline Pinckney Seabrook, 18 March 1865, *Leverett Letters*, 390.

117. William T. Sherman to Ellen Sherman, 16 December 1864, *Home Letters*, 318.

118. William T. Sherman to Hugh Judson Kilpatrick, 23 February 1865, *OR*, Ser. 1, Vol. 47, pt. 2: 543–44.

119. William T. Sherman to Ellen Sherman, 12 March 1865, *Sherman's Civil War*, 823–24.

120. Henry Halleck to William T. Sherman, 18 December 1864, *Supplemental Report of Joint Commission on the Conduct of the War*, 1:287.

121. James A. Connolly to Wife, 12 March 1865, *Three Years in the Army of the Cumberland*, 384.

122. Edward Allen to James and Emily Allen, 18 February 1865, Allen Papers, SHC.

123. Sherman to John A. Rawlins, 9 May 1865, *OR*, Ser. 1, Vol. 47, pt. 1: 38.

124. Holmes, 10 February 1865, *52d Ohio Volunteer Infantry*, 20. See also Thomas J. Myers to Wife, 26 February 1865, Myers Papers, SHC.

125. James Stillwell to Wife, 12 March 1865, as quoted in Grimsley, *Hard Hand of War*, 202.

126. Jesse S. Bean, 8 March 1865, Bean Diary, SHC.

127. William T. Sherman to H. W. Slocum, 6 March 1865, *OR*, Ser. 1, Vol. 47, pt. 2: 704; William T. Sherman to Judson Kilpartrick, 7 March 1865, *OR*, Ser. 1, Vol. 47, pt. 2: 721.

128. James A. Connolly to Wife, 12 March 1865, *Three Years in the Army of the Cumberland*, 384. Marszalek argues that when Sherman's troops entered North Carolina "the wholesale destruction they had practiced in South Carolina ceased." However, he admits that "the soldiers did not stop all pillaging; they simply toned it down." Marszalek, *Sher-

man, 327. Grimsley asserts that "the Tarheel State received much the same treatment as Georgia—possibly even a bit milder, since North Carolina was not part of the Deep South, was known to harbor significant Unionist sentiment, and had been one of the last states to secede." Grimsley, *Hard Hand of War,* 202. Also see Barrett, *Civil War in North Carolina,* 291–300, 311–17, 328–49; McPherson, *Battle Cry of Freedom,* 826. However, Fellman acknowledges that "the men still stripped the countryside of food and livestock and burned public facilities. Some soldiers noted little difference between the overall results in the two Carolinas." Fellman, *Citizen Sherman,* 235.

129. Rufus Mead to Dear Folks Back Home, 7 March 1865, "With Sherman Through Georgia and the Carolinas," 74.

130. Nichols, 14 March 1865, *Story of the Great March,* 252–53.

131. Anonymous Woman [Fayetteville, NC], 22 March 1865, Emma Mordecai Diary, Mordecai Family Papers, SHC.

132. Horton, 14 March 1865, "Dairy of an Officer," 248.

133. Wills, 18 March 1865, *Army Life of an Illinois Soldier,* 364.

134. William T. Sherman to Ellen Sherman, 9 April 1865, *Home Letters,* 342.

135. Wills, 29 April 1865, *Army Life of an Illinois Soldier,* 373. The immediate change in behavior upon orders betrays many of the explanations historians have offered for the nonessential items destroyed on the march. Southerners, perhaps not surprisingly, believed that the widespread destruction was either a direct result of official directives or an unofficial policy to turn a blind eye. For example, the morning after the burning of Columbia, Mrs. E. L. L. watched as "the order to cease the terrible carnival was given, and the immediate quiet which followed was passing strange, yet it showed the thorough discipline of the mighty army; besides it proved most clearly that permission, if not expressed command, had been given to burn and sack the town." Mrs. E. L. L., in *Charleston Weekly Courier,* "Our Women in the War," 255.

136. Geer, 29 April 1865, *Civil War Diary,* 217.

3. WORKING FOR WAR

1. Sallie E. White to Mary Snowden, 17 January 1865, Snowden Papers, Caroliniana.

2. S. C. Goodwyn to Artemus Darby Goodwyn, 22 January 1865, Goodwyn Papers, Caroliniana.

3. LeConte, 18 January 1865, LeConte Diary, SHC.

4. S. C. Goodwyn to Husband, 22 January 1865, Artemus Darby Goodwyn Papers, Caroliniana.

5. Massey, *Women in the Civil War;* Rable, *Civil Wars;* Faust, "Altars of Sacrifice," 113–40; Faust, *Mothers of Invention;* Roberts, *Confederate Belle,* 47, 78.

6. Edmondston, 3 May 1861, *"Journal of a Secesh Lady,"* 60. Also see Caroline Gilman to Children, 16 April 1861, "Letters of a Confederate Mother," 507.

7. Northern women behaved similarly. Maria Ewing described how "Teresa as well as most of the young and some of the married Ladies are very busy making red & gray flannel

shirts for the Soldiers—they meet and sew at the City Hall—they had a Ball on Friday night for the benefit of the soldiers." Maria Ewing to Ellen Sherman, 2 May 1861, Ellen Sherman Collection, HEH.

8. Cullen, *Civil War in Popular Culture,* 96.

9. Whites, *Civil War as a Crisis in Gender,* and *Gender Matters.*

10. Faust and Rable both conclude that Confederate womanhood, as a new gender ideology, could not be accepted. Faust states that it was primarily a creation of the male press unsuccessfully imposed on women. The wartime stress on female sacrifice "promoted the notion of an archetypal 'Confederate woman' as a form of false consciousness." Faust, "Altars of Sacrifice," 114, and *Mothers of Invention,* 17–19; Rable, *Civil Wars,* 113.

11. Faust, *Mothers of Invention,* 24. Southern Ladies' Aid Societies helped the Confederacy in many ways. For examples of membership lists, constitutions, meeting announcements, and executive boards of societies formed in areas that Sherman would later invade, see Ladies' Association of Columbia for the Relief and Comfort of the Families of Absent Soldiers in this City & its Vicinity, Bryce Family Papers, Caroliniana; Minutes of the Proceedings of the "Greenville Ladies' Association in aid of the Volunteers of the Confederate Army," Greenville Ladies' Association, Caroliniana; Proceedings of Soldiers' Relief Association [Charleston], 24 July 1861, *Charleston Mercury;* Ladies' Auxiliary Christian Association [Charleston], 26 July 1861, *Charleston Mercury;* Ladies' Clothing Association [Charleston], 7 August 1861, *Charleston Mercury;* Organization of Georgetown Relief Association, 30 August 1861, *Charleston Mercury;* Minutes of the Ladies' Relief Association of Fairfield, in Connor, et al., *South Carolina Women,* 1: 36–53; Rules of the Eutawville Aid Association, in Connor et al., *South Carolina Women,* 1:59–63; Kershaw Ladies' Aid Association, in Connor et al., *South Carolina Women,* 1:66; Minutes of the Young Ladies' Hospital Association of Columbia, in Connor et al., *South Carolina Women,* 1:88–93; Ladies' Aid Society (Columbia, S.C.) Papers, Caroliniana; Ladies' Benevolent Society (Charleston) Papers, Caroliniana; Ladies' Relief Association of Plantersville Papers, Sparkman Papers, Caroliniana; Ladies' Relief Association (Spartanburg) Papers, Caroliniana; Ladies' Volunteer Aid Association Papers, Caroliniana; Minutes of Greenville, Georgia Soldiers' Aid Society, GDAC; Barrett, *Civil War in North Carolina,* 260–61. A postwar list of the "Women's Associations in South Carolina for the Relief of Soldiers" contains one hundred aid societies in the state. See Connor et al., *South Carolina Women,* 1:21–25.

12. Some Southern women recorded the formation of the aid societies in their diaries. For example, see Margaret Dailey [April 1861], Confederate Miscellany I, Emory.

13. Caroline Howard Gilman, January 1863, Gilman Collection, Caroliniana.

14. Women's roles as spies and soldiers in the North and South are discussed in Varon, *Southern Lady;* Massey, *Women in the Civil War,* 87–107; Faust, *Mothers of Invention,* 214–19; Sizer, "Acting Her Part," 114–33; Kinchen, *Women Who Spied.* Some female spies left accounts of their exploits. For example, see Edmondson, *Lost Heroine of the Confederacy;* Greenhow, *My Imprisonment;* Boyd, *Belle Boyd.*

15. Rufus W. Cater to Fannie S. Cater [1861], Cater Papers, LC. See also Eaton, *History of the Southern Confederacy,* 88.

16. Mary E. Tucker [1864], Beauregard Papers, Emory.

17. C. M. C., n.d., Walker Paper, GHS.

18. William Gilmore Simms's collection of wartime poetry offers examples of women's use of words to encourage enlistment and demonstrate their continued dedication to the Confederacy. See Simms, *War Poetry of the South*. Simms dedicated this collection to "the women of the South" who "have shown themselves worthy of any manhood . . . [and] of the best womanhood." See also Linderman, *Embattled Courage*, 88–89.

19. For examples of women's early work for the Confederate soldiers, see Mary H. Legge to Harriet R. Palmer, 26 September 1861 and 15 January 1862, in Towles, ed., *World Turned Upside Down*, 309, 320; Maria L. Garlington to Harriet R. Palmer, 8 December 1861, in Towles, ed., *World Turned Upside Down*, 316; Sarah J. Palmer to Harriet R. Palmer, 29 October 1862, in Towles, ed., *World Turned Upside Down*, 352.

20. For example, South Carolinian Esther B. Cheesborough organized her own Confederate aid efforts and played a role in the larger community efforts. Cheesborough kept a log of the various items and multiple shipments she sent to the "Southern Prisoners" at Fort Delaware. In addition, she preserved their notes of thanks. See J. A. Crocheron to Esther B. Cheesborough, 20 November 1862, Cheesborough Notebook, Caroliniana; H. S. Bantor to Esther B. Cheesborough, 23 April 1863, Cheesborough Notebook, Caroliniana; H. K. Gregg to Esther B. Cheesborough, 15 November 1862, Cheesborough Notebook, Caroliniana; [ ] to Esther B. Cheesborough, 21 September 1862, Cheesborough Notebook, Caroliniana; J. J. Gaines to Esther B. Cheesborough, 10 April 1863, Cheesborough Notebook, Caroliniana. Also see Bryce Family Papers, Caroliniana.

21. Maria L. Garlington to Harriet R. Palmer, 20 July 1862, in Towles, ed., *World Turned Upside Down*, 333.

22. Thousands of women served as Union nurses. The Women's Central Relief Association and the United States Sanitary Commission coordinated and enlisted white women's relief work. Attie, *Patriotic Toil*; Giesberg, *Civil War Sisterhood*. On Southern nurses, see Schroeder-Lein, *Confederate Hospitals on the Move*; Rable, *Civil Wars*, 121–28; Faust, *Mothers of Invention*, 92–113. Perhaps because of the lack of official organizations, and no centralized archive of primary materials, the local organizations and nursing efforts of the South remain relatively unexplored. For an effort to discuss the Northern and Southern experience, see Schultz, *Women at the Front*.

23. Rufus W. Cater to Fannie S. Cater [1861], Cater Papers, LC.

24. On women's adaptation to wartime shortages, see Massey, *Ersatz in the Confederacy*; Massey, "Food and Drink Shortage," 306–34. Women of limited means frequently resented the disruptions and troubles caused by the war. See Bynum, *Unruly Women*; Harris, *Plain Folk and Gentry*.

25. [?] to Sarah "Sade" Jones Lenoir, 22 January 1865, Lenoir Family Papers, SHC. For other descriptions of food riots, see "Agnes" to Mrs. Pryor, 4 April 1863, in Jones, ed., *Ladies of Richmond: Confederate Capital*, 155; Mary Waring, 12 April 1865, *Miss Waring's Journal*, 15.

26. On the boundaries circumscribing the lives of Southern ladies, see Scott, *Southern Lady*; Faust, *Mothers of Invention*, 245.

27. See Rable, *Civil Wars*, 110.

28. See Whites, "Civil War as a Crisis in Gender," 3–21, and *Civil War as a Crisis in Gender*, esp. 96–131; Rable, "'Missing in Action'" 134–46.

29. Sarah to Hattie Taylor Tennent, 9 January 1865, Tennent Papers, Caroliniana.

30. Mother to Daughters, 8 March 1865, Heyward Papers, Caroliniana. Other women used similarly damning terms when describing the Union invaders. For examples of individuals who used these terms repeatedly, see Sams Letter, Caroliniana; Edmondston, *"Journal of a Secesh Lady";* LeConte Diary, SHC; Minerva Leah Rowles McClatchey, McClatchey Family Papers, GDAH; Kate Crosland to Bea and Nellie, McIntosh Papers, Duke; Sarah to Hattie Taylor Tennent, Tennent Papers, Caroliniana; Fannie to Addie Worth, Jonathan Worth Papers, SHC; Louisa Jane Harllee Pearce to Amelia, Louisa Jane Harllee Pearce Letter, Teague Papers, 1846–1921, SCHS; Susan and Harriott Middleton Correspondence, Cheves-Middleton Papers, SCHS; Susan Bowen Lining to Sister, 16 March 1865, Lining Letter, SCHS; Hinsdale Family Papers, Duke.

31. Elmore, 24 December 1864, *Heritage of Woe*, 83.

32. LeeAnn Whites terms the movement of women's domestic labor outside of the household as "public domesticity." Whites, *Civil War as a Crisis in Gender*, 50.

33. The women of South Carolina, headed by Mary Snowden, received many thank-you letters from soldiers for clothes and other needs that the women supplied. They also received some requests for specific items. For examples, see P. G. T. Beauregard to [W. D. Porter], 25 July 1864, Snowden Papers, Caroliniana; A. G. Lane to Mary Amarinthia Snowden, 12 October 1864, Snowden Papers, Caroliniana; Thomas Y. Simons to Mary Snowden, 12 November 1864, Snowden Papers, Caroliniana; Robert E. Lee to Flora Matheson, Mary Snowden, Amy Burgess, Clara Cheesborough, Annie Mordicre, Gilbert Tennant, L. M. Stoney, C. P. Matheson, W. Coles Fisher, J. Gates Snowden, 25 November 1864, Snowden Papers, Caroliniana; Wm. C. Ravenel to Mary Snowden, 6 December 1864, Snowden Papers, Caroliniana; E. M. Seabrook to Mary Snowden, 14 December 1864, Snowden Papers, Caroliniana, Jas. H. Ri[on] to Mary Snowden, 25 January 1865, Snowden Papers, Caroliniana; S. C. [Cory] to Mary Snowden, 25 January 1865, Snowden Papers, Caroliniana; Thomas Y. Simons to Mary Snowden, 25 January 1865, Snowden Papers, Caroliniana; [G. B. Lartegue] to Mary Snowden, 26 January 1865, Snowden Papers, Caroliniana; Joseph Blyth Allston to Mary Snowden, 14 February 1865, Snowden Papers, Caroliniana.

34. Speech of President Davis in Columbia, 4 October 1864, *Jefferson Davis, Constitutionalist*, 6:354. See also Speech of President Davis at Macon, Georgia, 28 September 1864, *Jefferson Davis, Constitutionalist*, 6:341–43; Speech of President Davis at Augusta, 5 October 1864, *Jefferson Davis, Constitutionalist*, 6:359–60

35. On the use of and pride in homespun, see Massey, *Ersatz in the Confederacy*, 85–89.

36. A. E. D. to Brother, 6 December 1864, Confederate Miscellany I, Emory. Other women were similarly engaged in constant sewing. For example, see Carrie Fries Shaffner, 3 November 1864, Fries and Shaffner Family Papers, SHC; Anna Maria Cain to Harriet R. Palmer, 6 November 1864, in Towles, ed., *World Turned Upside Down*, 412.

37. Through their actions, countless Union soldiers acknowledged the important contribution of Confederate women through sewing. Soldiers confiscated or destroyed needles, thread, and cloth from the homes that they entered. For examples, see Sue to Jane Ann Smythe, 16 April 1865, Adger, Smythe, Flynn Family Papers, Caroliniana; Eliza Tillinghast to David R. Tillinghast, 3 May 1865, Tillinghast Family Papers, Duke.

38. Sarah Jane Sams to Randolph Sams, 5 February 1865, Sams Letter, Caroliniana.

39. *Charleston Courier,* 2 February 1865. Also see Greenville Ladies' Association, Caroliniana; Minutes of the Ladies' Relief Association of Fairfield, in Connor et al., *South Carolina Women,* 1:44; Minutes of the Young Ladies' Hospital Association of Columbia, in Connor et al., *South Carolina Women,* 1:93.

40. Connor et al., *South Carolina Women,* 90.

41. Mary Gayle Aiken, 20 January 1865, Aiken Family Papers, Caroliniana.

42. Mary Hanes Davis to Catherine E. Hanes, 27 March 1865, Hanes Papers, SHC.

43. Not all Confederate women were anxious to work in hospitals. For many, this work defied the comfort of class, race, and gender in the South. For example, North Carolinian Lucy Capehart wrote "I never in my life could go to one [hospital], & never expect to unless I am compelled. not that I am not willing to do everything I can for the Soldiers, but simply because I dont like so *much mess,* & so *many different odours*—it makes me sick to smell soldiers anyway." Lucy Capehart to [?], 23 March 1865, Capehart Family Papers, SHC.

44. Douglas J. Cater to Fannie Cater, 1 June 1864, Cater Papers, LC.

45. John Peter Kendall to Sarah and D. J. Kendall, 18 July 1864, Kendall Papers, HEH.

46. For example, see Kennett, *Marching through Georgia,* 88, 90.

47. Chesnut, 19 August 1864 and 28 October 1864, *Mary Chesnut's Civil War,* 637, 656. Also see Chesnut, 29 August 1864, 21 September 1864, 6 November 1864, 25 November 1864, 7 January 1865, *Mary Chesnut's Civil War,* 641, 644, 667–68, 677, 700.

48. Mary Jones to Susan M. Cumming, 29 September 1864, in Myers, ed., *Children of Pride,* 2:1208.

49. Howard, 25 December 1864, *In and Out of the Lines,* 185.

50. Ellen Devereux Hinsdale to Son, 25 February 1865, Hinsdale Family Papers, Duke.

51. Ellen Devereux Hinsdale to Child, 23 March 1865, Hinsdale Family Papers, Duke.

52. George G. Young to Sister, 13 February 1865, Young Family Papers, Caroliniana. Also see Barrett, *Civil War in North Carolina,* 260; Wilkinson, *Narrative of a Blockade Runner,* 200–201.

53. For examples, see Cheesborough Notebook, Caroliniana; Mary Amarinthia Snowden Papers, Caroliniana.

54. Louise Medway to Jefferson Davis, 13 September 1864, Davis Papers, Duke.

55. William C. Honnoll to Decater Honnoll, 11 December 1863, Honnoll Family Correspondence, Emory.

56. Mary Gayle Aiken, 7 February 1865, Aiken Family Papers, Caroliniana.

57. John Peter Kendall to Sarah and D. J. Kendall, 18 July 1864, Kendall Papers, HEH.

58. Edmondston, 15 March 1865, *"Journal of a Secesh Lady,"* 678–79.

59. M. Gregg to Mary Snowden, 29 August 1864 and 9 September 1865, Mary Amarinthia Snowden Papers, Caroliniana. See *New York Times,* 9 December 1864 and 10 December 1864; Blackett, *Divided Hearts,* 184–85; Sirett and Williams, "Liverpool and the American Civil War," 113–29.

60. Excerpt from *Journal of the House of Representatives of the State of South Carolina,* 8 December 1864, Snowden Papers, Caroliniana.

61. William E. Martin to Mary Snowden [8 December 1864], Snowden Papers, Caroliniana.

62. Sallie E. White to Mary Snowden, 17 January 1865, Snowden Papers, Caroliniana.

63. Throughout the Civil War, Confederate women, like their Northern counterparts, held bazaars, concerts, and other fundraisers for the benefit of the Confederacy. Judging Southern fairs as only "emotionally and symbolically significant," Beverly Gordon minimizes the practical importance of what she labels Southern "ladies' fairs." Gordon, *Bazaars and Fair Ladies,* 96–99.

64. M Gregg to Mary Snowden, 8 November 1864, Snowden Papers, Caroliniana.

65. Sallie E. White to Mary Snowden, 17 January 1865, Snowden Papers, Caroliniana.

66. James Montgomery to Mary Snowden, 10 January 1865, Snowden Papers, Caroliniana. See also Annie B. Fuller to Catharine O. Barnwell, 2 February 1864, Barnwell Family Papers, SCHS.

67. "To the Friends of the Southern Cause at Home," 5 November 1864, Snowden Collection, Caroliniana. Also see "To the Friends of the Cause of the Confederate States," 31 May 1864, Snowden Papers, Caroliniana.

68. Adelaide L. Stuart to [?], 7 November 1864, Dimitry Papers, Duke.

69. LeConte, 18 January 1865, LeConte Diary, SHC. Also see Chesnut, 17 January 1865, *Mary Chesnut's Civil War,* 705.

70. Elmore, 7 February 1865, *Heritage of Woe,* 93.

71. S. C. Goodwyn to Artemus Darby Goodwyn, 22 January 1865, Goodwyn Papers, Caroliniana.

72. Elmore, 7 February 1865, *Heritage of Woe,* 93.

73. LeConte, 18 January 1865, LeConte Diary, SHC. Also see Elmore, 7 February 1865, *Heritage of Woe,* 94.

74. LeConte, 18 January 1865, LeConte Diary, SHC.

75. Faust, *Mothers of Invention,* 3–8.

76. Sallie Lawton to Johnnie, 22 January 1865, Willingham and Lawton Families Papers, Caroliniana.

77. Mary Gayle Aiken, 17 January 1865, Aiken Family Papers, SHC. Emma LeConte similarly noted that "our great Bazaar opened last night and *such* a jam!" LeConte, 18 January 1865, LeConte Diary, SHC.

78. LeConte, 18 January 1865, LeConte Diary, SHC. LeConte later recorded that "Columbia is thought in so much danger that the ladies closed the Bazaar on Friday." LeConte, 21 January 1865, LeConte Diary, SHC.

79. S. C. Goodwyn to Husband, 22 January 1865, Artemus Darby Goodwyn Papers, Caroliniana.

80. See Annie B. Fuller to Catharine O. Barnwell, 2 February 1865, Barnwell Family Papers, SCHS.

81. William T. Sherman to Ellen Sherman, 25 December 1864, *Home Letters,* 319–20.

4. CONFRONTING THE ENEMY

1. Heyward, 18 February 1865, *Confederate Lady Comes of Age,* 66.
2. Heyward, 18 February 1865, *Confederate Lady Comes of Age,* 69.

3. Heyward, 18 February 1865, *Confederate Lady Comes of Age*, 65–68. Other women felt similar outrage at the insult of having their undergarments taken or displayed. For examples, see Mary Maxcy Leverett to Milton Maxcy Leverett, 24 February 1865, in Taylor, ed., *Leverett Letters*, 385; Esther Alden [Elizabeth Allston], 4 March 1865, "*Our Women in the War,*" 359–60; Mary Sharpe Jones, 3 January 1865, Jones and Mallard, *Yankees a'Coming*, 65.

4. Kennett, *Marching through Georgia*, chap. 14, 288–307.

5. Countless books on Sherman and the Civil War in general emphasize this point. For example, Marszalek wrote that "when the Confederacy could not prevent a Union army from moving unimpeded through its heartland, destroying its railroads, taking its food and personal goods, freeing its slaves, terrorizing its people, and shaming its military establishment, its days were numbered." See Marszalek, *Sherman*, 315.

6. See Marszalek, *Sherman*, esp. 331–33.

7. Mitchell, *Vacant Chair*, 89–113. When they confronted Union soldiers verbally, Confederate women understood their actions as being within the confines of the female domain. For a discussion of women's traditional use of gossip and language as a form of power within the household and community, see Brown, *Good Wives, Nasty Wenches, and Anxious Patriarchs*, 99–100; Kamensky, *Governing the Tongue*; Wyatt-Brown, *Southern Honor*, 52, 347–48.

8. James E. Edmonds Diary, 16–20 November 1864, as quoted in Kennett, *Marching through Georgia*, 300.

9. Strong, *Yankee Private's Civil War*, 45. Strong found Confederate women's use of language so shocking that he recalled the confrontations vividly years later. Also see Edward W. Benham to Jennie, 19 February 1865, Benham Papers, Duke.

10. Mitchell argues that Southern "'she-devils' failed to meet the demands of true womanhood . . . [and] their passion and demonstrativeness in an era that valued passionlessness made them like prostitutes in northern eyes." In addition, "Confederate women should not be regarded as exemplars of domesticity and feminized virtue. Instead, they were she-devils . . . [whose] misuses of paramount feminine influence parodied the notion of woman's sphere." Mitchell, *Vacant Chair*, 91, 100.

11. In the antebellum South, poor white women routinely used violence to protect themselves. See Edwards, "Law, Domestic Violence, and the Limits of Patriarchal Authority," esp., 742–53.

12. See Mitchell, *Vacant Chair*, 102; Strong, *Yankee Private's Civil War*, 45; Glatthaar, *March to the Sea and Beyond*, 71. Also see Hight, 18 November 1864, *History of the Fifty-Eighth Regiment*, 416. Similar problems occurred in other invaded areas, especially in New Orleans, where women avoided Union soldiers on the streets, spit at the occupiers, mooned enemy men from balconies, wore pins to support the Confederacy, and hung rebel flags out of their windows. When one New Orleans woman dumped the contents of her chamber pot out the window and onto the head of United States Admiral David Farragut, Benjamin Butler issued his "Woman Order" in the hopes of bringing female Confederates under his control. For a discussion of women in occupied New Orleans, see Long, "(Mis) Remembering General Order No. 28," 17–32; Rable, "'Missing in Action,'" 139–44; Hearn, *When the Devil Came Down to Dixie*, 101–9; Campbell, "There Is No Difference between a He and a She Adder in Their Venom," 5–24.

13. Some women, but usually not those of the slaveholding class, disguised themselves as men to fight in the Confederate army. Although an accurate count is impossible, scholars estimate that hundreds of women fought for the Confederacy and the Union. See Blanton and Cook, *They Fought Like Demons*, 6–7.

14. "Speech of President Davis in Columbia," 4 October 1864, *Jefferson Davis, Constitutionalist*, 6:355. As Wyatt-Brown argues, "Women's expression of valor . . . was to be in the form of stoical acceptance of fate or, if their protectors were unavailable, fierce defense of hearth," *Southern Honor*, 234.

15. William T. Sherman to Ellen Sherman, 25 December 1864, *Home Letters*, 319–20.

16. Mother to Daughters, 8 March 1865, Heyward Papers, Caroliniana.

17. Loula to Poss, 22 May 1865, Graves Family Papers, SHC.

18. Anonymous Woman [Fayetteville], 22 March 1865, Emma Mordecai Diary, Mordecai Family Papers, SHC.

19. S. McCain to Daughter, 5 March 1865, Snowden Papers, Caroliniana. See also Elizabeth Collier, 20 April 1865, Elizabeth Collier Diary, SHC; [Laura?] to [?], 6 January 1865, Ferebee, Gregory, and McPherson Papers, SHC.

20. Mrs. E. A. Steele to Tody, 15 February 1865, in Jones, *When Sherman Came*, 135. Also see E. N. B. to Kate Taylor, 1 April 1865, Tennant Papers, Caroliniana; Elizabeth Palmer Porcher to Philip E. Porcher, 23 March 1865, in Towles, ed., *World Turned Upside Down*, 450; Sue Sample, 29 November 1864, in Jones, *When Sherman Came*, 47.

21. See Price, "'Such Are the Changes of Life.'"

22. Eliza Tillinghast to David R. Tillinghast, 3 May 1865, Tillinghast Family Papers, Duke. See also Caroline Gilman to Eliza [1865], "Letters of a Confederate Mother," 511.

23. Heyward, 18 February 1865, *Confederate Lady Comes of Age*, 65–68.

24. Heyward, 18 February 1865, *Confederate Lady Comes of Age*, 65–68.

25. Heyward, 18 February 1865, *Confederate Lady Comes of Age*, 65–68.

26. Strong, *Yankee Private's Civil War*, 62–63.

27. Burge, 19 November 1864, *Diary*, 159. See also Mary Noble to Lelia Montan, 20 November 1864, Noble Papers, SHC.

28. Eliza Tillinghast to David R. Tillinghast, 3 May 1865, Tillinghast Family Papers, Duke.

29. [Dorrie] Davis to Brother, 31 December 1865, Confederate Miscellany I, Emory.

30. On "imagined communities" built from shared experiences, see Anderson, *Imagined Communities*.

For opposing views of women's roles in the creation of Confederate nationalism, see Gallagher, *Confederate War*; Rubin, *A Shattered Nation*; Campbell, *When Sherman Marched North*; Faust, "Altars of Sacrifice," 114, and *Creation of Southern Nationalism*; McCardell, *Idea of a Southern Nation*; Potter, *South and the Sectional Conflict*, 34–83.

31. Burge, 19 November 1864, *Diary*, 161–62.

32. McClatchey, 15 November 1864, Diary of Minerva Leah Rowles McClatchey, 1864–1866, McClatchey Family Papers, 71–601, GDAH.

33. See Minutes of the Proceedings of the Greenville Ladies Association, Duke.

34. Jones, 7 January 1865, *Yankees a'Coming*, 73.

35. Sister R. to Iverson Louis Harris, [30 November 1864], Harris Collection, Duke. Jane E. Schultz asserts that the white women who confronted Sherman refrained from

verbal confrontations, but found outlets for their anger. "Mute Fury," 59–79. Perhaps this bias results from her selection of memoirs, reminiscences, and letters published many years after the march.

36. Ellis, 24 February 1865, Ellis Diary, Caroliniana.

37. Elmore, 26 November 1864, *Heritage of Woe*, 81–82. For examples of other women's fear of rape and threats of rape, see Edmondston, 11 July 1864, "*Journal of a Secesh Lady*," 587; LeConte, 10 March 1865, LeConte Diary, SHC; Sister A. to Willie, 11 April 1865, Southall and Bowen Family Papers, SHC; Mrs. W. K. Bachman to Kate Bachman, 27 March 1865, Bachman Papers, Caroliniana.

38. Sister R. to Iverson Louis Harris, [30 November 1864], Harris Collection, Duke.

39. Heyward, 18 February 1865, *Confederate Lady Comes of Age*, 69.

40. Mallard, 29 December 1864, Jones and Mallard, *Yankees a'Coming*, 63.

41. Louise Caroline Reese Cornwell Diary, [November 1864], in Jones, *When Sherman Came*, 22.

42. Mary Bull Maxcy Leverett to Caroline Pinckney Seabrook, 18 March 1865, Leverett Letter, Caroliniana.

43. Burge, 19 November 1864, *Diary*, 162.

44. Mallard, 19 December 1864, Jones and Mallard, *Yankees a'Coming*, 52.

45. Sister R. to Iverson Louis Harris, [30 November 1864], Harris Collection, Duke.

46. See Clinton, "'Southern Dishonor," 52–68; Stevenson, *Life In Black and White*, 138, 236–38; Schwalm, *Hard Fight for We*, 44–45.

47. Sue to Jane Ann Smythe, 14 April 1865, Adger, Smythe, Flynn Family Papers, Caroliniana.

48. S. McCain to Daughter, 7 March 1865, Snowden Papers, Caroliniana. Also see O. O. Howard to E. P. Blair, Jr., 10 January 1865, *OR*, Ser. 1, Vol. 47, Pt 2: 256; Bailey, *Chessboard of War*, 64; Weiner, *Mistresses and Slaves*, 186.

49. Brownmiller, *Against Our Will*, 88. Lowry came to a similar conclusion in *Stories the Soldiers Wouldn't Tell*, 123–131. However, in their work, E. Susan Barber and Charles F. Ritter have argued that soldiers committed sexual crimes against women of all classes and races. See Barber and Ritter, "'Physical Abuse . . . and Rough Handling,'" 49–64. See also Feimster, "General Benjamin Butler and the Threat of Sexual Violence during the American Civil War," 126–134, and "'How are the Daughters of Eve Punished?': Rape during the Civil War," 64–81.

50. Julia Frances Gott to Sister, 27 February 1865, Gott Collection, Caroliniana.

51. Loula to Poss, 22 May 1865, Graves Family Papers, SHC.

52. *Savannah Daily Morning News*, 6 December 1864.

53. Mary Baxter to Sallie Bird, [December 1864], in Rozier, ed., *Granite Farm Letters*, 223.

54. Cook, 17 November 1864, *Journal of a Milledgeville Girl*, 63. The editor noted an "attempt has been made to obliterate this name."

55. Early in the war, Mary Boykin Chesnut acknowledged her belief that Union soldiers would do anything. "Women can only stay at home, and every paper reminds us that women are to be violated, ravished, and all manner of humiliation." Chesnut, 29 August 1861, *Mary Chesnut's Civil War*, 172. See also Lavender R. Ray to Brother, 9 March 1865, Ray Letters and Diary, GDAH.

56. On the prosecution of sexual crimes by military courts, see Barber and Ritter, "'Physical Abuse ... and Rough Handling,'" 49–64.

57. Charles Brown Tomkins to Mollie Tomkins, 2 April 1865, Tomkins Papers, Duke. John "General Jack" Casement told a similar story. "One poor fellow was Shot the day I arrived here for Committing a Rape." John "General Jack" Casement to Francis Marion Jennings Casement, 2 April 1865, Casement Collection, HEH. Also see Esther Hill Hawks, [February 1864], *Woman Doctor's Civil War,* 61.

58. Hight, 17 November 1864, *History of the Fifty-Eighth Regiment of Indiana,* 416.

59. See Bailey, *Chessboard of War,* 65.

60. Charlotte St. Julien Ravenel to Meta Heyward, 8 April 1865, Charlotte St. Julien Ravenel Diary, Ravenel Family Papers, SCHS.

61. Jones, 17 January 1865, *Yankees a'Coming,* 81–82.

62. Mary Bull Maxcy Leverett to Caroline Pinckney Seabrook, 18 March 1865, Leverett Letter, Caroliniana. See also Esther Alden [Elizabeth Allston], 1 March 1865, *"Our Women in the War,"* 359; Mother to Gracia, 3 March 1865, Anonymous Mother to Daughter, Heyward Papers, Caroliniana.

63. Hitchcock, 17 November 1864, *Marching with Sherman,* 67.

64. Heyward, 18 February 1865, *Confederate Lady Comes of Age,* 66.

65. Heyward, 18 February 1865, *Confederate Lady Comes of Age,* 66–67.

66. Sister R. to Iverson Louis Harris, [30 November 1864], Harris Collection, Duke.

67. Sister R. to Iverson Louis Harris, [30 November 1864], Harris Collection, Duke.

68. LeConte, 26 February 1865, LeConte Diary, SHC.

69. In March she had a similar story to tell. "Mr Pope says all the Yankees he talked with concurred in unqualified admiration for the pluck and dignity of the Columbia women. Through all the frightful night they did not see a tear or hear one complaint and they did not think they could ever conquer the South if the men were animated by the same spirit as the women of South Carolina." LeConte, 18 March 1865, LeConte Diary, SHC.

70. Loula to Poss, 22 May 1865, Graves Family Papers, Caroliniana.

71. Loula to Poss, 22 May 1865, Graves Family Papers, Caroliniana; Howard, 21 January 1865, *In and Out of the Lines,* 196. See also Raleigh Spinks Camp to Sister, 10 October 1864, Camp Family Papers, Emory. For a discussion of mourning as female ritual, see Loughridge and Campbell, *Women and Mourning;* Kete, *Sentimental Collaborations;* Masson and Reveley, "When Life's Brief Sun Was Set," 32–56.

72. Jones, 17 January 1865, *Yankees a'Coming,* 81.

73. Nichols, *Story of the Great March,* 21–22.

74. Howard, 25 December 1864 and 27 December 1864, *In and Out of the Lines,* 191. See also Catherine (Kate) Douglas DeRossett Meares to Mother, 28 March 1865, DeRossett Family Papers, SHC.

75. Holmes, 4 March 1865, *Diary,* 402.

76. Harriott Middleton to Susan Middleton, 2 March 1865, "Middleton Correspondence, 1861–1865," 103. Also see Marrie to Sallie Lawton, 15 April 1865, Willingham and Lawton Families Papers, Caroliniana.

77. Ellen Devereux Hinsdale to Child, 23 March 1865, Hinsdale Family Papers, Duke. Also see Sue Sample, 29 November 1864, in *When Sherman Came,* 48.

78. Hitchcock, 25 November 1864, *Marching with Sherman*, 92.
79. Holmes, 4 March 1865, *Diary*, 402.
80. Harriott Middleton to Susan Middleton, 2 March 1865, "Middleton Correspondence," 103–4.
81. This sixty-day reference echoes the early boasts of Union supporters that they would subdue the South quickly. McPherson, *Battle Cry*, 333.
82. Burge, 19 November 1864, *Diary*, 160–61. Other Southerners similarly criticized the Union as hypocritical in its treatment of slaves. For examples, see Jones, 3 January 1865 and 5 January 1865, *Yankees a'Coming*, 65, 68; Martha Battey to Robert Battey, 17 November 1865, Battey Papers, Emory; Sue to Jane Ann Smythe, 14 April 1865, Adger, Smythe, Flynn Family Papers, Caroliniana.
83. Jones, 3 January 1865 and 5 January 1865, *Yankees a'Coming*, 65, 68.
84. See Penningroth, "Slavery, Freedom, and Social Claims," 405–36. Major General Oliver O. Howard worried about the Union mistreatment of slaves. "Many depredations ... would disgrace us even in the enemies country, e.g. the robbing of some negroes and abusing their women." O. O. Howard to E. P. Blair, Jr., 10 January 1865, *OR*, Ser. 1, Vol. 47, pt 2: 256.
85. LeConte, 18 February 1865, LeConte Diary, SHC. For a similar episode, see Nellie Worth to Cousin, 21 March 1865, North Carolina Collection, SHC. Another woman recorded a Union soldier's taunts. "The Yankees [told] Mrs Notts that their present treatment of the rebels, entitled them to a seat in Heaven, & that each rebels killed was a sure passport thither." Marrie to Sallie Lawton, 15 April 1865, Willingham and Lawton Families Papers, Caroliniana. Union Major Henry Hitchcock recorded a similar plea against war on "helpless women." When he confronted a Confederate woman of "eighteen or nineteen, [and a] good rebel, [she] was quite sharp on us." This woman criticized Union tactics, asserting that they "'had no right to punish helpless women who had never done anything, etc., etc.'" Hitchcock, 25 November 1864, *Marching with Sherman*, 92.
86. Confederate women maintained their belief that the Union soldiers would not shoot a woman. Before the soldiers arrived, Carolina Ravenel told a friend that such tactics "'tis only done to alarm." Caroline R. Ravenel to Isabell Middleton Smith, 31 March 1865, in *Mason Smith Family Letters*, 187.
87. Mary Bull Maxcy Leverett to Caroline Pinckney Seabrook, 18 March 1865, Leverett Letter, Caroliniana.
88. Mary Maxcy Leverett to Milton Leverett, 24 February [1865], in Taylor, ed., *Leverett Letters*, 387.
89. Anonymous woman [Fayetteville, NC], 22 March 1865, Emma Mordecai Diary, Mordecai Family Papers, SHC.

5. ASSERTING CONFEDERATE WOMANHOOD

1. Rogers, 17 November 1864, Rogers Papers, Emory.
2. Rogers, 11 May 1865, Rogers Papers, Emory.
3. Rogers, 18 April 1865, Rogers Papers, Emory.

4. Rogers, 30 April 1865, Rogers Papers, Emory.

5. Rogers, 11 May 1865, Rogers Papers, Emory.

6. Rogers, 30 April 1865, Rogers Papers, Emory.

7. Holmes, 22 April 1865, *Diary*, 436–37. Blair found similar reactions to confrontations with Union soldiers by Virginia women. Blair, *Virginia's Private War*, esp. 56, 78, 143–44.

8. On the importance of kin connections in the South, see Friedman, *Enclosed Garden*; Wyatt-Brown, *Southern Honor*, esp. 117–48; Bardaglio, *Reconstructing the Household*; Rose, *Victorian America*, 145–92; Cashin, "Structure of Antebellum Families," 55–70.

9. Like their male counterparts, few Southern women had a unified conception of "the South" when the war began. Instead, most saw their state as one of their defining markers of identity before nation or region. However, as the secession crisis intensified and regional issues came to the forefront, Southerners began to rally together against what they saw as Northern colonialism. For example, see Thomas, *Confederate Nation*, 19; O'Leary, *To Die For*, 11.

10. Mary Ann Cobb to Howell Cobb, 28 June 1864, in Coleman, ed., *Athens, 1861–1865*, 93.

11. Faust also writes that "the Confederacy did not endure longer.... because so many women did not want it to." Faust, "Altars of Sacrifice," 139–40. Rable, *Civil Wars*, x. Also see Faust, *Mothers of Invention*. Most recent military historians do not accept the idea that women lost the war for the Confederacy. For example, see Gallagher, *Confederate War*, esp. 24; Campbell, *When Sherman Marched North*.

12. Faust, *Mothers of Invention*; Faust, "Altars of Sacrifice," 113–40; Rable, *Civil Wars*; McCurry, *Confederate Reckoning*. See also Edwards, *Scarlett Doesn't Live Here Anymore*, 82–83; Bryant, *How Curious a Land*, 82–83. See also Stiehm, "The Protected, the Protector, the Defender," 367–76, esp. 374; Huston, "Tales of War and Tears of Women," 271–83.

Faust suggests that this reaction resulted from a feminine aversion to war, asserting that "the erosion of women's patriotism simply represented a reversion to conventional female concerns, an almost reactionary reassertion of the private and domestic and a rejection of the more public and political burdens women had been urged to assume." Faust, *Mothers of Invention*, 242. In many ways Faust's conclusions seem to be a backlash against feminist scholars, such as Anne Firor Scott, who painted women's roles in the Civil War as a liberating step toward the feminist movement. Instead, Faust emphasizes Southern women's desires—during and after the Civil War—to return to the traditionally female domestic sphere. Faust emphasizes how women's difficulties in carrying out men's roles inspired in them a longing for a world of the past. For the classic study of the Civil War as a revolutionary experience for Southern women, see Scott, *Southern Lady*.

13. The editor of the Georgia *Countryman* came to this conclusion in January 1865. "Those of us who have suffered can hardly be expected to love our tormentors, and persecutors, and we can hardly be expected to look with much favor upon anything that has the remotest resemblance to reunion with the Yankees." Joseph Addison Turner, 10 January 1865, "A Bitter Draught We Had to Quaff," 326.

14. Elliot Welch to Mother, 20 March 1865, Welch Papers, Duke. Historians have agreed. For examples, see Blair, *Virginia's Private War*, 6, 143; McPherson, *What They Fought For*, 18; Jimerson, *Private Civil War*, 165–69.

15. Mary Ann Cobb to Howell Cobb, 28 June 1864, in Coleman, ed., *Athens, 1861–1865*, 93.

16. For discussions of renewed dedication to the Southern cause in the face of adversity, see Blair, *Virginia's Private War*; Gallagher, *Confederate War*; Campbell, *When Sherman Marched North*; Frank, "War Comes Home."

17. Ellen Devereux Hinsdale to Child, 23 March 1865, Hinsdale Family Papers, Duke. After a lengthy description of the destruction by the Union soldiers and her reactions to it, Hinsdale felt she had not done the events justice. The litany of destruction could continue indefinitely, but Hinsdale had more pressing issues to attend to. "I could fill many sheets with their doings but have not time."

Many Confederate women voiced a frustration with their status as females. A large number of them wrote of their desire to be men so that they could fight. Others disguised themselves as men and enlisted. For examples of women wishing to be men, see Holmes, 21 November 1864, *Diary*, 323; Elmore, 21 February 1865, *Heritage of Woe*, 102; Morgan, 23 January 1863, *Sarah Morgan*, 411; Alice Ready, 13 April 1862 and 19 April 1862, Ready Diary, SHC; Catherine Barnes Rowland, 3 January 1865, as quoted in Whites, *Civil War as a Crisis in Gender*, 106.

18. For more information on Sherman's tenure in Savannah, see Marszalek, *Sherman*, 309–18; Kennett, *Marching through Georgia*, 308–9.

19. Cohen, 26 December 1864, "Fanny Cohen's Journal," 413, emphasis added.

20. Howard, 21 January 1865, *In and Out of the Lines*, 196.

21. LeConte, 19 February 1865, LeConte Diary, SHC.

22. LeConte, 17 February 1865, LeConte Diary, SHC.

23. Ellen Mordecai to Emma Mordecai [1865], Mordecai Family Papers, SHC.

24. Burge, 20 November 1864, *Diary*, 162.

25. Margaret Dailey, 12 January 1865, Confederate Miscellany I, Emory.

26. Sister R to Iverson Louis Harris, Jr., 1 December 1864, Harris Collection, Duke. For a similar statement made by a Confederate man, see Melvin Dwinell to Albert Dwinell, 30 September 1865, in "Vermonter in Gray," 229.

27. Jill Lepore states that during warfare, "the fundamental differences [between warring societies] are brought into sharp relief. Warring societies may even exaggerate their differences to make the killing easier; the more foreign the enemy, the better." By creating these differences, Confederate women may have found it easier to hate the enemy. Lepore, *Name of War*, 113–14.

28. LeConte, 21 February 1865, LeConte Diary, SHC.

29. Elmore, 4 March 1865, *Heritage of Woe*, 108.

30. LeConte, 23 February 1865, LeConte Diary, SHC.

31. Elmore, 21 February 1865, *Heritage of Woe*, 102.

32. LeConte, 26 February 1865, LeConte Diary, SHC.

33. Harriott Middleton to Susan Middleton, 10 March 1865, Susan and Harriott Middleton Correspondence, Cheves-Middleton Papers, SCHS.

34. Andrews, 17 April 1865, *War-Time Journal of a Georgia Girl*, 149.

35. Harriott Middleton to Susan Middleton, 21 March 1865, Susan and Harriott Middleton Correspondence, Cheves-Middleton Papers, SCHS.

36. Nellie Worth to Cousin, 21 March 1865, North Carolina Collection, SHC.

37. Elmore, 21 February 1865, *Heritage of Woe*, 103.

38. Janie Smith to Janie Robeson, 12 April, 1865, Lenoir Family Papers, SHC. Emma LeConte voiced a similar demand for vengeance. "I wonder if the vengeance of heaven will not pursue such fiends! Before they came here, I thought I hated them as much as was possible—now I know there are no limits to the feeling of hatred." LeConte Diary, 21 February 1865, SHC. See also Martha Caroline Marshal to Brother, 6 December 1864, Walraven Family Papers, AHC.

39. Catherine Barnes Rowland, 3 January 1865, as quoted in Whites, *Civil War as a Crisis in Gender*, 105–6.

40. Andrews, 21 April 1865, *War-Time Journal of a Georgia Girl*, 172.

41. Loula to Poss, 22 May 1865, Graves Family Papers, SHC.

42. Joe Varner, 24 November 1864, Sanders Collection, GDAH.

43. Esther Alden [Elizabeth Allston], 6 March 1865, Esther Alden Diary, *"Our Women in the War,"* 360.

44. Annie B. Fuller to Catharine O. Barnwell, 20 February 1865, Barnwell Family Papers, SCHS.

45. Cook, 19 November 1864, *Journal of a Milledgeville Girl*, 63.

46. Elmore, 21 February 1865, *Heritage of Woe*, 103.

47. Mary Maxcy Leverett to Milton, 24 February 1865, *Leverett Letters*, 384.

48. Mrs. W. H. Stiles to William Stiles, 2 March 1865, Mackay-Stiles Papers, SHC.

49. A. E. D. to Brother, 6 December 1864, Confederate Miscellany I, Emory. LeConte echoed these sentiments. LeConte, 21 February 1865, LeConte Diary, SHC.

50. Ellen Devereux Hinsdale to Child, 23 March 1865, Hinsdale Family Papers, Duke.

51. Nellie Worth to Cousin, 21 March 1865, North Carolina Collection, SHC. Also see Mary Noble to Lelia Montan, 20 November 1864, Noble Papers, SHC.

52. Sue Thermutis Montgomery to Moultrie Reid Wilson, 23 February 1865, Wilson Papers, Caroliniana.

53. Mrs. Alston Pringle to Mrs. William Mason Smith, 30 March 1865, *Mason Smith Family Letters*, 186. See also Mrs. William McKenzie Parker to Mrs. William Mason Smith, 30 March 1865, *Mason Smith Family Letters*, 183.

54. Lily Logan to Thomas M. Logan, 2 March 1865, *My Confederate Girlhood*, 80–81.

55. Fiction reflected the persistence of Confederate womanhood, especially William Faulkner's *The Unvanquished*. Faulkner's Bayard Sartoris observes that after the Civil War ended "the men had given in and admitted that they belonged to the United States but the women had never surrendered." Faulkner, *Unvanquished*, 188.

56. Bradley, *Star Corps*, 186.

57. LeConte, 20 April 1865, LeConte Diary, SHC.

58. Holmes, 22 April 1865, *Diary*, 436. See also William M. Post to Mary Snowden, 17 June 1865, Snowden Papers, Caroliniana; Susan Cornwall, 22 August 1865, Cornwall Journal, SHC.

59. Charlotte Burckmyer to Cornelius Burckmyer, 13 April 1865, in Holmes, ed., *Burckmyer Letters*, 473.

NOTES TO PAGES 136-142

60. Mrs. W. H. Stiles of Milledgeville voiced frustrations with the shortages faced by Confederate troops. "Had our army half their implements the tale would be very different." Mrs. W. H. Stiles to William Stiles, 2 March 1865, Mackay-Stiles Papers, SHC.

61. When stating, "The South is *not whipped*," Tillinghast underlined "not" four times to further emphasize her confidence in the Confederacy and Southern people. Eliza Tillinghast to David R. Tillinghast, 3 May 1865, Tillinghast Family Papers, Duke.

62. Collier, 20 April 1865, Collier Diary, SHC.

63. Eliza Tillinghast to David R. Tillinghast, 3 May 1865, Tillinghast Family Papers, Duke.

64. Mollie Cunningham to George A. Cunningham, 16 January 1865, Cunningham Family Papers, UGA.

65. On gender's role in the Lost Cause tradition, see Cox, *Dixie's Daughters*, 3.

66. LeConte, 20 April 1865, LeConte Diary, SHC. Also see Pellona Alexander to Manning Alexander, 24 April 1865, Alexander Letters, UGA.

67. Holmes, 22 April 1865, *Diary*, 436-37. On postwar tensions between the North and South, see Silber, *Romance of Reunion*.

68. Rogers, 11 May 1865, Rogers Papers, Emory.

69. Edmondston, 16 April 1865, *"Journal of a Secesh Lady,"* 696.

70. Eliza Tillinghast to David R. Tillinghast, 3 May 1865, Tillinghast Family Papers, Duke.

71. Rogers, 11 May 1865, Rogers Papers, Emory.

72. LeConte, 20 April 1865, LeConte Diary, SHC. Women in other parts of the Confederacy had similar reactions to the news of surrender. For example, Louisianan Kate Stone wrote that "most seem to think it useless to struggle longer, now that we are subjugated. I say, 'Never, never, though we perish in the track of their endeavor!'" Later, she continued in this tone: "it would be better for us to resist as long as there is a man left to load a gun." Stone, 28 April 1865 and 20 May 1865, *Brokenburn*, 334, 342.

73. Eliza Tillinghast to David R. Tillinghast, 3 May 1865, Tillinghast Family Papers, Duke.

74. Rogers, 11 May 1865, Rogers Papers, Emory.

75. Cook, 1 May 1865, *Journal of a Milledgeville Girl*, 74. See also Jorantha Semmes to Benedict J. Semmes, 3 November 1864, Semmes Papers, SHC.

76. LeConte, [20 April 1865], LeConte Diary, SHC.

77. Eliza Tillinghast to David R. Tillinghast, 3 May 1865, Tillinghast Family Papers, Duke.

78. Cook, 1 May 1865, *Journal of a Milledgeville Girl*, 74. On the disappointment of surrender and the uncertainty that would follow, see also Carrie Fries Shaffner, 17 April [1865], Carrie Shaffner Journal, Fries and Shaffner Family Papers, SHC; Minerva McClatchey, April [1865], Diary of Minerva Leah Rowles McClatchey, McClatchey Family Papers, GDAH; Sabina Elliott Wells to Mrs. Thomas L. Wells, 10 April [1865], *Mason Smith Family Letters*, 194.

79. Elizabeth Collier Diary, 25 April 1865, Collier Papers, SHC.

80. LeConte, 28 May 1865, LeConte Diary, SHC.

81. Eliza Tillinghast to David R. Tillinghast, 3 May 1865, Tillinghast Family Papers, Duke. Southerners did not necessarily concoct the stories of Sherman's threats of further devastation. Union soldiers overheard Sherman declare to a Methodist preacher on the

March to the Sea that "there is a class of persons at the South who must be exterminated before there can be peace in the land." Nichols, *Story of the Great March,* 119. Union lieutenant George Wise reported that in Cheraw Sherman asserted that "when the rebels took Sumpter, an army ought to have been sent against Charleston and every building burned & leveled to the ground, more than this I would have killed every man[,] woman & child found in it." In addition, Sherman asserted that "this people [of South Carolina] are possessed with devils & when we fight the devil we must fight him with fire." Wise, "Marching through South Carolina," 194.

82. Harriet R. Palmer Diary, 3 May 1865, *World Turned Upside Down,* 474.

83. Charlotte St. Julien Ravenel to Meta Heyward, 22 April 1865, in Jervey and Ravenel, *Two Diaries,* 45.

84. LeConte, 22 April 1865, LeConte Diary, SHC.

85. Rogers, 30 April 1865, Rogers Papers, Emory.

86. Cumming, 7 May 1865, *Kate,* 283.

87. LeConte, 22 April 1865, LeConte Diary, SHC.

88. LeConte, 22 April 1865, LeConte Diary, SHC.

89. Holmes, [end of May 1865], *Diary,* 443–44.

90. Rogers, 11 May 1865, Rogers Papers, Emory. Other took solace from the revolutionary struggles and believed that the fight could still be won. Writing from "Where Home Use to Be" Janie Smith recognized that "our political sky does seem darkened by a fearful cloud; but when compared with the situation of our fore-fathers, I can but take courage." Janie Smith to Janie Robeson, 12 April 1865, Lenoir Family Papers, SHC.

91. Loula to Poss, 22 May 1865, Graves Family Papers, Caroliniana.

92. E[llen] [Maria] R[avenel] to R[osa] M. Pringle, 23 April 1865, E[llen] [Maria] R[avenel] Letter, Caroliniana.

93. Edmondston, 26 June 1865, *"Journal of a Secesh Lady,"* 714.

94. Ellen Mordecai to Emma Mordecai, [1865], Mordecai Family Papers, SHC.

95. LeConte, 23 April 1865, LeConte Diary, SHC.

96. Loula to Poss, 22 May 1865, Graves Family Papers, Caroliniana.

97. Andrews, 7 May 1865, *War-Time Journal of a Georgia Girl,* 228.

98. Rogers, 13 May 1865, Rogers Papers, Emory.

99. Mrs. William Mason Smith [Eliza Huger Smith] to Daughters, [November–December 1864], *Mason Smith Family Letters,* 150. See also Edmondston, 26 June 1865, *"Journal of a Secesh Lady,"* 714.

100. Sue to Jane Ann Smythe, 29 April 1865, Adger, Smythe, Flynn Family Papers, Caroliniana.

101. Foster noted that "women who right after the war had displayed greater hatred than men for the Yankees who had exposed their vulnerability and denied them respect apparently not only continued to harbor their resentments but passed them on to their daughters. Especially for them, but for all Daughters, the preservation and promulgation of the southern view of the war became and remained their goal and passion." Foster, *Ghosts of the Confederacy,* 172. Also see Cox, *Dixie's Daughters.*

102. Julia to Friend, 26 September 1865, Graves Family Papers, Caroliniana.

103. Loula to Fannie, 6 June 1865, Graves Family Papers, Caroliniana.

104. Elmore, 9 September 1868, *Heritage of Woe*, 176.
105. Rogers, 11 May 1865, Rogers Papers, Emory.
106. LeConte, 22 April 1865, LeConte Diary, SHC.
107. On women's continued support of the Confederacy in the postwar era, see Janney, *Burying the Dead*, and *Remembering the Civil War*; Cox, *Dixie's Daughters*.

EPILOGUE: SHAMING SOUTHERN SOLDIERS

1. Samuel Wiley to Eliza DeWitt Wiley, 26 November 1864, Rozier, ed., *Granite Farm Letters*, 214–15.
2. Samuel Wiley to Eliza DeWitt Wiley, 26 November 1864, Rozier, ed., *Granite Farm Letters*, 214–15.
3. William T. Sherman to Ellen Sherman, 23 March 1865, 829. (Comments about working at the sanitary fair are in the same letter.)
4. John Alfred Feister Coleman, 21 [February 1865], Confederate Miscellany I, Emory.
5. Turner, 10 January 1865, "'A Bitter Draught We Had to Quaff,'" 326.
6. Floyd King to Lin Capterton, 21 January 1865, King Papers, SHC.
7. Cash, *Mind of the South*, 86. Rotundo, *American Manhood*, and "Body and Soul," 23–38; Carnes, *Secret Ritual and Manhood*; Cott, "On Men's History and Women's History," 205–11; Glover, *Southern Sons*, 182–83; Tosh, *Man's Place*; Wyatt-Brown, *A Warring Nation*. On the Civil War creating for Southern white men a "crisis in their understanding of their manhood," see Whites, *Civil War as a Crisis in Gender* (quotation, 9); Silber, *Romance of Reunion*. McPherson notes that "for many Confederate soldiers [the concept of Southern nationalism] took a concrete, visceral form: the defense of home and heart against an invading enemy. This purpose in turn became transformed for many southern soldiers into hatred and a desire for revenge." McPherson, *What They Fought For*, 18. See Wyatt-Brown, *Southern Honor*.
8. Samuel Hoey Walkup, 6 March 1865, Walkup Diary, Duke.
9. J. M. Sharp to Eliza Sharp, 9 August 1864, Confederate Miscellany I, Emory.
10. J. M. Sharp to Eliza Sharp, 9 August 1864, Confederate Miscellany I, Emory.
11. J. M. Sharp to Eliza Sharp, 16 August 1864, Confederate Miscellany I, Emory.
12. J. M. Sharp to Eliza Sharp, 16 August 1864, Confederate Miscellany I, Emory.
13. J. M. Sharp to Eliza Sharp, 11 September 1864, Confederate Miscellany I, Emory.
14. J. M. Sharp to Eliza Sharp, 24 January 1865, Confederate Miscellany I, Emory.
15. J. M. Sharp to Eliza Sharp, 24 January 1865, Confederate Miscellany I, Emory.
16. Harry Hammond to Emily Hammond, 27 November 1864, Hammond, Bryan, and Cumming Families Papers, Caroliniana.
17. Harry Hammond to Emily Hammond, 14 February [1865], Hammond, Bryan, and Cumming Families Papers, Caroliniana.
18. Frank Coker to Wife, 26 November 1864, in Lane, ed., *"Dear Mother,"* 336–37. For other examples, see Harry Hammond to Emily C. Hammond, 5 August 1864 and 8 October 1864, Hammond, Bryan, and Cumming Families Papers, Caroliniana; Marion Hill Fitzpatrick to Amanda White Fitzpatrick, 8 December 1864, *Letters to Amanda*, 187; William M. Murray

to Mrs. John Jenkins, 31 December 1864, John Jenkins Papers, Caroliniana; Edward McCrady Jr. to Edward McCrady, 5 January 1865, McCrady Family Papers, Caroliniana; W. A. Clarkson to Mrs. Campbell R. Bryce, 18 March 1865, Bryce Family Papers, Caroliniana; John A. Taylor to Kate Taylor, 22 March 1865, Tennent, Caroliniana.

19. [Duncan Alexander Buie] to Kate McGeachy, 9 April 1865, Buie Papers, Duke.

20. Tom to Sister, 17 September 1864, Bomar Family Papers, Emory.

21. John Alfred Feister Coleman, 4 March 1865, Confederate Miscellany I, Emory. Also see John Alfred Feister Coleman, 28 February 1865, Confederate Miscellany I, Emory.

22. John Alfred Feister Coleman, 1 March 1865, Confederate Miscellany I, Emory. On desertion from the Confederate ranks, see Doyle, "Understanding the Desertion of South Carolinian Soldiers," 657–79; Weitz, *More Damning than Slaughter,* and *A Higher Duty.*

23. B. F. Mason to Mrs. Turner Mason, 4 January 1865, Mason Civil War Letter, GDAH.

24. John Jenkins to Wife, 15 December 1864, John Jenkins Papers, Caroliniana.

25. Felix Prior to Nancy Prior, 10 August 1864, Prior Civil War Letters, GDAH.

26. Felix Prior to Nancy Prior, 23 November 1864, Prior Civil War Letters, GDAH.

27. John Craig Evans to Annie Evans, 18 January 1865, "War Letters of John Craig Evans," United Daughters of the Confederacy Papers, Emory.

28. John Craig Evans to Annie Evans, [6 March 1865], "War Letters of John Craig Evans," United Daughters of the Confederacy Papers, Emory. Also see John Craig Evans to Annie Evans, 20 January 1865, 5 March 1865, and 7 March 1865, "War Letters of John Craig Evans," United Daughters of the Confederacy Papers, Emory.

29. William Chunn to Mother, 11 September 1864, William Augustus Chunn Letters, Emory.

30. Reverend John Jones to Mary Jones, 23 September 1864, *Children of Pride,* 1203.

31. H. T. Howard to Wife, 11 August 1864, Civil War Miscellaneous Correspondence, 3–2728, GDAH. Also see John Bratton to Bettie Bratton, 17 February 1865, Confederate War Letters of Dr. John Bratton, SCDAH; Henry Lea Graves to Sarah Dutton Graves, 5 September 1864, Graves Family Papers, SHC; John H. Boyce to Mother, 4 August 1864, Civil War Miscellaneous Correspondence, 3–2717, GDAH; R. L. Burn to Mother, 16 February 1865, Burn Family Papers, Caroliniana.

32. Edgeworth Bird to Sallie Bird, 3 September 1864, Rozier, ed., *Granite Farm Letters,* 196.

33. Edgeworth Bird to Sallie Bird, 22 September 1864, Rozier, ed., *Granite Farm Letters,* 203.

34. Sallie Bird to Sallie (Saida) Bird, 21 November 1864, Rozier, ed., *Granite Farm Letters,* 208.

35. Edward Spann Hammond to Harry Hammond, 13 November 1864, *The Hammonds of Redcliffe,* 129.

36. Tom Hightower to Lou, 28 November 1864, *"Dear Mother,"* 337–38.

37. John Alfred Feister Coleman, 13 March 1865, Confederate Miscellany I, Emory.

38. John Craig Evans to Annie Evans, 16 March 1865, "War Letters of John Craig Evans," United Daughters of the Confederacy Papers, Emory.

39. Felix W. Prior to Nancy Prior, 23 November 1864, Felix W. Prior Civil War Letters, GDAH.

40. Harry Hammond to Emily Hammond, 5 August 1864, Hammond, Bryan, and Cumming Families Papers, Caroliniana.

41. Harry Hammond to Emily Hammond, 27 March 1865, Hammond, Bryan, and Cumming Families Papers, Caroliniana.

42. *Augusta Register,* 6 December 1864.

43. Andrew Gordon Magrath [1865], "The Governor of the State, To the People of South Carolina," Magrath Papers, SCDAH, emphasis added.

44. As historian Bertram Wyatt-Brown has noted, in this type of situation, "the intensity of feeling arose from the social fact that a male's moral bearing resided not in him alone, but also in his women's standing. To attack his wife, mother, or sister was to assault the man himself." Wyatt-Brown, *Southern Honor,* 53.

45. Robert Hill to His Sister, 8 January 1865, as quoted in Kennett, *Marching through Georgia,* 313.

46. Thomas Caffey to Sister, 15 January 1865, as cited in Wiley, *Life of Johnny Reb,* 134.

47. Alexander Couper to Floyd King, 27 December 1864, King Papers, SHC.

48. Iverson Dutton "Dutt" Graves to Sarah Dutton Graves, 27 January 1865, Graves Family Papers, SHC.

49. H. L. Bebow to Clara Dargan, 3 March 1865, Maclean Papers, Duke.

50. Wyatt-Brown, *Southern Honor,* 53. Also see Wyatt-Brown, *Shaping of Southern Culture,* 255–69.

51. C. F. Holst to Isabella Ann Woodruff, 11 March 1865, Woodruff Papers, Duke.

52. Raleigh Spinks Camp to Sister, 10 October 1864, Camp Family Papers, Emory.

53. Harry Hammond to Emily Hammond, 12 September 1864, Hammond, Bryan, and Cumming Families Papers, Caroliniana.

54. Henry Lea Graves to Sarah Dutton Graves, 28 December 1864, Graves Family Papers, SHC.

55. G. Dunbar to Cousin, 14 January 1865, Baber-Blackshear Papers, UGA.

56. W. A. Clarkson to Mrs. Campbell R. Bryce, 18 March 1865, Bryce Family Papers, Caroliniana.

57. Emile Sternberg to Clara Dargan, 19 June 1865, Clara Victoria (Dargan) Maclean Papers, Duke.

58. *Augusta Daily Constitutionalist,* 27 January 1865. As quoted in Whites, *Civil War as a Crisis in Gender,* 110.

59. William T. Sherman to James M. Calhoun, Mayor, E. E. Rawson, and S. C. Wells, 12 September 1865, *Hero's Own Story,* 60.

BIBLIOGRAPHY

MANUSCRIPTS

Atlanta History Center Archives, Atlanta, Georgia.
    Civil War Letters.
    Rawson-Collier-Harris Papers.
    Walraven Family Papers.

Duke University Library, David M. Rubenstein Rare Book and Manuscript Library, Durham, North Carolina.
    Benham, Edward W. Papers.
    Brown, Charles S. Papers.
    Buie, Catherine Jane (McGeachy). Papers.
    Davis, Jefferson. Papers.
    Dimitry, John B. S. Papers.
    Harden Family Papers.
    Harris, Iverson L. Collection.
    Herr, John. Papers.
    Hinsdale Family Papers.
    Hoadley, R. B. Papers.
    Maclean, Clara Victoria (Dargan). Papers.
    McBride, Andrew Jay. Papers.
    McIntosh, Thomas M. Papers.
    Minutes of the Proceedings of the Greenville Ladies Association.
    Smith, Joseph Belknap. Papers.
    Thomas, Ella Gertrude Clanton. Papers.
    Tillinghast Family Papers.
    Tomkins, Charles Brown. Papers.
    United Daughters of the Confederacy, South Carolina Division, Edgefield Chapter Papers.
    Van Duzer, John C. Diary.

Walkup, Samuel Hoey. Diary.
Welch, Elliot Stephen. Papers.
Woodruff, Isabellana Roberts. Papers, 1768–1865.

Emory University, Special Collections Department, Robert W. Woodruff Library, Atlanta, Georgia.
    Battey, Robert. Papers.
    Baurdick, Anthony J. Papers.
    Beauregard, Pierre Gustave Toutant. Papers.
    Bomar Family Papers.
    Camp Family Papers.
    Champion, Sidney S. Papers.
    Chunn, William Augustus. Letters.
    Confederate Miscellany I.
    Honnoll Family Correspondence.
    Rogers, Loula Kendall. Papers.
    Taylor, Thomas T. Collection.
    United Daughters of the Confederacy, Alfred Holt Colquitt Chapter.
    Wiley, Bell Irvin. Files.

Georgia Department of Archives and History, Atlanta.
    Akin, Warren. Civil War Letters.
    Civil War Miscellaneous Correspondence, Georgia Microfilm Record Group 3-2728.
    Fletcher, Louisa Warren Patch (Mrs. Dix). Journal.
    Lamar, Charles Augustus Lafayette. Family Papers.
    Mason, B. F. Civil War Letter.
    McClatchey Family Papers.
    Minutes of Greenville, Georgia Soldiers' Aid Society, United Daughters of the Confederacy, LaGrange Chapter.
    Prior, Felix W. Civil War Letters.
    Ray, Lieut. Lavender R. Letters and Diary, 1861–65, Typescript, Georgia Department of Archives and History, Atlanta.
    Sanders, Birdie Varner. Collection.
    Wilson Family Papers.

Georgia Historical Society, Savannah.
    Everett, J. H. Papers.
    Habersham, Leila [Elliott]. Paper, 1861–62.
    Lawrence, Alexander A. Papers.

Lawton Protectors. Paper, 1864.
United Daughters of the Confederacy Colquitt Chapter Papers.
Walker, Mattie Jane. Paper, 1858–62.
Wray, Henry and Drucilla. Paper.

Henry E. Huntington Library and Art Gallery, San Marino, California.
Bowen Papers.
Casement Collection.
Daniels, Sylvester Diary. Typescript.
Kendall, William Devereux. Papers.
Leath, James. A Journal of Movements & Incidents of the 3rd Brig, 4th Div, 15th A.C. During the March from Rome to Savannah Georgia, Commencing November 10th 1864 and ending December 23, 1864.
Lieber Papers.
Sherman File.
Sherman, Ellen Boyle Ewing. Collection.
Simkins, Eldred J. Collection.
Van Deusen, Delos. Papers.

Library of Congress, Washington, D.C.
Cater, Douglas J. and Rufus W. Papers.
Cotton, J. Dexter. Papers.
Hitchcock, Henry. Collection.
Mordecai, Alfred. Papers.
Phillips, Eugenia. "Journal of Mrs. Eugenia Phillips Wife of Philip Phillips of the City of Washington, Counselor at Law," 23 August 1861–26 September 1861.

North Carolina Department of Archives and History, Raleigh.
Myers, Thomas J. Letter.

South Carolina Department of Archives and History, Columbia.
Bratton, Dr. John. Confederate War Letters.
Magrath, Governor Andrew. Papers.

South Carolina Historical Society, Charleston.
Barnwell Family Papers.
Cheves-Middleton Papers.
Ford, Tho[mas] R. Letter.
Lining, Susan Bowen. Letter.

BIBLIOGRAPHY

Ravenel Family Papers, 1828–1937.
Teague, Benjamin H. Papers, 1846–1921.

South Caroliniana Library, University of South Carolina, Columbia.
Adger, Smythe, Flynn. Family Papers.
Aiken Family Papers.
Bachman Family Papers.
Bryce Family Papers.
Burn Family Papers.
Cheesborough, Esther B. Notebook.
Ellis, Mrs. Emily Caroline. Diary.
Ford, Thomas. Letter.
Gilman, Caroline Howard. Collection.
Goodwyn, Artemus Darby. Papers.
Goodwyn, Thomas Jefferson. Letter.
Gott, Julia. Collection.
Graves Family Papers.
Greenville Ladies' Association in Aid of the Volunteers of the Confederate Army Papers.
Hammond, Bryan, and Cumming Families. Papers.
Heyward, Mrs. Albert Rhett (Sallie Coles Green). Papers.
Jenkins, John. Papers.
Jenkins, Micah. Papers.
Ladies' Aid Society (Columbia, S.C.) Papers.
Ladies' Benevolent Society (Charleston) Papers.
Ladies' Relief Association (Spartanburg) Papers.
Ladies' Volunteer Aid Association Papers.
Leverett, Mary Maxcy. Letter.
Macfarlan, Allan. Papers.
Marcy, Henry Orlando. Diary.
McCrady Family Papers.
Padgett, J[ames] D. Papers.
Palmer, Harriet. Diary.
R[avenel], E[llen] [Maria]. Letter.
Sams, Sarah Jane. Letter.
Scofield, William. Papers.
Sherman, William Tecumseh. Papers.
Snowden, Mary Amarinthia. Papers.
Sparkman, James Ritchie. Papers.

BIBLIOGRAPHY

Tennent, Edward Smith. Papers.
Ward, Charles G. Diary.
Willingham and Lawton Families. Papers.
Wilson, Moultrie Reid. Papers.
Young Family Papers.

Southern Historical Collection, University of North Carolina, Chapel Hill.
Allen, Edward W. Papers.
Bean, Jesse S. Diary.
Capehart Family Papers.
Collection of Heiskell, McCampbell, Wilkes, and Steel Family Materials.
Collier, Elizabeth. Diary.
Cornwall, Susan. Journal.
DeRossett Family Papers.
Ferebee, Gregory, and McPherson Family Papers.
Finley, Robert Stuart. Papers.
Fries and Shaffner Family Papers.
Graves Family Papers.
Hanes, Catherine E. Papers.
Haynsworth, Maria L. Letter.
Jones, Cadwallader. Papers.
King, Thomas Butler. Papers.
LeConte, Emma. Diary.
Lenoir Family Papers.
Mackay-Stiles Papers.
Mordecai Family Papers.
Myers, Thomas J. Papers.
Noble, Mary. Papers.
North Carolina Collection.
Ready, Alice. Diary.
Semmes, Benedict J. Papers.
Southall and Bowen Family Papers.
Worth, Jonathan. Papers.

University of Georgia, Hargrett Rare Book and Manuscript Library, Athens.
Alexander, Manning P. and Pellona David. Letters.
Baber-Blackshear Papers.
Cobb-Erwin-Lamar Collection.
Cunningham Family Papers.

Platter, C. C. Journal.
Sexton, Margaret Branch. Collection.
Stanley Letters (Reproductions).

NEWSPAPERS

Augusta Chronicle and Georgia Advertiser.
Augusta Chronicle & Georgia Gazette.
Augusta Chronicle-Sentinel.
Augusta Daily Constitutionalist.
Augusta Register.
Charleston Courier.
Charleston Mercury.
Georgia Journal (Milledgeville, Ga.).
New York Times.
Savannah Daily Morning News.
Southern Recorder.

PUBLISHED PRIMARY SOURCES

Andrews, Eliza Frances. *The War-Time Journal of a Georgia Girl, 1864–65.* Edited by Spencer Bidwell King, Jr. 1908. Reprint, Atlanta: Cherokee Publishing Company, 1976.

Bacot, Ada W. *A Confederate Nurse: The Diary of Ada W. Bacot, 1860–1863.* Edited by Jean V. Berlin. Columbia: University of South Carolina Press, 1994.

Bartness, Jacob W. "Jacob W. Bartness Civil War Letters." Edited by Donald F. Carmony. *Indiana Magazine of History* 52 (June 1956): 157–86.

Boggs, Marion Alexander, ed. *The Alexander Letters, 1787–1900.* Savannah, GA: George J. Baldwin, 1910.

Boyd, Belle. *Belle Boyd in Camp and Prison, Written by Herself.* Edited by Curtis Carroll Davis. 1865. Reprint, New York: Thomas Yoseloff, 1968.

Bradley, G. S. *The Star Corps: or Notes of an Army Chaplain During Sherman's Famous "March to the Sea."* Milwaukee: Jermain & Brightman, 1865.

Brockett, L. P., and Mary C. Vaughan. *Women's Work in the Civil War: A Record of Heroism, Patriotism, and Patience.* Philadelphia: Zeigler, McCurdy, 1867.

Burge, Dolly Lunt. *The Diary of Dolly Lunt Burge, 1848–1879.* Edited by Christine Jacobson Carter. Athens: University of Georgia Press, 1997.

Burton, E. P. *Diary of E. P. Burton, Surgeon 7th Reg. Ill., 3rd Brig. 2nd Div. 16 A. C.*

Des Moines, IA: Historical Records Survey, 1939.

Chapman, Horatio Dana. *Civil War Diary: Diary of a Forty-Niner.* Hartford, CT: Allis, 1929.

Charleston Weekly News and Courier. *"Our Women in the War": The Lives they Lived, the Deaths they Died, from the Weekly News and Courier, Charleston, S.C.* Charleston: News & Courier Book Presses, 1885.

Chesnut, Mary Boykin. *Mary Chesnut's Civil War.* Edited by C. Vann Woodward. New Haven, CT: Yale University Press, 1981.

———. *The Private Mary Chesnut: The Unpublished Civil War Diaries.* Edited by C. Vann Woodward and Elisabeth Muhlenfeld. New York: Oxford University Press, 1984.

Cohen, Fanny Yates. "Fanny Cohen's Journal of Sherman's Occupation of Savannah." Edited by Spencer B. King. *Georgia Historical Quarterly* 41 (December 1957): 407–16.

Coleman, Kenneth, ed. *Athens, 1861–1865: As Seen through Letters in the University of Georgia Libraries.* Athens: University of Georgia Press, 1969.

Confederate Women of Arkansas in the Civil War. Little Rock, AR: H. G. Pugh, 1907.

Conner, Mrs. James, Mrs. Thomas Taylor, Mrs. A. T. Smythe, Mrs. August Kohn, Miss Mary B. Poppenheim, Miss Martha B. Washington, eds. *South Carolina Women in the Confederacy: Volume 2.* Columbia, SC: The State Company, 1907.

Connolly, James A. *Three Years in the Army of the Cumberland: The Letters and Diary of Major James A. Connolly.* Bloomington: Indiana University Press, 1959.

Conyngham, David P. *Sherman's March Through the South with Sketches and Incidents of the Campaign.* New York: Sheldon & Company, 1865.

Cook, Anna Maria Green. *The Journal of a Milledgeville Girl, 1861–1867.* Edited by James C. Bonner. Athens: University of Georgia Press, 1964.

Cox, Charles. "'Gone for a Soldier': The Civil War Letters of Charles Harding Cox." Edited by Lorna Lutes Sylvester. *Indiana Magazine of History* 68 (September 1972): 181–239.

Cumming, Kate. *Kate: The Journal of a Confederate Nurse.* Edited by Richard Barksdale Harwell. Baton Rouge: Louisiana State University Press, 1959.

Davis, Jefferson. *Jefferson Davis, Constitutionalist, His Letters, Papers and Speeches.* 10 vols. Edited by Dunbar Rowland. Jackson: Mississippi Department of Archives and History, 1923.

Edmonds, S. Emma E. *Nurse and Spy in the Union Army: Comprising the Adventures and Experiences of a Woman in Hospitals, Camps, and Battle-Fields.* Hartford, CT: W. S. Williams & Co., 1865.

———. *Unsexed; or, The Female Soldier: The Thrilling Adventures, Experiences and Escapes of a Woman, as Nurse, Spy and Scout, in Hospitals, Camp and Battlefields.* Philadelphia: Philadelphia Publishing, 1864.

Edmondson, Belle. *A Lost Heroine of the Confederacy: The Diaries and Letters of Belle Edmondson*. Edited by William and Loretta Galbraith. Jackson: University Press of Mississippi, 1991.

Edmondston, Catherine Ann Devereux. *"Journal of a Secesh Lady": The Diary of Catherine Ann Devereux Edmondston, 1860–1866*. Edited by Beth G. Crabtree and James W. Patton. Raleigh: North Carolina Division of Archives and History, 1979.

Elmore, Grace Brown. *A Heritage of Woe: The Civil War Diary of Grace Brown Elmore, 1861–1868*. Edited by Marli F. Weiner. Athens: University of Georgia Press, 1997.

Evans, Augusta Jane. *Macaria; or, Altars of Sacrifice*. With an introduction by Drew Gilpin Faust. 1864. Reprint, Baton Rouge: Louisiana State University Press, 1992.

Ewing, Charles. "Sherman's March through Georgia: Letters from Charles Ewing to His Father Thomas Ewing." Edited by George C. Osborn. *Georgia Historical Quarterly* 42 (September 1958): 323–27.

Fitzpatrick, Marion Hill. *Letters to Amanda: The Civil War Letters of Marion Hill Fitzpatrick, Army of Northern Virginia*. Edited by Jeffrey C. Lowe and Sam Hodges. Macon, GA: Mercer University Press, 1998.

Geer, Allen Morgan. *The Civil War Diary of Allen Morgan Geer, Twentieth Regiment, Illinois Volunteers*. Edited by Mary Ann Anderson. Bloomington, IL: Robert C. Appleman, 1977.

Georgia Division, United Daughters of the Confederacy. *Confederate Reminiscences and Letters, 1861–1865*, 7 vols. Atlanta: Georgia Division United Daughters of the Confederacy, 1997.

Gilman, Caroline Howard. "Letters of a Confederate Mother: Charleston in the Sixties." *Atlantic Monthly* 137 (April 1926): 503–15.

Glidden, John M. "A Yankee Views the Agony of Savannah." Edited by Frank Otto Gatell. *Georgia Historical Quarterly* 43 (December 1959): 428–31.

Gray, John Chipman, and John Codman Ropes. *War Letters, 1862–1865, of John Chipman Gray and John Codman Ropes, With Portraits*. Cambridge, MA: Riverside Press, 1927.

Greenhow, Rose O'Neal. *My Imprisonment and the First Year of Abolition Rule in Washington*. London: n.p., 1863.

Hanger, G. W. "With Sherman in Georgia—A Letter from the Coast." Edited by F. B. Joyner. *Georgia Historical Quarterly* 42 (December 1958): 440–41.

Hawks, Esther Hill. *A Woman Doctor's Civil War: Esther Hill Hawks' Diary*. Edited by Gerald Schwartz. Columbia: University of South Carolina Press, 1989.

Heyward, Pauline DeCaradeuc. *A Confederate Lady Comes of Age: The Journal of Pauline DeCaradeuc Heyward, 1863–1888*. Edited by Mary D. Robertson. Columbia: University of South Carolina Press, 1992.

Hight, John J. *History of the Fifty-Eighth Regiment of Indiana Volunteer Infantry. Its Organization, Campaigns and Battles from 1861 to 1865. From the Manuscript Prepared by the Late Chaplain John J. Hight During His Service with the Regiment in the Field.* Edited by Gilbert R. Stormont. Princeton, NJ: Press of the Clarion, 1895.

Hitchcock, Henry. *Marching with Sherman: Passages from the Letters and Campaign Diaries of Henry Hitchcock, Major Assistant Adjutant General of Volunteers, November 1864–May 1865.* Edited by M. A. DeWolfe Howe. Lincoln: University of Nebraska Press, 1995.

Holmes, Charlotte R., ed. *The Burckmyer Letters, March, 1865–June, 1865.* Columbia, SC: The State Company, 1926.

Holmes, Emma. *The Diary of Miss Emma Holmes, 1861–1866.* Edited by John F. Marszalek. Baton Rouge: Louisiana State University Press, 1979.

Holmes, J. Taylor. *52d Ohio Volunteer Infantry, Then and Now.* Columbus, OH: Berlin Print, 1898.

Horton, Dexter. "Dairy of an Officer in Sherman's Army Marching through the Carolinas." Edited by Clement Eaton. *Journal of Southern History* 9 (May 1943): 238–54.

Howard, Frances Thomas. *In and Out of the Lines: An Accurate Account of the Incidents during the Occupation of Georgia by Federal Troops in 1864–65.* New York: Neale Publishing Company, 1905.

Hubert, Charles F. *History of the Fiftieth Regiment Illinois Volunteer Infantry.* Kansas City, MO: Western Veteran Publishing Company, 1894.

Huff, Lawrence. "'A Bitter Draught We Had to Quaff': Sherman's March through the Eyes of Joseph Addison Turner." *Georgia Historical Quarterly* 72 (Summer 1988): 306–26.

Jackson, Isaac. *"Some of the Boys . . .": The Civil War Letters of Isaac Jackson, 1862–1865.* Edited by Joseph Orville Jackson. Carbondale: Southern Illinois University Press, 1960.

Jackson, Oscar L. *The Colonel's Diary.* Sharon, PA: N.p., 1922.

Jervey, Susan Ravenel, and Charlotte St. Julien Ravenel. *Two Diaries from Middle St. John's, Berkeley, South Carolina, February–May, 1865. Journals Kept by Miss Susan R. Jervey and Miss Charlotte St. Julien Ravenel, at Northampton and Pooshee Plantations, and Reminiscences of Mrs. Waring Henegan. With Two Contemporary Reports from Federal Officials.* Pinopolis, SC: St. John's Hunting Club, 1921.

Jones, Katherine M., ed. *Ladies of Richmond: Confederate Capital.* New York: Bobbs-Merrill, 1962.

———. *When Sherman Came: Southern Women and the "Great March."* New York: Bobbs-Merrill, 1964.

Jones, Mary Sharpe, and Mary Jones Mallard. *Yankees a'Coming: One Month's Experience during the Invasion of Liberty County, Georgia, 1864–1865.* Edited by Haskell Monroe. Tuscaloosa, AL: Confederate Publishing, 1959.

Joslyn, Mauriel Phillips, ed. *Charlotte's Boys: Civil War Letters of the Branch Family of Savannah.* Berryville, VA: Rockbridge Publishers, 1996.

Lane, Mills, ed. *"Dear Mother: Don't grieve about me. If I get killed, I'll only be dead.": Letters from Georgia Soldiers in the Civil War.* 1977. Reprint, Savannah, GA: Beehive Press, 1990.

LeConte, Emma. *When the World Ended: The Diary of Emma LeConte.* Edited by Earl Schenck Miers. New York: Oxford University Press, 1957.

Logan, Kate Virginia Cox, *My Confederate Girlhood: The Memoirs of Kate Virginia Cox Logan.* Edited by Lily Logan Morrill. Richmond, VA: Garrett & Massie, 1932.

Mahon, Samuel. "The Civil War Letters of Samuel Mahon." Edited by John K. Mahon. *Iowa Journal of History* 51 (July 1953): 233–66.

McGuire, Judith White. *Diary of a Southern Refugee, During the War.* Richmond, VA: J. W. Randolph & English, Publishers, 1889.

Mead, Rufus. "With Sherman through Georgia and the Carolinas: Letters of a Federal Soldier." Edited by James A. Padgett. *Georgia Historical Quarterly* 33 (March 1949): 49–81.

Middleton, Harriott, and Susan Middleton. "Middleton Correspondence, 1861–1865." Edited by Isabella Middleton Leland. *South Carolina Historical Magazine* 63 (April 1962): 61–70; 65 (April 1964): 95–104.

Mitchell, Margaret. *Gone with the Wind.* 1936. Reprint, New York: Avon Books, 1973.

Moore, Frank. *Women of the War: Their Heroism and Self-Sacrifice.* Hartford, CT: S. S. Scranton, 1866.

Morgan, Sarah. *Sarah Morgan: The Civil War Diary of a Southern Woman.* Edited by Charles East. New York: Simon & Schuster, 1991.

Myers, Robert Manson, ed. *The Children of Pride,* 3 vols. New York: Popular Library, 1972.

Nichols, George Ward. *The Story of the Great March from the Diary of a Staff Officer.* New York: Harper & Brothers, 1865.

Noble, Vett, "Vett Noble of Ypsilanti: A Clerk for General Sherman." Edited by Donald W. Disbrow. *Civil War History* 14 (March 1968): 15–39.

Osborn, Thomas W. *The Fiery Trail: A Union Officer's Account of Sherman's Last Campaigns.* Edited by Richard Harwell and Philip N. Racine. Knoxville: University of Tennessee Press, 1986.

Painter, Nell Irvin. "The Journal of Gertrude Clanton Thomas: An Educated White Woman in the Eras of Slavery, War, and Reconstruction." Introduction to *The Secret Eye: The Journal of Gertrude Clanton Thomas, 1848-1889*, 1-67. Edited by Virginia Ingraham Burr. Chapel Hill: University of North Carolina Press, 1990.

Rowe, Mary. "A Southern Girl's Diary." *Confederate Veteran* 40 (July 1932): 264-65.

Rozier, John, ed. *The Granite Farm Letters: The Civil War Correspondence of Edgeworth & Sallie Bird*. Athens: University of Georgia Press, 1988.

Sherlock, E. J. *Memorabilia of the Marches and Battles in Which the One Hundredth Regiment of Indiana Infantry Volunteers Took an Active Part: War of the Rebellion, 1861-5*. Kansas City, MO: Gerard-Woody Printing Co., 1896.

Sherman, William T. *The Hero's Own Story: General Sherman's Official Account of His Great March Through Georgia and the Carolinas, From his Departure from Chattanooga to the Surrender of General Johnston, and the Confederate Forces Under his Command, To Which are Added General Sherman's Evidence before the Congressional Committee on the Conduct of the War; the Animadversions of Secretary Stanton and General Halleck; with a Defence of his Proceedings, &c.* New York: Bunce & Huntington, Publishers, 1865.

———. *Home Letters of General Sherman*. Edited by M. A. DeWolfe Howe. New York: Charles Scribner's Sons, 1909.

———. *Memoirs of General W. T. Sherman*. Edited by Michael Fellman. New York: Penguin Books, 2000.

———. *The Sherman Letters: Correspondence Between General and Senator Sherman from 1837-1891*. Edited by Rachel Sherman Thorndike. New York: Charles Scribner's Sons, 1894.

———. *Sherman's Civil War: Selected Correspondence of William T. Sherman, 1860-1865*. Edited by Brooks D. Simpson and Jean V. Berlin. Chapel Hill: University of North Carolina Press, 1999.

Silber, Nina, and Mary Beth Sievens, eds. *Yankee Correspondence: Civil War Letters between New England Soldiers and the Home Front*. Charlottesville: University Press of Virginia, 1996.

Simkins, Francis Butler, and James Welch Patton. *The Women of the Confederacy*. New York: Garrett & Massie, 1936.

Simms, William Gilmore, ed. *War Poetry of the South*. 1866. Reprint, New York: Arno Press, 1972.

Smith, Daniel E. Huger, Alice R. Huger Smith, and Arney R. Childs, eds. *Mason Smith Family Letters, 1860-1868*. Columbia: University of South Carolina Press, 1950.

Sterkx, H. E. *Partners in Rebellion: Alabama Women and the Civil War*. Rutherford, NJ: Farleigh Dickinson University Press, 1970.

Stevenson, William. *Thirteen Months in the Rebel Army: Being a Narrative of Personal Adventures in the Infantry, Ordnance, Cavalry, Courier, and Hospital

Service; With an Exhibition of the Power, Purposes, Earnestness, Military Despotism, and Demoralization of the South. New York: A. S. Barnes & Burr, 1862.

Stone, Kate. *Brokenburn: The Journal of Kate Stone, 1861–1868*. Edited by John Q. Anderson. Baton Rouge: Louisiana State University Press, 1972.

Strong, Robert Hale. *A Yankee Private's Civil War*. Edited by Ashley Halsey. Chicago: Saturday Evening Post, 1961.

Taylor, Frances Wallace, Catherine Taylor Matthews, and J. Tracy Power, eds. *The Leverett Letters: Correspondence of a South Carolina Family, 1851–1868*. Columbia: University of South Carolina Press, 2000.

Taylor, Mrs. Thomas, Mrs. A. T. Smythe, Mrs. August Kohn, Miss M. B. Poppenheim, Miss Martha B. Washington, eds. *South Carolina Women in the Confederacy: Volume 1*. Columbia, SC: The State Company, 1903.

Thomas, Ella Gertrude Clanton. *The Secret Eye: The Journal of Ella Gertrude Clanton Thomas, 1848–1889*. Edited by Virginia Ingraham Burr. Chapel Hill: University of North Carolina Press, 1990.

Towles, Louis P., ed. *A World Turned Upside Down: The Palmers of South Santee, 1818–1881*. Columbia: University of South Carolina Press, 1996.

Underwood, John Levi. *The Women of the Confederacy: In which is presented the heroism of the women of the Confederacy with accounts of their trials during the War and the period of Reconstruction, with their ultimate triumph over adversity. Their motives and their achievements as told by writers and orators now preserved in permanent form*. New York: Neale Publishing Company, 1906.

Wakeman, Sarah Rosetta. *An Uncommon Soldier: The Civil War Letters of Sarah Rosetta Wakeman, alias Pvt. Lyons Wakeman, 153rd Regiment, New York State Volunteers, 1862–1864*. Edited by Lauren Cook Burgess. New York: Oxford University Press, 1994.

The War of the Rebellion: A Compilation of the Official Records of the Union and Confederate Armies. 130 vols. Washington, DC: Government Printing Office, 1881–1902.

Waring, Mary. *Miss Waring's Journal, 1863 and 1865: Being the Diary of Miss Mary Waring of Mobile, during the final days of the War Between the States*. Edited by Thad Holt, Jr. Chicago: The Wyvern Press of S. F. E., 1964.

Wilkinson, J. *Narrative of a Blockade Runner*. New York: Sheldon & Co., 1877.

Wills, Charles W. *Army Life of an Illinois Soldier Including a Day-by-Day Record of Sherman's March to the Sea: Letters and Diary of Charles W. Wills*. Edited by Mary E. Kellogg. Carbondale: Southern Illinois University Press, 1996.

Wise, George M. "Marching through South Carolina: Another Civil War Letter of George M. Wise." Edited by Wilfred W. Black. *Ohio Historical Quarterly* 46 (April 1957): 193–94.

BIBLIOGRAPHY

SELECTED SECONDARY SOURCES

Books

Adams, Michael C. C. *Living Hell: The Dark Side of the Civil War.* Baltimore: Johns Hopkins University Press, 2014.

Anderson, Benedict. *Imagined Communities: Reflections on the Origin and Spread of Nationalism.* New York: Verso, 1991.

Ash, Stephen V. *Middle Tennessee Society Transformed, 1860–1870: War and Peace in the Upper South.* Baton Rouge: Louisiana State University Press, 1988.

———. *When the Yankees Came: Conflict and Chaos in the Occupied South, 1861–1865.* Chapel Hill: University of North Carolina Press, 1995.

Attie, Jeanie. *Patriotic Toil: Northern Women and the American Civil War.* Ithaca, NY: Cornell University Press, 1998.

Ayers, Edward L. *Vengeance and Justice: Crime and Punishment in the Nineteenth-Century American South.* New York: Oxford University Press, 1984.

———. *In the Presence of Mine Enemies: War in the Heart of America, 1859–1863.* New York: W. W. Norton, 2003.

Bailey, Anne J. *The Chessboard of War: Sherman and Hood in the Autumn Campaigns of 1864.* Lincoln: University of Nebraska Press, 2000.

———. *War and Ruin: William T. Sherman and the Savannah Campaign.* Wilmington, DE: Scholarly Resources, 2003.

Bardaglio, Peter. *Reconstructing the Household: Families, Sex, and the Law in the Nineteenth-Century South.* Chapel Hill: University of North Carolina Press, 1995.

Barrett, John G. *The Civil War in North Carolina.* Chapel Hill: University of North Carolina Press, 1963.

———. *Sherman's March through the Carolinas.* Chapel Hill: University of North Carolina Press, 1956.

Baym, Nina. *Woman's Fiction: A Guide to Novels by and about Women in America, 1820–70.* 1978. Reprint, Chicago: University of Illinois Press, 1993.

Beringer, Richard E., Herman Hattaway, Archer Jones, and William N. Still, Jr. *Why the South Lost the Civil War.* Athens: University of Georgia Press, 1986.

Berlin, Ira, Barbara J. Fields, Steven F. Miller, Joseph F. Miller, Joseph P. Reidy, and Leslie S. Rowland, eds. *Free at Last: A Documentary History of Slavery, Freedom, and the Civil War.* New York: New Press, 1992.

Berry, Stephen, ed. *Weirding the War: Stories from the Civil War's Ragged Edges.* Athens: University of Georgia Press, 2011.

Berry, Stephen W., II. *All That Makes a Man: Love and Ambition in the Civil War South.* New York: Oxford University Press, 2003.

Blackett, R. J. M. *Divided Hearts: Britain and the American Civil War.* Baton Rouge: Louisiana University Press, 2001.

Blair, William. *Virginia's Private War: Feeding Body and Soul in the Confederacy, 1861–1865*. New York: Oxford University Press, 1998.

Blanton, DeAnne, and Lauren M. Cook, *They Fought Like Demons: Women Soldiers in the American Civil War*. Baton Rouge: Louisiana State University Press, 2002.

Bleser, Carol, ed. *In Joy and In Sorrow: Women, Family, and Marriage in the Victorian South*. New York: Oxford University Press, 1991.

Blight, David. *Race and Reunion: The Civil War in American Memory*. Cambridge: Belknap Press of Harvard University Press, 2001.

Bodnar, John, ed. *Bonds of Affection: Americans Define Their Patriotism*. Princeton, NJ: Princeton University Press, 1996.

Brady, Lisa M. *War upon the Land: Military Strategy and the Transformation of Southern Landscapes during the American Civil War*. Athens: University of Georgia Press, 2012.

Brown, Kathleen M. *Good Wives, Nasty Wenches, and Anxious Patriarchs: Gender, Race, and Power in Colonial Virginia*. Chapel Hill: University of North Carolina Press, 1996.

Browning, Judkin. *Shifting Loyalties: The Union Occupation of Eastern North Carolina*. Chapel Hill: University of North Carolina Press, 2011.

Brownmiller, Susan. *Against Our Will: Men, Women and Rape*. New York: Simon & Schuster, 1975.

Bryant, Jonathan. *How Curious a Land: Conflict and Change in Greene County, Georgia, 1850–1885*. Chapel Hill: University of North Carolina Press, 1996.

Burton, Orville Vernon. *In My Father's House Are Many Mansions: Family and Community in Edgefield, South Carolina*. Chapel Hill: University of North Carolina Press, 1985.

Bynum, Victoria E. *The Long Shadow of the Civil War: Southern Dissent and Its Legacies*. Chapel Hill: University of North Carolina Press, 2010.

———. *Unruly Women: The Politics of Social and Sexual Control in the Old South*. Chapel Hill: University of North Carolina Press, 1992.

Camp, Stephanie M. H. *Closer to Freedom: Enslaved Women and Everyday Resistance in the Plantation South*. Chapel Hill: University of North Carolina Press, 2004.

Campbell, Edward D., Jr., and Kym S. Rice, eds. *A Woman's War: Southern Women, Civil War, and the Confederate Legacy*. Charlottesville: University Press of Virginia, 1996.

Campbell, Jacqueline Glass. *When Sherman Marched North from the Sea: Resistance on the Confederate Home Front*. Chapel Hill: University of North Carolina Press, 2003.

Capers, Gerald M. *Occupied City: New Orleans under the Federals, 1862–1865*. Lexington: University of Kentucky Press, 1965.

Carnes, Mark C. *Secret Ritual and Manhood in Victorian America*. New Haven, CT: Yale University Press, 1989.

Cash, W. J. *The Mind of the South*. With an introduction by Bertram Wyatt-Brown. 1941. Reprint, New York: Vintage, 1991.

Cashin, Joan E. *Our Common Affairs*. Baltimore: Johns Hopkins University Press, 1996.

Caudill, Edward, and Paul Ashdown, *Sherman's March in Myth and Memory*. Lanham, MD: Rowan & Littlefield, 2008.

Censer, Jane Turner. *North Carolina Planters and Their Children, 1800–1860*. Baton Rouge: Louisiana State University Press, 1987.

———. *The Reconstruction of White Southern Womanhood, 1865–1895*. Baton Rouge, Louisiana State University Press, 2003.

Channing, Stephen A. *Crisis of Fear: Secession in South Carolina*. New York: W. W. Norton, 1974.

Cimbala, Paul. *Soldiers North and South: The Everyday Experiences of the Men Who Fought America's Civil War*. New York: Fordham University Press, 2010.

Cisco, Walter Brian. *War Crimes against Southern Civilians*. Gretna, LA: Pelican Press, 2007.

Clampitt, Bradley R. *The Confederate Heartland: Military and Civilian Morale in the Western Confederacy*. Baton Rouge: Louisiana State University Press, 2011.

Clinton, Catherine. *The Plantation Mistress: Woman's World in the Old South*. New York: Pantheon, 1982.

———. *Tara Revisited: Women, War, and the Plantation Legend*. New York: Abbeville Press, 1995.

Clinton, Catherine, ed. *Southern Families at War: Loyalty and Conflict in the Civil War South*. New York: Oxford University Press, 2000.

Clinton, Catherine, and Nina Silber, eds. *Divided Houses: Gender and the Civil War*. New York: Oxford University Press, 1992.

———. *Battle Scars: Gender and Sexuality in the American Civil War*. New York: Oxford University Press, 2006.

Cogan, Frances. *All-American Girl: The Ideal of Real Womanhood in Mid-Nineteenth-Century America*. Athens: University of Georgia Press, 1989.

Cooke, Miriam, and Angela Walcott, eds. *Gendering War Talk*. Princeton, NJ: Princeton University Press, 1993.

Cott, Nancy F. *The Bonds of Womanhood: "Woman's Sphere" in New England, 1780–1835*. New Haven, CT: Yale University Press, 1977.

Cox, Karen L. *Dixie's Daughters: The United Daughters of the Confederacy and the Preservation of Confederate Culture*. Gainesville: University Press of Florida, 2003.

Crofts, Daniel W. *Reluctant Confederates: Upper South Unionists in the Secession Crisis*. Chapel Hill: University of North Carolina Press, 1989.

Cullen, Jim. *The Civil War in Popular Culture: A Reusable Past*. Washington, DC: Smithsonian Press, 1995.

Cushman, Steven. *Bloody Promenade: Reflections on a Civil War Battle*. Charlottesville: University Press of Virginia, 1999.

Davis, Stephen. *What the Yankees Did to Us: Sherman's Bombardment and Wrecking of Atlanta*. Macon, GA: Mercer University Press, 2012.

Dew, Charles B. *Apostles of Disunion: Southern Secession Commissioners and the Causes of the Civil War*. Charlottesville: University of Virginia Press, 2001.

Dorsey, Bruce. *Reforming Men and Women: Gender in the Antebellum City*. Ithaca, NY: Cornell University Press, 2006.

Dunkelman, Mark H. *Marching with Sherman: Through Georgia and the Carolinas with the 154th New York*. Baton Rouge: Louisiana State University Press, 2012.

Durrill, Wayne K. *War of Another Kind: A Southern Community in the Great Rebellion*. New York: Oxford University Press, 1990.

Dyer, Thomas G. *Secret Yankees: The Union Circle in Confederate Atlanta*. Baltimore: Johns Hopkins University Press, 1999.

Eaton, Clement. *A History of the Southern Confederacy*. 1954. Reprint, New York: Free Press, 1965.

Edwards, Laura F. *People and Their Peace*. Chapel Hill: University of North Carolina Press, 2009.

———. *Scarlett Doesn't Live Here Anymore: Southern Women in the Civil War Era*. Urbana: University of Illinois Press, 2000.

Edwards, Rebecca. *Angels in the Machinery: Gender in American Party Politics from the Civil War to the Progressive Era*. New York: Oxford University Press, 1997.

Fahs, Alice. *The Imagined Civil War: Popular Literature of the North and South, 1861–1865*. Chapel Hill: University of North Carolina Press, 2001.

Fahs, Alice and Joan Waugh, eds. *The Memory of the Civil War in American Culture*. Chapel Hill: University of North Carolina Press, 2004.

Farnham, Christie Anne. *The Education of the Southern Belle: Higher Education and Student Socialization in the Antebellum South*. New York: New York University Press, 1994.

Faulkner, William. *The Unvanquished*. 1934. Reprint, New York: Vintage International, 1991.

Faust, Drew Gilpin. *The Creation of Confederate Nationalism: Ideology and Identity in the Civil War South*. Baton Rouge: Louisiana State University Press, 1988.

———. *Mothers of Invention: Women of the Slaveholding South in the American Civil War*. Chapel Hill: University of North Carolina Press, 1996.

———. *Southern Stories: Slaveholders in Peace and War.* Columbia: University of Missouri Press, 1992.

———. *This Republic of Suffering: Death and the American Civil War.* New York: Vintage, 2009.

Fellman, Michael. *Citizen Sherman: A Life of William Tecumseh Sherman.* New York: Random House, 1995.

———. *Inside War: The Guerrilla Conflict in Missouri during the American Civil War.* New York: Oxford University Press, 1989.

Foote, Lorien. *The Gentlemen and the Roughs: Violence, Honor, and Manhood in the Union Army.* New York: New York University Press, 2010.

Foster, Gaines M. *Ghosts of the Confederacy: Defeat, the Lost Cause, and the Emergence of the New South, 1865 to 1913.* New York: Oxford University Press, 1987.

Fowler, John D., and David B. Parker, eds. *Breaking the Heartland: The Civil War in Georgia.* Macon, GA: Mercer University Press, 2011.

Fox-Genovese, Elizabeth. *Within the Plantation Household: Black and White Women of the Old South.* Chapel Hill: University of North Carolina Press, 1988.

Freedman, Estelle B. *Redefining Rape: Sexual Violence in the Era of Suffrage and Segregation.* Cambridge, MA: Harvard University Press, 2013.

Freehling, William W. *The South vs. the South: How Anti-Confederate Southerners Shaped the Course of the Civil War.* New York: Oxford University Press, 2001.

Friedman, Jean E. *The Enclosed Garden: Women and Community in the Evangelical South, 1830–1900.* Chapel Hill: University of North Carolina Press, 1985.

Friend, Craig Thompson, and Lorri Glover, eds. *Southern Manhood: Perspectives on Masculinity in the Old South.* Athens: University of Georgia Press, 2004.

Gallagher, Gary W. *Becoming Confederates: Paths to a New National Loyalty.* Athens: University of Georgia Press, 2013.

———. *The Confederate War: How Popular Will, Nationalism, and Military Strategy Could Not Stave Off Defeat.* Cambridge, MA: Harvard University Press, 1997.

———. *The Union War.* Cambridge, MA: Harvard University Press, 2011.

Gallagher, Gary W., and Alan T. Nolan, eds. *The Myth of the Lost Cause and Civil War History.* Bloomington: Indiana University Press, 2000.

Gardner, Sarah E. *Blood and Irony: Southern White Women's Narratives of the Civil War, 1861–1937.* Chapel Hill: University of North Carolina Press, 2004.

Giesberg, Judith Ann. *Army at Home: Women and the Civil War on the Northern Home Front.* Chapel Hill: University of North Carolina Press, 2009.

———. *Civil War Sisterhood: The U.S. Sanitary Commission and Women's Politics in Transition.* Boston: Northeastern University Press, 2000.

Ginzberg, Lori D. *Women and the Work of Benevolence: Morality, Politics, and Class in the Nineteenth-Century United States.* New Haven, CT: Yale University Press, 1990.

Glatthaar, Joseph T. *The March to the Sea and Beyond: Sherman's Troops in the Savannah and Carolinas Campaigns*. Baton Rouge: Louisiana State University Press, 1985.

Glover, Lorri. *Southern Sons: Becoming Men in the New Nation*. Baltimore: Johns Hopkins University Press, 2010.

Gordon, Beverly. *Bazaars and Fair Ladies: The History of the American Fundraising Fair*. Knoxville: University of Tennessee Press, 1998.

Greenberg, Kenneth. *Honor and Slavery: Lies, Duels, Noses, Masks, Dressing as a Woman, Gifts, Strangers, Humanitarianism, Death, Slave Rebellions, the Proslavery Argument, Baseball, Hunting, and Gambling in the Old South*. Princeton, NJ: Princeton University Press, 1996.

Griffith, Paddy. *Battle Tactics of the Civil War*. New Haven, CT: Yale University Press, 1989.

Grimsley, Mark. *The Hard Hand of War: Union Military Policy toward Southern Civilians, 1861–1865*. New York: Cambridge University Press, 1995.

Grimsley, Mark, and Clifford J. Rogers, eds. *Civilians in the Path of War*. Lincoln: University of Nebraska Press, 2002.

Grimsley, Mark, and Brooks D. Simpson, eds. *The Collapse of the Confederacy*. Lincoln: University of Nebraska Press, 2001.

Hall, Richard. *Patriots in Disguise: Women Warriors of the Civil War*. New York: Paragon House, 1993.

Hearn, Chester G. *When the Devil Came Down to Dixie: Ben Butler in New Orleans*. Baton Rouge: Louisiana State University Press, 1997.

Hilde, Libra R. *Worth a Dozen Men: Women and Nursing in the Civil War South*. Charlottesville: University of Virginia Press, 2012.

Hirshson, Stanley P. *The White Tecumseh: A Biography of William T. Sherman*. New York: John Wiley & Sons, 1997.

Hoehling, A. A. *Last Train from Atlanta*. New York: Thomas Yoseloff, 1958.

Inscoe, John. *Race, War, and Remembrance in the Appalachian South*. Lexington: University Press of Kentucky, 2008.

Jabour, Anya. *Scarlett's Sisters: Young Women in the Old South*. Chapel Hill: University of North Carolina Press, 2007.

Janney, Caroline E. *Burying the Dead but Not the Past: Ladies' Memorial Associations and the Lost Cause*. Chapel Hill: University of North Carolina Press, 2008.

———. *Remembering the Civil War: Reunion and the Limits of Reconciliation*. Chapel Hill: University of North Carolina Press, 2013.

Jimerson, Randall C. *The Private Civil War: Popular Thought during the Sectional Conflict*. Baton Rouge: Louisiana State University Press, 1988.

Jones, Anne Goodwyn. *Tomorrow Is Another Day: The Woman Writer in the South, 1859–1936*. Baton Rouge: Louisiana State University Press, 1981.

Jones, Jacqueline. *Saving Savannah: The City and the Civil War.* New York: Knopf, 2008.

Kamensky, Jane. *Governing the Tongue: The Politics of Speech in Early New England.* New York: Oxford University Press, 1997.

Kelley, Mary. *Learning to Stand and Speak: Women, Education, and Public Life in America's Republic.* Chapel Hill: University of North Carolina Press, 2008.

———. *Private Woman, Public Stage: Literary Domesticity in Nineteenth-Century America.* New York: Oxford University Press, 1984.

Kennett, Lee B. *Marching through Georgia: The Story of Soldiers and Civilians during Sherman's Campaign.* New York: HarperCollins, 1995.

———. *Sherman: A Soldier's Life.* New York: HarperCollins, 2001.

Kenzer, Robert C. *Kinship and Neighborhood in a Southern Community: Orange County, North Carolina, 1849–1881.* Knoxville: University of Tennessee Press, 1987.

Kete, Mary Louise. *Sentimental Collaborations: Mourning and Middle-Class Identity in Nineteenth-Century America.* Durham, NC: Duke University Press, 2000.

Kierner, Cynthia A. *Beyond the Household: Women's Place in the Early South, 1700–1835.* Ithaca, NY: Cornell University Press, 1998.

Kinchen, Oscar A. *Women Who Spied for the Blue and the Gray.* Philadelphia: Dorrance & Company, 1972.

Lebsock, Suzanne. *The Free Women of Petersburg: Status and Culture in a Southern Town, 1784–1860.* New York: W. W. Norton, 1984.

Leonard, Elizabeth D. *All the Daring of the Soldier: Women of the Civil War Armies.* New York: W. W. Norton, 1999.

———. *Yankee Women: Gender Battles in the Civil War.* New York: W. W. Norton, 1994.

Lepore, Jill. *The Name of War: King Philip's War and the Origins of American Identity.* New York: Vintage, 1998.

Lewis, Lloyd. *Sherman: Fighting Prophet.* New York: Harcourt, Brace, 1932.

Linderman, Gerald. *Embattled Courage: The Experience of Combat in the Civil War.* New York: Free Press, 1987.

Loughridge, Patricia R., and Edward D. C. Campbell, Jr. *Women and Mourning.* Richmond, VA: Museum of the Confederacy, 1985.

Lowry, Thomas P. *The Stories the Soldiers Wouldn't Tell: Sex in the Civil War.* Mechanicsburg, PA: Stackpole Books, 1994.

Lucas, Marion B. *Sherman and the Burning of Columbia.* 1976. Reprint, Columbia: University of South Carolina Press, 2000.

Maher, Mary Denis. *To Bind Up Their Wounds: Catholic Sister Nurses in the U.S. Civil War.* New York: Greenwood Press, 1989.

Manning, Chandra. *What This Cruel War Was Over: Soldiers, Slavery, and the Civil War.* New York: Vintage, 2008.
Marten, James, ed. *Children and Youth during the Civil War Era.* New York: New York University Press, 2012.
Marszalek, John F. *Sherman: A Soldier's Passion for Order.* New York: Vintage, 1994.
———. *Sherman's March to the Sea.* Abilene, TX: McWhiney Foundation Press, 2005.
Massey, Mary Elizabeth. *Ersatz in the Confederacy: Shortages and Substitution on the Southern Homefront.* 1952. Reprint, Columbia: University of South Carolina Press, 1993.
———. *Refugee Life in the Confederacy.* Baton Rouge: Louisiana State University Press, 1964.
———. *Women in the Civil War.* Lincoln: University of Nebraska Press, 1994. Originally published as *Bonnet Brigades,* New York: A. A. Knopf, 1966.
McCardell, John. *The Idea of a Southern Nation: Southern Nationalists and Southern Nationalism, 1830–1860.* New York: W. W. Norton, 1979.
McCurry, Stephanie. *Confederate Reckoning: Power and Politics in the Civil War South.* Cambridge, MA: Harvard University Press, 2010.
———. *Masters of Small Worlds: Yeoman Households, Gender Relations, & the Political Culture of the Antebellum South Carolina Low Country.* New York: Oxford University Press, 1995.
McDonough, James Lee, and James Pickett Jones. *War So Terrible: Sherman and Atlanta.* New York: W. W. Norton, 1987.
McPherson, James M. *Battle Cry of Freedom: The Civil War Era.* New York: Ballantine, 1988.
———. *For Cause and Comrades: Why Men Fought in the Civil War.* New York: Oxford University Press, 1997.
———. *What They Fought For, 1861–1865.* Baton Rouge: Louisiana State University Press, 1994.
Mitchell, Reid. *Civil War Soldiers.* New York: Viking Press, 1988.
———. *The Vacant Chair: The Northern Soldier Leaves Home.* New York: Oxford University Press, 1993.
Mohr, Clarence L. *On the Threshold of Freedom: Masters and Slaves in Civil War Georgia.* Athens: University of Georgia Press, 1986.
Moody, Wesley. *Demon of the Civil War: Sherman and Civil War History.* Columbia: University of Missouri Press, 2011.
Morris, Roy, Jr. *Sheridan: The Life and Wars of General Phil Sheridan.* New York: Crown Publishers, 1992.
Morton, Patricia, ed. *Discovering the Women in Slavery: Emancipating Perspectives of the American Past.* Athens: University of Georgia Press, 1996.

Moss, Elizabeth. *Domestic Novelists in the Old South: Defenders of Southern Culture*. Baton Rouge: Louisiana State University Press, 1992.

Mountcastle, Clay. *Punitive War: Confederate Guerrillas and Union Reprisals*. Lawrence: University Press of Kansas, 2009.

Murphy, Kim. *I Had Rather Die: Rape in the Civil War*. Batesville, VA: Coachlight Press, 2014.

Neely, Mark E., Jr. *The Civil War and the Limits of Destruction*. Cambridge, MA: Harvard University Press, 2007.

Nelson, Megan Kate. *Ruin Nation: Destruction and the American Civil War*. Athens: University of Georgia Press, 2012.

Nudelman, Franny. *John Brown's Body: Slavery, Violence, and the Culture of War*. Chapel Hill: University of North Carolina Press, 2004.

O'Leary, Cecilia Elizabeth. *To Die For: Paradox of American Patriotism*. Princeton, NJ: Princeton University Press, 1999.

Pease, Jane H., and William H. Pease. *A Family of Women: The Carolina Petigrus in Peace and War*. Chapel Hill: University of North Carolina Press, 1999.

Penningroth, Dylan C. *The Claims of Kinfolk: African American Property and Community in the Nineteenth-Century South*. Chapel Hill: University of North Carolina Press, 2002.

Phillips, Jason. *Diehard Rebels: The Confederate Culture of Invincibility*. Athens: University of Georgia Press, 2010.

Potter, David. *The South and the Sectional Conflict*. Baton Rouge: Louisiana State University Press, 1968.

Quigley, Paul. *Shifting Grounds: Nationalism and the American South, 1848–1865*. New York: Oxford University Press, 2012.

Rable, George C. *Civil Wars: Women and the Crisis of Southern Nationalism*. Urbana: University of Illinois Press, 1989.

———. *The Confederate Republic: A Revolution against Politics*. Chapel Hill: University of North Carolina Press, 1994.

Ramold, Steven J. *Across the Divide: Union Soldiers View the Northern Home Front*. New York: New York University Press, 2013.

Reston, James, Jr. *Sherman's March and Vietnam*. New York: MacMillan, 1984.

Roberts, Giselle. *The Confederate Belle*. Columbia: University of Missouri Press, 2003.

Rose, Anne C. *Victorian America and the Civil War*. New York: Cambridge University Press, 1992.

Rose, Willie Lee. *Rehearsal for Reconstruction: The Port Royal Experiment*. New York: Bobbs-Merrill, 1964.

Rotundo, E. Anthony. *American Manhood: Transformations in Masculinity from the Revolution to the Modern Era*. New York: Basic Books, 1993.

Royster, Charles. *The Destructive War: William Tecumseh Sherman, Stonewall Jackson, and the Americans*. New York: Vintage, 1993.

Rubin, Anne Sarah. *A Shattered Nation: The Rise and Fall of the Confederacy, 1861–1868*. Chapel Hill: University of North Carolina Press, 2005.

———. *Through the Heart of Dixie: Sherman's March and America*. Chapel Hill: University of North Carolina Press, 2014.

Ryan, Mary P. *Cradle of the Middle Class: The Family in Oneida County, New York, 1790–1865*. New York: Cambridge University Press, 1981.

Scarborough, Ruth. *Belle Boyd: Siren of the South*. Macon, GA: Mercer University Press, 1983.

Schroeder-Lein, Glenna R. *Confederate Hospitals on the Move: Samuel H. Stout and the Army of Tennessee*. Columbia: University of South Carolina Press, 1994.

Schwalm, Leslie A. *A Hard Fight for We: Women's Transition from Slavery to Freedom in South Carolina*. Urbana: University of Illinois Press, 1997.

Schweninger, Loren. *Families in Crisis in the Old South: Divorce, Slavery, and the Law*. Chapel Hill: University of North Carolina Press, 2012.

Scott, Anne Firor. *The Southern Lady: From Pedestal to Politics, 1830–1930*. Chicago: University of Chicago Press, 1970.

Scott, Joan Wallach. *Gender and the Politics of History*. New York: Columbia University Press, 1988.

Shammas, Carole. *A History of Household Government in America*. Charlottesville: University of Virginia Press, 2002.

Silber, Nana. *Daughters of the Union: Northern Women Fight the Civil War*. Cambridge, MA: Harvard University Press, 2005.

———. *Gender and the Sectional Conflict*. Chapel Hill: University of North Carolina Press, 2009.

———. *The Romance of Reunion: Northerners and the South, 1865–1900*. Chapel Hill: University of North Carolina Press, 1993.

Sizer, Lyde Cullen. *The Political Work of Northern Women Writers and the Civil War, 1850–1872*. Chapel Hill: University of North Carolina Press, 2000.

Smith-Rosenberg, Caroll. *Disorderly Conduct: Visions of Gender in Victorian America*. New York: Alfred A. Knopf, 1985.

Sternhell, Yael A. *Routes of War: The World of Movement in the Confederate South*. Cambridge, MA: Harvard University Press, 2012.

Stevenson, Brenda E. *Life in Black and White: Family and Community in the Slave South*. New York: Oxford University Press, 1996.

Stowe, Steven M. *Intimacy and Power in the Old South: Ritual in the Lives of the Planters*. Baltimore: Johns Hopkins University Press, 1987.

Sutherland, Daniel E. *The Emergence of Total War*. Fort Worth, TX: Ryan Place Publishers, 1996.

——. *A Savage Conflict: The Decisive Role of Guerrillas in the American Civil War*. Chapel Hill: University of North Carolina Press, 2013.

——. *Seasons of War: The Ordeal of a Confederate Community, 1861–1865*. New York: Free Press, 1995.

Thomas, Emory M. *The Confederate Nation: 1861–1865*. New York: Harper Torchbooks, 1979.

Tosh, John. *A Man's Place: Masculinity and the Middle-Class Home in Victorian England*. New Haven, CT: Yale University Press, 1999.

Trudeau, Noah Andre. *Southern Storm: Sherman's March to the Sea*. New York: Harper Collins, 2009.

Varon, Elizabeth R. *Appomattox: Victory, Defeat, and Freedom at the End of the Civil War*. New York: Oxford University Press, 2013.

——. *Southern Lady, Yankee Spy: The True Story of Elizabeth Van Lew, a Union Agent in the Heart of the Confederacy*. New York: Oxford University Press, 2003.

——. *We Mean to Be Counted: White Women and Politics in Antebellum Virginia*. Chapel Hill: University of North Carolina Press, 1998.

Walters, John Bennett. *Merchant of Terror: General Sherman and Total War*. New York: Bobbs-Merrill, 1973.

Wallenstein, Peter, and Bertram Wyatt-Brown, eds. *Virginians and the Civil War*. Charlottesville: University of Virginia Press, 2005.

Weigley, Russell F. *A Great Civil War: A Military and Political History, 1861–1865*. Bloomington: Indiana University Press, 2000.

Weiner, Marli F. *Mistresses and Slaves: Plantation Women in South Carolina, 1830–80*. Urbana: University of Illinois Press, 1998.

Weitz, Mark A. *A Higher Duty: Desertion among Georgia Troops during the Civil War*. Lincoln: University of Nebraska Press, 2001.

——. *More Damning than Slaughter: Desertion in the Confederate Army*. Lincoln: University of Nebraska Press, 2005.

Wells, Jonathan Daniel. *Origins of the Southern Middle Class, 1800–1861*. Chapel Hill: University of North Carolina Press, 2003.

Wells, Jonathan Daniel, and Jennifer R. Green. *The Southern Middle Class in the Long Nineteenth Century*. Baton Rouge: Louisiana State University Press, 2011.

Welter, Barbara. *Dimity Convictions: The American Woman in the Nineteenth Century*. Athens: Ohio University Press, 1976.

Wheeler, Richard. *Sherman's March*. New York: Thomas Y. Crowell Publishers, 1978.

Whites, LeeAnn. *The Civil War as a Crisis in Gender: Augusta, Georgia, 1860–1890*. Athens: University of Georgia Press, 1995.

——. *Gender Matters: Civil War, Reconstruction, and the Making of the New South*. New York: Palgrave Macmillan, 2005.

Whites, LeeAnn, and Alecia P. Long. *Occupied Women: Gender, Military Occupation, and the American Civil War.* Baton Rouge: Louisiana State University Press, 2009.

Wiley, Bell Irvin. *The Life of Billy Yank: The Common Soldier of the Union.* 1952. Reprint, Baton Rouge: Louisiana State University Press, 1971.

———. *The Life of Johnny Reb: The Common Soldier of the Confederacy.* 1943. Reprint, Baton Rouge: Louisiana State University Press, 1971.

Witt, John Fabian. *Lincoln's Code: The Laws of War in American History.* New York: Free Press, 2013.

Wood, Kirsten E. *Masterful Women: Slaveholding Widows from the American Revolution through the Civil War.* Chapel Hill: University of North Carolina Press, 2004.

Wyatt-Brown, Bertram. *House of Percy: Honor, Melancholy, and Imagination in a Southern Family.* New York: Oxford University Press, 1997.

———. *The Shaping of Southern Culture: Honor, Grace, and War, 1760s–1880s.* Chapel Hill: University of North Carolina Press, 2001.

———. *Southern Honor: Ethics and Behavior in the Old South.* New York: Oxford University Press, 1982.

———. *A Warring Nation: Honor, Race, and Humiliation in America and Abroad.* Charlottesville: University of Virginia Press, 2013.

———. *Yankee Saints and Southern Sinners.* Baton Rouge: Louisiana State University Press, 1985.

Articles

Atkinson, Maxine P., and Jacqueline Boles, "The Shaky Pedestal: Southern Ladies Yesterday and Today." *Southern Studies* 24 (Winter 1985): 398–406.

Attie, Jeanie. "Warwork and the Crisis of Domesticity in the North." In *Divided Houses: Gender and the Civil War,* edited by Catherine Clinton and Nina Silber, 247–59. New York: Oxford University Press, 1992.

Baker, Paula. "The Domestication of Politics: Women and American Political Society, 1780–1900." *American Historical Review* 89 (June 1984): 620–47.

Barber, E. Susan, and Charles F. Ritter. "'Physical Abuse . . . and Rough Handing': Race, Gender, and Sexual Justice in the Occupied South." In *Occupied Women: Gender, Military Occupation, and the American Civil War,* edited by LeeAnn Whites and Alecia P. Long, 49–64. Baton Rouge: Louisiana State University Press, 2009.

———. "'Unlawfully and Against Her Consent': Sexual Violence and the Military during the American Civil War." In *Sexual Violence in Conflict Zones: From the*

BIBLIOGRAPHY

Ancient World to the Era of Human Rights, edited by Elizabeth D. Heineman. Philadelphia: University of Pennsylvania Press, 2011.

Berlin, Jean V. "Did Confederate Women Lose the War? Deprivation, Destruction, and Despair on the Homefront." In *The Collapse of the Confederacy*, edited by Mark Grimsley and Brooks D. Simpson, 168–93. Lincoln: University of Nebraska Press, 2001.

Blanton, DeAnne. "Women Soldiers of the Civil War." *Prologue: The Journal of the National Archives* 25 (Spring 1993): 27–35.

Bode, Frederick A. "A Common Sphere: White Evangelicals and Gender in Antebellum Georgia." *Georgia Historical Quarterly* 79 (Winter 1995): 775–809.

Bonner, James C. "Sherman at Milledgeville in 1864." *Journal of Southern History* 22 (January 1931): 41–54.

Brinsfield, John W. "The Military Ethics of General William T. Sherman: A Reassessment." *Parameters* 12:2 (1982): 36–48.

Broussard, Joyce L. "Occupied Natchez, Elite Women, and the Feminization of the Civil War." *Journal of Mississippi* 70 (Summer 2008): 179–207.

Campbell, Jacqueline Glass. "There Is No Difference between a He and a She Adder in Their Venom: Benjamin Butler, William T. Sherman, and Confederate Women." *Louisiana History.* 50:1 (Winter 2009): 5–24.

———. "'The Unmeaning Twaddle about Order 28': Benjamin Butler and Confederate Women in Occupied New Orleans, 1862." *Journal of the Civil War Era* 2 (March 2012): 11–30.

Cashin, Joan E. "The Structure of Antebellum Families: 'The Ties That Bound Us Was Strong,'" *Journal of Southern History* 56 (February 1990): 55–70.

Clampitt, Bradley R. "'Not Intended to Dispossess Females': Southern Women and Civil War Amnesty." *Civil War History* 56 (December 2010): 325–49.

Clinton, Catherine. "'Southern Dishonor': Flesh, Blood, Race, and Bondage." In *In Joy and in Sorrow: Women, Family, and Marriage in the Victorian South*, edited by Carol Bleser, 52–68. New York: Oxford University Press, 1991.

Cott, Nancy F. "On Men's History and Women's History." In *Meaning for Manhood: Constructions of Masculinity in Victorian America*, edited by Mark C. Carnes and Clyde Griffen, 205–11. Chicago: University of Chicago Press, 1990.

Doyle, Patrick J. "Understanding the Desertion of South Carolinian Soldiers during the Final Years of the Confederacy." *Historical Journal* 56 (September 2013): 657–79.

Drago, Edmund L. "How Sherman's March through Georgia Affected the Slaves." *Georgia Historical Quarterly* 57 (Fall 1973): 361–75.

Dwinell, Harold A., ed. "Vermonter in Gray: The Story of Melvin Dwinell." *Vermont History* 30 (July 1962): 220–37.

Edwards, Laura F. "Law, Domestic Violence, and the Limits of Patriarchal Authority in the Antebellum South." *Journal of Southern History* 65 (November 1999): 733–70.

Escott, Paul D. "The Failure of Confederate Nationalism: The Old South's Class System in the Crucible of War." In *The Old South in the Crucible of War,* edited by Harry P. Owens and James J. Cooke. Jackson: University Press of Mississippi, 1983.

Faust, Drew Gilpin. "Altars of Sacrifice: Confederate Women and the Narratives of War." In *Southern Stories: Slaveholders in Peace and War,* 113–140. Columbia: University of Missouri Press, 1992.

———. "Race, Gender, and Confederate Nationalism: William D. Washington's *Burial of Latane.*" *Southern Review* 25 (Spring 1989): 297–307.

Feimster, Crystal N. "General Benjamin Butler and the Threat of Sexual Violence during the American Civil War." *Daedalus* (Spring 2009): 126–34.

———."'How Are the Daughters of Eve Punished?': Rape during the Civil War." In *Writing Women's History: A Tribute to Anne Firor Scott,* edited by Elizabeth Anne Payne, 64–81. Jackson: University Press of Mississippi, 2011.

———. "The Impact of Racial and Sexual Politics on Women's History." *Journal of American History* 99 (December 2012): 822–26.

Fellman, Michael. "Women and Guerrilla Warfare." In *Divided Houses: Gender and the Civil War,* edited by Catherine Clinton and Nina Silber, 147–65. New York: Oxford University Press, 1992.

Frank, Lisa Tendrich. "Bedrooms as Battlefields: The Role of Gender Politics in Sherman's March." In *Occupied Women: Gender, Military Occupation, and the American Civil War,* edited by LeeAnn Whites and Alecia P. Long, 33–48. Baton Rouge: Louisiana State University Press, 2009.

———. "'Between Death and Dishonor': Defending Confederate Womanhood during Sherman's March." In *Southern Character: Essays in Honor of Bertram Wyatt-Brown,* edited by Lisa Tendrich Frank and Daniel Kilbride, 116–27. Gainesville: University Press of Florida, 2011.

———. "Children of the March: Confederate Girls and Sherman's Home Front Campaign." In *Children and Youth in the Civil War Era,* edited by James Marten, 110–24. New York: New York University Press, 2012.

———. "War Comes Home: Confederate Women and Union Soldiers." In *Virginia's Civil War,* edited by Peter Wallenstein and Bertram Wyatt-Brown, 123–36. Charlottesville: University of Virginia Press, 2005.

Gallagher, Gary W. "Shaping Public Memory of the Civil War: Robert E. Lee, Jubal A. Early, and Douglas Southall Freeman." In *The Memory of the Civil War in American Culture,* edited by Alice Fahs and Joan Waugh, 39–63. Chapel Hill: University of North Carolina Press, 2004.

Genovese, Eugene D. "Toward a Kinder and Gentler America: The Southern Lady in the Greening of the Politics of the Old South." In *In Joy and in Sorrow: Women, Family, and Marriage in the Victorian South,* edited by Carol Bleser, 125–34. New York: Oxford University Press, 1991.

Hagler, D. Harland. "The Ideal Woman in the Antebellum South: Lady or Farmwife?" *Journal of Southern History* 46 (August 1980): 405–18.

Harris, William. "East Tennessee's Civil War Refugees and the Impact of the War on Civilians." *Journal of East Tennessee History* 64 (1992): 3–19.

Hume, Janice, and Amber Roessner. "Surviving Sherman's March: Press, Public Memory, and Georgia's Salvation Mythology." *Journalism & Mass Communication Quarterly* 86 (Spring 2009): 119–37.

Huston, Nancy. "Tales of War and Tears of Women." *Women's Studies International Forum* 5 (1982): 271–83.

Inscoe, John. "Coping in Confederate Appalachia: A Portrait of a Mountain Woman and Her Community at War." *North Carolina Historical Review* 69 (October 1992): 388–413.

Junker, Clara. "Behind Confederate Lines: Sarah Morgan Dawson." *Southern Quarterly* 30 (Fall 1991): 7–18.

Kelley, Mary. "The Literary Domestics: Private Women on a Public Stage." In *Ideas in America's Cultures: From Republic to Mass Society,* edited by Hamilton Cravens, 83–102. Ames: Iowa State University Press, 1982.

Kerber, Linda K. "Separate Spheres, Female Worlds, Women's Place: The Rhetoric of Women's History." *Journal of American History* 75 (June 1988): 9–39.

Kierner, Cynthia A. "Hospitality, Sociability, and Gender in the Southern Colonies." *Journal of Southern History* 62 (August 1996): 449–80.

———. "Women's Piety within Patriarchy: The Religious Life of Martha Hancock Wheat of Bedford County." *Virginia Magazine of History and Biography* 100 (January 1992): 79–98.

Kilbride, Daniel. "Cultivation, Conservatism, and the Early National Gentry: The Manigault Family and Their Circle." *Journal of the Early Republic* 19 (Summer 1999): 221–56.

Larson, Kay C. "Bonnie Yank and Ginnie Reb." *Minerva* 8 (Spring 1990): 33–48.

Leonard, Elizabeth D. "Civil War Nurse, Civil War Nursing: Rebecca Usher of Maine." *Civil War History* 41 (September 1995): 190–207.

Long, Alecia P. "(Mis)Remembering General Order No. 28: Benjamin Butler, The Woman Order, and Historical Memory." In *Occupied Women: Gender, Military Occupation, and the American Civil War,* edited by LeeAnn Whites and Alecia P. Long, 17–32. Baton Rouge: Louisiana State University Press, 2009.

Marrs, Aaron W. "Desertion and Loyalty in the South Carolina Infantry, 1861–1865." *Civil War History* 50 (March 2004): 47–65.

Marszalek, John F. "Sherman Called It the Way He Saw It." *Civil War History* 40 (March 1995): 72–78.
Massey, Mary Elizabeth. "The Food and Drink Shortage on the Confederate Homefront." *North Carolina Historical Review* 26 (July 1949): 306–34.
Masson, Ann, and Bryce Reveley. "When Life's Brief Sun Was Set: Portraits of Southern Women in Mourning, 1830–1860." *Southern Quarterly* (Winter 1988): 32–56.
McClintock, Megan J. "Civil War Pensions and the Reconstruction of Union Families." *Journal of American History* 83 (September 1996): 456–80.
McCurry, Stephanie. "The Politics of Yeoman Households in South Carolina." In *Divided Houses: Gender and the Civil War*, edited by Catherine Clinton and Nina Silber, 22–38. New York: Oxford University Press, 1992.
Murrell, Amy E. "'Of Necessity and Public Benefit': Southern Families and Their Appeals for Protection." In *Southern Families at War: Loyalty and Conflict in the Civil War South*, edited by Catherine Clinton, 77–100. New York: Oxford University Press, 2000.
Ogelsby, Catherine. "Gender and the History of the Postbellum South." *History Compass* 12 (December 2010): 1369–79.
Olsen, Christopher J. "Respecting 'The Wise Allotment of Our Sphere': White Women and Politics in Mississippi, 1840–1860." *Journal of Women's History* 11:3 (Autumn 1999): 104–25.
Penningroth, Dylan C. "Slavery, Freedom, and Social Claims to Property among African Americans in Liberty Country, Georgia, 1850–1880." *Journal of American History* 84 (September 1997): 405–36.
Powell, Lawrence N., and Michael S. Wayne. "Self-Interest and the Decline of Confederate Nationalism." In *The Old South in the Crucible of War*, edited by Harry P. Owens and James J. Cooke, 29–45. Jackson: University Press of Mississippi, 1983.
Price, Michael. "'Such Are the Changes of Life': The Literary Response on the Home Front to the Civil War." *Journal of the Georgia Association of Historians* 15 (1994): 162–91.
Rable, George C. "Despair, Hope, and Delusion: The Collapse of Confederate Morale Reexamined." In *The Collapse of the Confederacy*, edited by Mark Grimsley and Brooks D. Simpson, 129–67. Lincoln: University of Nebraska Press, 2001.
———. "'Missing in Action': Women of the Confederacy." In *Divided Houses: Gender and the Civil War*, edited by Catherine Clinton and Nina Silber, 134–46. New York: Oxford University Press, 1992.
Reid, Brian Holden. "William T. Sherman and the South." *American Nineteenth Century History* 11:1 (March 2010): 1–16.
Rhodes, James Ford. "Sherman's March to the Sea." *American Historical Review* 6 (April 1901): 466–74.

Ross, Kristie. "Arranging a Doll's House: Refined Women as Union Nurses." In *Divided Houses: Gender and the Civil War,* edited by Catherine Clinton and Nina Silber, 97–113. New York: Oxford University Press, 1992.

Rotundo, E. Anthony. "Body and Soul: Changing Ideals of American Middle-Class Manhood, 1770–1920." *Journal of Social History* 16 (Summer 1983): 23–38.

Samuelson, Nancy. "Employment of Female Spies in the American Civil War." *Minerva* 7 (Spring 1989): 57–66.

Schultz, Jane E. "The Inhospitable Hospital: Gender and Professionalism in Civil War Medicine." *Signs* 17 (Winter 1992): 363–92.

———. "Mute Fury: Southern Women's Diaries of Sherman's March to the Sea." In *Arms and the Woman: War, Gender, and Literary Representation,* edited by Helen M. Cooper, Adrienne Auslander Munich, and Susan Merrill Squier, 59–79. Chapel Hill: University of North Carolina Press, 1989.

———. "Race, Gender and Bureaucracy: Civil War Army Nurses and the Pension Bureau." *Journal of Women's History* 6 (Summer 1994): 45–69.

———. *Women at the Front: Hospital Workers in Civil War America.* Chapel Hill: University of North Carolina Press, 2004.

Scott, Anne Firor. "Women's Perspective on the Patriarchy." *Journal of American History* 61 (June 1974): 52–64.

Shy, John. "The Cultural Approach to the History of War." *Journal of Military History* 57 (October 1993): 13–26.

Sirott, K. F., and K. J. Williams. "Liverpool and the American Civil War: A Confederate Heritage in England." *Journal of Confederate History* 4 (1989): 113–29.

Sizer, Lyde Cullen. "Acting Her Part: Narratives of Union Women Spies." In *Divided Houses: Gender and the Civil War,* edited by Catherine Clinton and Nina Silber, 114–33. New York: Oxford University Press, 1992.

Smith, Mark A. "Sherman's Unexpected Companions: Marching through Georgia with Jomini and Clausewitz." *Georgia Historical Quarterly* 81 (Spring 1997): 1–24.

Sternhell, Yael A. "Revisionism Reinvented? The Antiwar Turn in Civil War Scholarship. *Journal of the Civil War Era* (June 2013): 239–56.

Stiehm, Judith Hicks. "The Protected, the Protector, the Defender." *Women's Studies International Forum* 5 (1982): 367–76.

Stutzman, Maureen. "Rape in the American Civil War: Race, Class, and Gender in the Case of Harriet McKinley and Perry Pierson." *Transcending Silence* (Spring 2009). http://www.albany.edu/womensstudies/journal/2009/stutzman.html.

Sutherland, Daniel E. "Introduction to War: The Civilians of Culpepper County, Virginia." *Civil War History* 37 (June 1991): 120–37.

Varon, Elizabeth R. "Tippecanoe and the Ladies, Too: White Women and Party Politics in Antebellum Virginia." *Journal of American History* 82 (September 1995): 494–521.

Walters, John Bennett. "General William T. Sherman and Total War." *Journal of Southern History* 14 (November 1948): 447–80.

Weiner, Marli F. "Mistresses, Morality, and the Dilemmas of Slaveholding: The Ideology and Behavior of Elite Antebellum Women." In *Discovering the Women in Slavery,* edited by Patricia Morton, 278–98. Athens: University of Georgia Press, 1996.

Welter, Barbara. "The Cult of True Womanhood, 1820–1860." In *Dimity Convictions: The American Woman in the Nineteenth Century,* 21–41. Athens: Ohio University Press, 1976. First published in *American Quarterly* 18 (Summer 1966): 151–74.

Whites, LeeAnn. "Forty Shirts and a Wagonload of Wheat: Women, the Domestic Supply Line, and the Civil War on the Western Border." *Journal of the Civil War Era.* 1:1 (March 2011): 56–78.

———. "The Tale of Three Kates: Outlaw Women, Loyalty, and Missouri's Long Civil War." In *Weirding the War: Stories from the Civil War's Ragged Edges,* edited by Stephen Berry, 73–94. Athens: University of Georgia Press, 2011.

Wiley, Bell Irvin. "Southern Reaction to Federal Invasion." *Journal of Southern History* 16 (November 1950): 491–510.

Williams, Julieanna. "The Homefront: 'For Our Boys—the Ladies' Aid Societies.'" In *Valor and Lace: The Roles of Confederate Women 1861–1865,* edited by Mauriel Phillips Joslyn, 16–33. Murfreesboro, TN: Southern Heritage Press, 1996.

Wolfe, Margaret Ripley. "The Southern Lady: Long Suffering Counterpart of the Good Ole' Boy." *Journal of Popular Culture* 11 (Summer 1977): 18–27.

Wood, Kirsten E. "'One Woman So Dangerous': Gender and Power in the Eaton Affair." *Journal of the Early Republic* 17 (Summer 1997): 237–75.

INDEX

17th South Carolina Regiment, 154

African Americans, enslaved, 12, 46, 65–66, 110–11, 120, 178n68
Aid societies, 77–79, 85, 183n11. *See also* Greenville Ladies' Association in Aid of the Volunteers of the Confederate Army; Ladies' Association of Columbia for the Relief and Comfort of the Families of Absent Soldiers; Ladies' Relief Association of Spartanburg, South Carolina; Soldiers' Relief Association of Charleston; Wilmington's Ladies' Soldiers' Aid Society; Women's Central Relief Association
Aiken, Mary Gayle, 42, 86, 94–95
Aiken, S.C., 97, 103
Allen, Edward, 57, 60–61, 67, 68, 72
Allston, Elizabeth, 133
Andrews, Eliza Frances, 131, 132, 145
Athens, Ga., 36
Atlanta, Ga., 3–5, 7, 33–36, 53, 54–58, 62, 63, 83, 84, 87, 117, 127, 134, 148, 151, 155, 156, 157, 161; burning of, 11, 38–39, 56; eviction of civilians, 5, 21, 33, 34, 48–49, 53–56
Augusta, Ga., 33, 35, 36, 38, 88, 132, 153, 159, 163
Averasboro, N.C., 74

Bandages, rolling of, 16, 77, 79
Barnwell, S.C., 68

Bean, Jesse, 73
Beauregard, P. G. T., 30
Bebow, H. L., 160
Beds and bedrooms, 1, 3, 4, 7, 11, 13, 17, 45, 46, 51, 68, 75, 98, 102–5, 110, 114, 139, 151, 157, 163. *See also* Cribs; Mattresses
Bentonville, N.C., 74
Bird, Edgeworth, 156–57
Blackville, S.C., 68, 153
Blockade, Union, 81–82, 91, 94
Booth, John Wilkes, 143
Bowen, Edwin, 70
Branch, Charlotte, 26
Bread riots, 82
Brown, Charles, 59, 61, 63, 70
Buie, Duncan, 154
Burckmyer, Charlotte, 136
Burge, Dolly Lunt, 24, 105, 106, 110, 119–20, 130
Burton, E. P., 56
Butler, Benjamin, 20, 28, 29, 44, 46, 48

Camden, S.C., 72
Camp, Raleigh Spinks, 161
Cash, W. J., 150
Cater, Douglas J., 87
Cater, Rufus, 81
Cemeteries, 116–17
Champion, Matilda, 46
Chapman, Horatio Dana, 54, 58
Charleston, S.C., 39, 42, 43, 44, 66, 69, 85, 136; burning of, 72, 73

INDEX

Cheraw, S.C., 72, 158
Chesnut, James, 28
Chesnut, Mary Boykin, 25, 28, 29, 88
Chester, S.C., 111
Chesterfield, S.C., 72
Cheves, John, 69
Children, southern, 1, 2, 5, 17, 20–23, 32–34, 44–45, 48, 50, 54–57, 60, 70–71, 92, 99, 119–20, 128, 132–33, 137, 144, 148, 149, 151–55, 157–58, 173n74; treated as enemies, 21, 71
Christianity, rhetoric of, 32, 131
Chunn, William, 156
Cities and towns, burning of, 11, 55, 56, 68, 69, 70, 72–73. *See also under* Atlanta, Ga.; Charleston, S.C.; Columbia, S.C.
Clarkson, W. A., 161
Clothes, destruction and theft of, 11, 17, 22, 35, 45, 51, 60, 63, 83, 97, 98, 102, 104, 109, 128, 134, 151, 158, 163; women's gowns, 7, 8, 13, 45, 63, 75
Cobb, Howell, 62
Cobb, Mary Ann, 127
Cohen, Fanny Yates, 128–29
Coker, Frank, 153–54
Coleman, John Alfred Feister, 154, 157–58
Collier, Elizabeth, 137, 138, 142
Columbia, S.C., 1, 2, 36, 37, 41, 46, 60, 69–72, 76, 77, 79, 83, 88, 92–95, 102, 107, 109, 113, 117, 121, 129–30, 132, 160; burning of, 11, 69–70, 73, 130, 134, 157–58, 180n95, 180n105, 181n109, 182n135
Columbia Bazaar, 76–77, 92–95
Conyers, Ga., 112
Cook, Anna Maria Green, 25, 133, 134, 141
Cornwell, Louise Caroline Reese, 109
Cotton, J. Dexter, 54
Couper, Alexander, 159
Cribs, 13, 17. *See also* Beds and bedrooms
Crosland, Kate, 40, 41
Cult of domesticity, 52
Cumming, Kate, 143
Cunningham, Mollie, 137

Dailey, Margaret, 130
Davis, Dorrie, 105–6
Davis, Jefferson, 19, 43, 56, 59, 63, 71, 84, 89–90, 101, 134, 142
Davis, Mary "Mollie," 86
Death of loved ones, 22–23, 26, 81, 98. *See also* Mourning
DeCaradeuc (Heyward), Pauline, 39, 69, 97–98, 103–4, 109, 114–15
Deserters and desertion, 135, 143, 154, 163
Destruction of private property, 1, 6–9, 11, 13, 17–18, 31–32, 35, 50–52, 56–63, 67–68, 71–75, 97–98, 102–10, 112–17, 120–22, 130–33, 137–42
Diaries and letters, protection of, 20, 24, 36–37, 42, 75, 98, 124, 127
Domesticity, 8, 12, 15–16, 23, 32, 36, 38–39, 51–52, 63, 66, 70, 75, 83–84, 96, 98–99, 123, 125, 127, 129, 131, 133, 139, 146–47
Douglas, Stephen A., 19
Draft, Confederate, 50
Dresbach, Michael, 60
Dunbar, G., 161
Duncan, Sebastian, 68
Durham Station, N.C., 3, 74

Editorials, women's, 24
Edmonds, James, 100
Edmondston, Catherine, 19, 20, 21, 29, 32, 33, 34, 37, 44, 78–79, 82, 90–91, 138, 144
Election of 1860, 19, 24–25
Ellis, Emily Caroline, 108
Elmore, Grace Brown, 41, 42, 44, 83, 93, 94, 108, 130–32, 134, 146
Emancipation, 6, 11, 13, 65, 66, 150
Enlistment, 5, 16, 26, 49, 50, 77, 80, 84, 171n31
Evans, John Craig, 155–56

Fayetteville, N.C., 73–74, 103, 163
Fire Eaters, 19, 24
Fisher, Jane Coles, 88

INDEX

Flags, 1, 76, 93, 115, 129, 133, 146, 159
Food drives, community, 22, 78–79, 81–82, 89
Foraging, 4, 14, 17, 51–52, 55–60
Fuller, Annie, 133
Fundraising, women's, 16, 20, 77–79, 81–84, 90–92, 107. *See also* Columbia Bazaar; Liverpool (Eng.) Bazaar

Garlington, Maria L., 81
Geer, Allen Morgan, 74
Gender: behavior, 53, 54; behavior, of soldiers, 139; boundaries, 28, 31, 33, 38, 44–45, 46–47, 55, 64, 78, 100, 105, 124, 125, 130; centrality to Civil War experience, 6–13; ideals, 101, 118, 127; identities, 55, 75, 99, 123; insults, 157–58; privileges of, 34, 43–44; roles, 78, 82; space, 45; tactics, 142, 157, 163; war as crisis in, 12, 150–51; warfare, 34, 49, 51, 55, 120; wartime expectations and, 56, 58, 70, 84, 105; and women's expectations of protection, 98, 101. *See also* Cult of domesticity; Fundraising, women's; Manhood, crisis of; Masculinity; Nurses and nursing; Womanhood, true
General Order 28 (Woman Order), 20, 28, 29, 30, 46–47, 172n44, 172n48, 188n12. *See also* Butler, Benjamin; New Orleans, La.
Georgia, 3, 5, 7, 10, 12, 15, 16, 17, 22, 24, 25, 26, 28, 29, 31, 32, 33, 34, 36, 37, 38, 39, 40, 41, 43, 46, 48–49, 50–59, 62–66, 67, 71, 74, 75, 78, 80, 82, 85, 86, 87, 89, 90, 95, 98, 100, 101, 102, 105, 106, 107, 108, 112, 113, 115, 117, 120, 121, 122–25, 130–34, 136–38, 140–44, 146, 148–51, 153, 155–59, 161, 163–64
Gibson, William, 56–60
Gillisonville, S.C., 68
Gilman, Caroline Howard, 79
Glidden, John, 65
Goodwyn, Thomas Jefferson, 69

Goodwyn, S. C., 41, 93, 94
Gott, Julia, 111
Graffiti, 62–63
Grahamville, S.C., 68
Grant, Ulysses S., 31, 32, 74, 136
Graves, Henry Lea, 161
Graves, Iverson Dutton, 159
Green, Anna Maria, 111–12
Greenhow, Rose O'Neal, 20, 27, 28
Greenville, S.C., 133
Greenville Ladies' Association in Aid of the Volunteers of the Confederate Army, 79, 85, 107
Gregg, Maxcy, 69, 91–92

Halleck, Henry, 53, 72
Hammond, Harry, 153, 158, 161
Hammond, James Henry, 157
"Hard war," 7, 8, 68, 96
Hardee, William J., 61
Hardeeville, S.C., 68
Herr, John, 61, 66–67
Hight, John J., 60, 112
Hightower, Tom, 157
Hinsdale, Ellen Devereux, 118–28
Historians' interpretations: of Confederate defeat, 126; of gender and Civil War, 11–14, 21, 78; of Sherman's March, 6–10, 17, 99, 111; of women in public, 24
Hitchcock, Henry, 9, 53, 65, 113–14, 118
Holmes, Emma, 25, 26–27, 42, 117, 118, 136, 138, 143
Holst, C. F., 160
Home front, as feminized, 28, 40, 50
Home guards, female, 13, 38
Homespun, 77–78, 84, 92, 142
Honor, 13, 17, 25–26, 30, 42, 44, 57, 80, 86, 101, 103, 108, 124, 136, 139, 140, 148, 150, 159–63. *See also* Shame
Hood, John Bell, 54, 55, 56, 63
Horton, Dexter, 74
Hospitals, 77, 81, 84–90, 92, 186n43. *See also* Nurses and nursing

INDEX

Howard, Frances Thomas, 88, 116
Howard, H. T., 156
Howard, Oliver O., 56

Indian Springs, Ga., 133
Indians, use of imagery concerning, 29, 98, 118, 142
Izard, Mrs. Allen S., 26

Jackson, Oscar L., 70
Jenkins, Jeremiah W., 70–71
Jenkins, John, 155
Jewelry, donation of, 25, 76, 85, 89, 91, 93
Johnson, Andrew, 143–44
Johnston, Joseph, 3, 74
Jones, John, 156
Jones, Mary, 88
Jones, Mary Sharpe, 107–8, 113, 117, 120
Jonesboro, Ga., 62, 117
Jonesville, N.C., 82

Kendall, John Peter, 90
Kitchens, 13, 17, 101, 105

Ladies' Association of Columbia for the Relief and Comfort of the Families of Absent Soldiers, 79
Ladies' Asylum (Columbia), 2
Ladies' Relief Association of Spartanburg, South Carolina, 79
Lancaster, S.C., 72
Language, profane, 100, 102–3
Lark, M. A., 36
Lawton Protectors (Ga.), 38
Lawtonville, S.C., 68
Leath, James, 57
LeConte, Emma, 37, 45–46, 76, 94–95, 115–16, 120–21, 129–31, 136, 138–43, 146
Lee, Robert E., 74, 123, 136, 137, 138, 141, 143, 145, 162
Leverett, Mary Maxcy, 1–2, 36, 109–10, 113, 121–22, 134
Lexington, S.C., 68
Liberty County, Ga., 37

Lincoln, Abraham, 19, 24, 27, 62, 142–43
Linens, 60, 104
Lingerie, 1, 7, 13, 79, 98, 104, 139
Liverpool (Eng.) Bazaar, 91–92
Logan, Lily, 135
Logan, Thomas M., 135
Lost Cause, 5, 14, 139, 168n40

Macon, Ga., 155
Madison, Ga., 58, 130
Magrath, Andrew Gordon, 159
Mallard, Mary Jones, 109, 110
Manassas, First Battle of, 26
Manhood, crisis of, 150–51
Masculinity, 4, 8, 12–13, 23, 26, 30, 53, 71, 100, 127–28, 150–51, 160, 164
Mason, B. F., 154–55
Mattresses, 17, 45, 46, 102. *See also* Beds and bedrooms
McBride, Andrew, 62–63
McCain, S., 102
McClatchey, Minerva Leah Rowles, 35, 107
McPhersonville, S.C., 68
Medway, Louise, 89–90
Memoirs, 14–15
Middleton, Harriott, 117–19, 131
Midway, S.C., 68
Milledgeville, Ga., 59–60, 101, 108, 111, 115, 133, 159
Montgomery, Sue, 135
Moore, Thomas O., 30
Moral support, 5, 77
Morale, 9, 14, 22, 53–54, 56, 58, 77, 79–80, 88, 94–95, 126–27, 131, 135, 146, 149, 151, 154
Mordecai, Ellen, 129
Mordecai, Emma, 144
Mourning, 116
Music, sheet, 61, 98

New Market, Va., 157
New Orleans, La., 20, 28–31, 48, 188n12
Nichols, George Ward, 68, 117
Nichols, Kate Latimer, 111–12

INDEX

North Carolina, 3, 5, 6, 7, 10, 15, 16, 19, 20, 22, 28, 29, 31, 32, 33, 34, 36, 37, 39, 43, 49, 50–52, 64, 65, 73, 74, 75, 78, 79, 82–84, 88–90, 95, 98, 102, 103, 105, 116, 122, 123, 126, 130, 131, 134–35, 138, 143, 145, 146, 149, 151, 159, 161–64, 181n128
Nurses and nursing, 11, 16, 77, 84, 86–89. *See also* Hospitals

Occupied areas, 3, 27, 33, 48. *See also* Atlanta, Ga.; Savannah, Ga.
Orangeburg, S.C., 68
Orphans, 132. *See also* Children, southern

Palmer, Harriet, 24
Parlors, 3, 63, 114, 144, 158
Pearce, Louisa, 40
Petersburg, Va., 67, 155
Phillips, Eugenia Yates Levy, 20, 27, 28
Pianos, destruction of, 7, 13, 63
Pocotaligo, S.C., 155
Poe, O. M., 67
Poetry, 26, 73, 80
Pringle, Mrs. Alston, 135
Prior, Felix, 155, 158
Private property, burning of, 2, 4, 7, 13, 31, 32, 35, 36, 56, 57–58, 60, 61, 68, 69, 72–73, 75, 78, 83, 96, 99, 104, 106, 107, 109, 115, 116, 120, 128, 132, 133, 137, 149, 151, 160, 163, 173n72, 179n93, 181–82n128. *See also* Cities and towns, burning of

Race, 4, 10, 11, 34, 39, 111, 161
Racism, 50, 66
Railroads, 7, 11, 55, 57, 74, 99, 121, 126. *See also* Sherman neckties
Raleigh, N.C., 74
Ravenel, Charlotte St. Julien, 46, 112–13, 142
Ravenswood, Ga., 33
Recruitment. *See* Enlistment
Refugees, 35, 40, 48, 56, 87, 131, 154–55
Relics of the dead, 13, 116–17. *See also* Cemeteries

Respectability, 5, 8, 13, 54, 98, 104, 111
Richmond, Va., 82, 148
Roads, destruction of, 11, 51
Robertsville, S.C., 68
Robeson, Janie, 132
Rogers, Loula Kendall, 35–37, 124–25, 138–40, 143, 145
Rome, Ga., 101
Rowland, Catherine, 35, 132
Rules of war, 48–49
Rumors, 26, 27, 36, 38, 39, 44, 45, 46, 75, 95, 105, 111, 142, 148, 151, 153–54, 158

Sacrifice, 14, 26–27, 40, 42–43, 78–79, 81–84, 86–87, 89, 91, 98, 103, 126, 132, 134, 136, 138, 140, 144, 168n40
Sams, Sarah Jane, 45–46, 85
Sanitary Fair, Chicago, 53
Savannah, Ga., 3, 6, 38–42, 56, 59–67, 83, 88, 102, 117, 128–29, 153–54, 159, 161; as Christmas gift to Lincoln, 62
Schofield, John M., 56
Secession, 5, 19, 20, 22, 24, 25, 39–40, 42–43, 48–50, 55, 58, 60, 65, 68, 72, 75, 77, 79, 86, 104, 116, 129, 143
Separate spheres, 23. *See also* Womanhood, true
Seward, William H., 142
Sewing, 16, 79, 84–88, 120; importance of sewing supplies, 100, 109, 185n37
Sexual violence, 4, 13, 29, 30, 44, 51, 83, 97–98, 108–9, 110–12, 158–59; language of, 46, 159. *See also under* Women, white southern
Sexuality, used as weapon of resistance, 44–45, 47. *See also* Gender
Shame, 2, 17, 22, 26, 28–29, 35, 42–44, 51, 60, 63, 70, 96, 98, 108, 128, 137, 148–51, 158–61, 164. *See also* Honor
Sharp, J. M., 151
Shenandoah Valley, Va., 20, 31, 32, 33, 47
Sheridan, Philip H., 20, 31, 32, 33, 47
Sherman, Ellen, 1, 54, 55, 71–72
Sherman, John, 5

235

INDEX

Sherman, William Tecumseh: aims of campaign, 10, 49, 55, 75, 102, 123, 149; burning of Charleston, 72; and destruction, 52, 57, 64, 66, 180n105; and domesticity, 52–53; domestic war campaign, 33–34, 75, 102; and elite Southerners, 5; on making Confederacy "howl," 34, 51, 53, 55, 123, 143, 164, 176n6; and North Carolina, 73, 181–82n128; orders to burn, 179n93, 182n135; plan for campaign, 53–54; and Savannah, 62, 63; and suffering, 71–72, 74; tactics of, 59, 61, 167n21; war on slaveholders, 50, 62, 67, 69; and women's role in war, 48–52, 64, 118

Sherman neckties, 3, 11, 57, 99. *See also* Railroads

Sherman's March: as assault on domesticity, 4, 15, 16, 27, 32, 34, 38, 50, 51, 52, 56, 65, 66, 70, 72, 75, 96, 98, 99, 103, 116, 120, 126, 127, 131, 132, 137, 139, 146–47, 150, 159, 160, 163; food enjoyed by soldiers, 58–59, 61, 69–70, 83; official aims, 9, 10. *See also* Destruction of private property

"Sherman's sentinels," 3, 57

Shortages, on Confederate home front, 23, 48, 50, 83–84, 91–92, 94, 98, 127, 146

Sims, Leora, 24

Sleep, fear of, 106

Slocum, Henry W., 56, 74

Smith, Eliza Middleton Huger, 145

Smith, Janie, 132

Smith, Mrs. John, 88

Smythe, Jane Ann, 145

Snowden, Mary, 91

Soldiers, Confederate, 2, 5, 9, 14, 15, 17, 26, 30, 38, 44, 49, 53, 59, 61, 67, 71, 74, 76–82, 85, 87, 88, 90, 133, 136, 137, 138, 141, 148–64; desire for furlough, 156

Soldiers, female, 11

Soldiers, Union: attitudes toward campaign, 54–55, 56, 73–75; behavior along march, 2, 3, 4, 17, 56–57, 59–63, 65, 67, 74, 98–123, 179n93; and class envy, 58, 69; desire for vengeance, 67–69, 72–73, 167n21, 180n97; destruction of pianos, 7, 13, 63; opinions of, toward slaveholders, 50, 62; seen as devils, 2, 17, 41, 44, 62, 65, 98, 103, 105, 111, 112, 127–28, 131, 134, 135, 142, 195n38; taking of souvenirs, 60–61; theft of personal items, 37, 51, 59–62, 70–71, 180n105; treatment of female enemies, 10–11, 13, 58, 70–73, 74, 75; in Virginia, 31

Soldiers' Relief Association of Charleston, 79, 85

South Carolina, 1, 3, 5, 6, 7, 10, 15, 16, 17, 19, 22, 24, 25, 26, 28, 29, 31, 32, 33–34, 36–44, 46–49, 50–52, 60, 61, 64, 65–76, 77–79, 80, 81–86, 97–98, 103–4, 107–8, 111, 112, 115–16, 117–19, 123, 126, 129–31, 133–36, 138, 140, 143, 146, 149, 151, 153, 157, 159–61, 163–64; State House, 92, 129

Special Field Orders № 15 (Sea Islands), 65–66

Special Field Orders № 67 (Atlanta). *See under* Atlanta, Ga.

Spies, female, 11, 20, 27, 78–79

Springfield, S.C., 68

Sternberg, Emile, 162

Stillwell, James, 73

Strong, Robert Hale, 104

Summerville, S.C., 85, 136, 155

Surrender, Confederate military, 3, 44, 74, 118, 129, 131, 133, 136, 138, 140, 141, 144, 145, 161, 162

Taylor, Tom, 17–18

Teachers, female, 23, 78

Tennent, Sarah, 42–43

Thomas, George H., 56, 64

Thomas, Gertrude Clanton, 29–30, 33

Tillinghast, Eliza, 103, 105, 136, 137, 139–42

Tomkins, Charles Brown, 112

Trescot, Eliza Josephine, 39

Tucker, Mary E., 80
Turner, Joseph Addison, 149–50

U.S. Sanitary Commission, 53, 81
Upson County, Ga., 124

Van Deusen, Delos, 58
Varner, Joe, 133
Vicksburg, Miss., 48

Wartime tactics, Union, 27–32. *See also under* Sherman, William T.
Washington, D.C., 27, 31, 143
Wayside Hospital (Columbia, S.C.), 88
White, Sallie, 92–93
Widows, 132
Wiley, Samuel, 148–49
Wills, Charles W., 74
Wilmington's Ladies' Soldiers' Aid Society, 89
Wine and spirits, 60, 63, 88, 104, 114, 116, 180n105
Winnsboro, S.C., 72
Wise, George M., 71
Womanhood, Confederate, 13, 17, 45, 78–79, 82, 84, 90, 110, 113, 115, 119–20, 124–47, 160, 183n10
Womanhood, true, 23, 52, 79, 115
Women, white southern: antipathy toward Union, 28–29; calling Yankees devils, 2, 41, 62, 65, 98, 105, 111, 128, 131, 134, 135; condemnation of Union tactics prior to Sherman's March, 32, 33, 34; Confederate patriotism of, 16, 24, 26–28, 33, 34, 36, 39–44, 81, 84, 86, 92, 94–96, 99–102, 106, 115–17, 122–47, 170n18; and Confederate war effort, 22–23, 25–26, 76–84, 85–96; confrontations with enemy, 12–13, 97–123; defiance of, 100–6, 114; desire for Confederate invasion of North, 132, 140–41, 159; desire for vengeance, 195n38; and domesticity, 23; expectations of protection, 28, 29, 32, 35, 43, 173n66; expressions of hatred of Union soldiers, 16, 26–30, 33, 35, 41, 44, 46, 72, 102, 105–6, 107, 113, 117, 124–47; fear of sexual assault, 108–9, 112, 190n55; feeding Confederate soldiers, 90–91; hiding valuables, 13, 36, 37, 41, 45, 46, 85, 114, 115; imprisonment of, 20, 27–28, 46; increased devotion to Confederate cause, 123–47; nationalism of, 58, 78, 84, 91, 94, 101–2, 106, 113, 117, 152, 170n18, 193n9; physical attacks by, 101; physical attacks on, 109–10, 111; political awareness of, 19–21, 23–26; preparation for invasion, 34–40, 41, 44–46, 83–84, 108–9; and secession, 24–25; as she-devils, 100, 188n10; on Sherman, 14, 32, 41, 43, 46, 54, 98, 99, 117, 142, 146, 181n116; stoicism of, 107–8, 191n69; and surrender, 196n72; thoughts of suicide, 108. *See also* Aid societies; Hospitals; Nurses and nursing; Separate spheres; Womanhood, true
Women's Central Relief Association, 81
Worth, Nellie, 131, 135
Wray, Drucilla, 25

www.ingramcontent.com/pod-product-compliance
Lightning Source LLC
Chambersburg PA
CBHW030619230426
43661CB00053B/2057